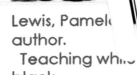

TEACHING WHILE BLACK

DATE DUE

W

TEACHING WHILE BLACK

A NEW VOICE ON RACE AND EDUCATION IN NEW YORK CITY

PAMELA LEWIS

Empire State Editions
An imprint of Fordham University Press
New York   2016

Fordham University Press has no responsibility for the persistence or accuracy
of URLs for external or third-party Internet websites referred to in this
publication and does not guarantee that any content on such websites is, or will
remain, accurate or appropriate.

Fordham University Press also publishes its books in a variety of electronic
formats. Some content that appears in print may not be available in electronic
books.

Visit us online at:
www.fordhampress.com
www.empirestateeditions.com

Library of Congress Cataloging-in-Publication Data
available online at catalog.loc.gov.

Printed in the United States of America

18 17 16   5 4 3 2 1
First edition

This book is dedicated to the many people who are responsible for my being the woman I am today. Thank you, Mom, for being my greatest teacher, for teaching me the value of hard work, and for all the love and support you have given me from the moment I was born. To my fiancé, Omar, thank you for reminding me of my first love, writing. Thank you, Doc, for teaching me that activism never dies, no matter how many people want you to shut up. To the parents and students who make my job easy, and even those who don't, you are my truth, and it is for you that I will always write in truth. To all my teachers, who have put their blood, sweat, and tears into teaching, loving, and shaping the minds of children, you rock. And finally, to the children who have forever changed me: This one's for you.

Contents

Preface

> When we revolt it's not for a particular
> culture. We revolt simply because, for many
> reasons, we can no longer breathe.
>
> —*Frantz Fanon*

Speaking up never came easily to me; one of my earliest memories proves as much. When I was four or five, I recall, I was awakened from a very peaceful slumber by my bickering parents. I don't remember exactly what they were fighting about, but I had seen them argue so often that I used to resort to putting my hands over my mother's mouth whenever she started to say anything to my father.

"Shhhh," I'd insist, shaking my head and trying to convince her that silence was best. She could have been ready to do something as innocent as ask for a glass of water, but I always assumed the worst.

My parents in turn decided to save their arguments for after my bedtime. But this particular night the fighting had escalated beyond their desire not to be overheard.

I lay there not knowing what to do. Should I say something? Cry? The intensity in their voices made me wonder if anything I did would make a difference. If my crying *did* make them stop, I'd be embarrassed, because then they'd realize that I'd been hurt by their decision to fight in front of me. I was also aware of how my crying would make my parents feel; they'd feel guilty, like unfit parents, and I didn't want them to feel that. I also felt slight contempt that I had to alert them to my presence at all. Didn't they realize that their fighting might wake me up? Didn't they care enough about my feelings to not fight at all? Feeling both worthless and powerless, I decided to fake sleep.

I took all the necessary precautions. I made sure not to move a muscle except for taking deep breaths that suggested deep sleep. I kept my eyes tightly shut. Opening my eyes to see my Strawberry Shortcake bed sheets, their loft bed above mine, the freshly waxed hardwood floors, or the Teddy Ruxpin talking bear that a friend of my dad's had bought me for Christmas would only make my presence more real. Or worse, opening my eyes would allow me to possibly catch a glimpse of them. I would be *there*, in the apartment where my parents were screaming at each other at the top of their lungs. Though I could still hear them, closing my eyes gave me the opportunity to not see them. As a child, I always believed that if I could not see you, you couldn't see me. I made myself invisible, no longer bearing witness to their dysfunction and leaving their dignity intact.

That night was the first time I experienced some sort of dual or double-consciousness. I was introduced to these terms through the writings of W. E. B. Du Bois and Frantz Fanon, whose work I had been introduced to by Yvette Christiansë, a professor of mine at Fordham University. The term *double-consciousness* had first been articulated by Du Bois, who used it to describe what he called the "peculiar sensation" or challenge that African Americans experience when they are forced to view themselves not only from their own perspective but also from the perspective of others. Du Bois theorized that whites do not face this challenge. Rather than acquire a double-consciousness, they are allowed to see the world from only their own perspective, thus making African Americans and our perspective invisible.

While that early memory of keeping my eyes shut while my parents fought does not pertain to race, the experience set the stage for the many times in my life in which double-consciousness would, first as a student of color who attended a mostly white college, and later as a public school teacher. Being employed in a public institution of learning that serves many students of color yet employs an overwhelming number of white teachers—82 percent at last count—often means looking at oneself through the eyes of another. My students were me, and I had no choice but to take personally the way my colleagues viewed them.

Still, my feelings were constantly conflicted because in many ways my lens was the same as that of my white-teacher peers. I constantly struggled with whom to defend. Was I a proponent of teachers' rights or was I for the people, *my* people—that is to say, students and parents from the community? What exactly did I stand for? Whom did I represent?

You might expect me to say I represented both, and that it was possible to support the people of my community as well as my colleagues, who were as weary and beaten down as I am. To some extent that is accurate, as illustrated in this book.

However, as I write this Preface in the wake of the deaths of Michael Brown in Ferguson, Missouri; Eric Garner on Staten Island, New York; Freddie Gray in Baltimore, Maryland; Sandra Bland in Waller County, Texas; and countless others, as much as I might have shared my fellow teachers' discomfort with education reform, I am certain that many of my colleagues did not gasp for air after learning that neither Darren Wilson nor Daniel Pantaleo, the officers involved in the first two aforementioned cases, respectively, was indicted. In fact, some wore T-shirts in support of the New York Police Department to school. They did not understand how such an action could be regarded as a conflict of interest. In their minds, Michael Brown and Eric Garner were criminals—they had broken the law. They did not see the race of these men, nor did they believe that the police officers had. They did not question the sheer ridiculousness of Freddie Gray severing his own spine. They condoned officer Brian Encinia's excessive force against a woman whose appropriate questions to the officer were too sassy for their liking. The story was always the same: They were criminals, they didn't follow orders, they resisted arrest, they did it to themselves. Race had *nothing* to do with it.

To be color-blind in the United States is to commit a grave injustice to us all. It deprives those who are still oppressed the right to be angry and, more important, the ability to overcome. Not seeing race preserves racism by implying that it doesn't exist, and thus there is no longer a need for a head start, a way to catch up to those who've always had one. Color-blindness impedes the progress of people of color because it makes us and our issues invisible. These issues run deep in the fabric of our history, and the problems that have resulted will not be solved overnight. However, the first step toward arriving at solutions is to acknowledge the problem.

Americans have yet to formally confront the reality of race in the classroom. Race is so sensitive a topic in the United States that we often choose to remain in a state of denial. We acknowledge that there is a gap between the academic achievements of black and white students, but we fail to include the notion of race in any of our solutions. Instead we look for the smartest teachers around, expecting their intelligence and academic credentials to serve as an antidote to poverty. Rarely do people consider how the race of one's teacher can affect a child's psyche, or how detrimental it can be to a child's belief in the ability and intelligence of his own people to have mostly white teachers throughout his school career.

Some attempts have been made to bridge the gap between teachers and parents, yet we as a society have yet to confront one of the real reasons so many inner-city parents do not trust the education system. In addition, few people will admit that race is often the reason for divisions among staff members within a school. While we conduct background checks on teachers, requiring fingerprints, proof of degrees, and certifications, we do not consider teachers' feelings about the race of students they may be teaching before hiring them in predominantly black and brown communities.

———————

In this book I use my experience working in the New York City school system to show how the issue of race has shaped my approach to teaching and informed my struggle to remain in love with this profession. I am deeply aware of how much teachers of color are needed in this system. My hope is to promote a formal dialogue among those who run school systems, hire teachers, and shape educational policy. My hope is that through such a dialogue, teachers such as I will begin to feel a sense of belonging and will be reminded of our importance.

We teachers of color can feel so torn, so defeated, so at a loss on how to reach some of our children and parents that we sometimes forget why we decided to teach in the first place, which was to uplift the people of our communities, to make students who feel invisible feel visible again, and to give them the confidence they need in order to want to achieve.

I hope that my story, which is riddled with just as many mistakes as victories, will remind teachers of color and those who stand in solidarity with them of their intended purpose. I hope to inspire you to lead the way toward culturally responsive teaching. I challenge teachers of color to speak up for the sake of our children, to not be afraid of hurting the feelings of your colleagues. We're all adults, and uncomfortable conversations can be had respectfully. We must remember who comes first. We must remember that the only group that should feel entitlement is our children. They are entitled to an education that considers their needs and desires. They are entitled to love themselves and to feel worthy of the best. They are entitled to understanding and respect.

I also hope to challenge the thousands of educators of other ethnic backgrounds to *not* be color-blind. Rather, I challenge you to consider ethnicity, race, *and* color in all that you do, to ensure that you are uplifting our children as much as humanly possible. I ask you to consider Du Bois's theory of double-consciousness in an effort to try to understand those who are different from you. I pray this book will help you to never be so naïve as to think that racism has no grip on your classroom. I also hope my words will help you consider the feelings of your black and brown colleagues who are struggling to survive in an atmosphere that continues to ignore both our expertise and the full needs of our children. I simply ask you to see us, and to promote our children's ability to see themselves. Instilling black pride is not a threat. It is a necessity.

TEACHING WHILE BLACK

1

Is This Love?

This is a love story. Thankfully, I'm still alive to tell it and, dare I say, proud to still be standing. I cannot say the same for large numbers of my colleagues, many of whom have left us, and the children, all alone.

I'm not talking about white flight. Sisters and brothers, not that we had too many to begin with in this profession, are leaving their communities to teach in others that are easier to deal with. Many are leaving the profession entirely. The focus has always been on white teachers who leave, particularly those in programs that grant free degrees. It is often assumed by members of the black community that these white teachers lack the commitment, the love, or the ache in their soul to make things better because these children are not *their* people. We are not surprised when they leave to teach in schools with white walls and white children. We are more angered when it is we who abandon our own. When a teacher of color leaves her children, we are bewildered. We do not understand how one can care so deeply and still flee. We do not consider the possibility that *having* these qualities is reason enough to walk away. There is such a thing as loving so hard it hurts.

Many who stay also run the risk of going numb. Over the years, I've met teachers who have grown so desensitized to the side effects of poverty and systemic dysfunction that they utter atrocities like, "Look, I'm going to be paid whether you learn or not."

I'm sure that just as many doctors, lawyers, and police officers have lost feeling in more than simply their fingers and toes. We've all heard of the doctor with the horrendous bedside manner, the one who feels no guilt

1

for saying, "Tina, your mother has only a few weeks to live," never once looking up from his paperwork. Or the lawyer who knows that his client is guilty but defends him anyway because the check is fat enough. And police officers? Growing up in public housing, I've seen more cops who don't care than cops who do.

So let us not be so quick to judge teachers who find themselves in that place. Consider this a "Dear John" letter of sorts. I could just leave with no explanation. But when you've put your all into something or someone, even when you fall out of love, you feel obliged to—at the very least—explain why.

My love affair with teaching started just over a decade ago. And as with all relationships, time zipped by like the Road Runner in the desert, leaving a dust cloud and me, looking like a bewildered Wile E. Coyote. It's as if I blinked while sitting in my Fordham dorm room reading my letter of acceptance to the New York City Teaching Fellowship, and now here I am writing these words in my apartment, enjoying a glass of merlot and a much-needed summer vacation. Actually, when I got that letter, I was home in my mother's apartment in Co-op City, a large cooperative housing development in the North Bronx. As my wonderful colleague Ms. Lake informed me after my first month of teaching: "Ms. Lewis, there are two things in life that will rob a woman of her memory: teaching and pregnancy." Let me begin again.

It was spring and I was graduating from Fordham University. As if my mom weren't proud enough of me already, my following in her footsteps by becoming a teacher was the icing on my graduation cake. She was beside herself as she ran up the hall to my bedroom clutching the letter that she had decided not to open in order to avoid another reprimand from me, her only child, who abhorred her intrusive ways. Though Fordham's campus was only a brief bus ride away, I had decided to live in the dorm for my last two years just to free myself of her.

My mother, usually so serious, was giddier than I had ever seen her. Here I was, a child of a single mother, a child who'd spent most of her life in the projects and had a father who had been in prison since she was a teenager and wasn't getting out until she probably had at least one child of her own, yet she had finished college—a pretty good one at that—and was graduating with a degree in English literature. When my mother introduces herself these days, she somehow manages to squeeze in that fact: "Hi, I'm Ms. Lewis, and my daughter, Pamela, is a Fordham graduate."

You'd think my mom had X-ray vision the way she danced around my boyfriend, Trey, and me with the good news. *How did she know it wasn't a rejection letter*? I myself had no such faith. I'd never planned on being a teacher. I'd applied to the fellowship program only because everyone was doing it, scared that we wouldn't get gigs after graduation upon hearing horror stories from *magna cum laude* graduates remaining unemployed for months, sometimes years, after graduation.

The New York City Teaching Fellowship is a program designed to produce a new kind of teacher for the city's neediest schools. Established in 2000, it hires primarily recent college graduates, along with people seeking to change careers. After an intensive summer training program, fellows spend two years working toward a master's degree while teaching during the day. They are assigned to schools in poor neighborhoods, mostly in Brooklyn and the Bronx, to teach such subjects as math, science, and English as a second language, as well as special education.

Currently, more than 8,700 fellows are teaching in the city's public schools, making up 12 percent of all New York public school teachers, and earning a starting salary of about $48,000. Unlike similar programs, in which many teachers leave after obtaining a free master's degree, the Teaching Fellowship program has a high retention rate. Among new teachers, 87 percent go on to teach after their second year, and more than half continue teaching after the fifth year. I knew I desperately wanted to help my people and my community, but teaching had never been an option. Even before college, when asked if I would follow in my mother's footsteps, I always said no, not in a million years. I had no younger brothers or sisters and was the definition of a spoiled brat. Applying to the fellowship program was just something I'd been advised to do by other students, fearful of what could happen to us after we stepped outside of Fordham's pristine walls, and of course, by my mother. If WASPy young men were terrified of being unemployed, I definitely had something to worry about.

"Open it, Pam! I know you got in! Who wouldn't want you?"

Secretly, I agreed with her. I was a shoo-in, I thought, given the other applicants I had competed against. The application process had had several parts, including an essay, a demonstration lesson in which we had to pretend we were teaching a class, and a group interview. The lesson was a sure shot because a colleague of my mother's had taught me how to "tap out" one-syllable CVC (consonant-vowel-consonant) words like *cat* or *dig*, a method used in the acclaimed Wilson Reading System for special-education students.

"Cuh-Ah-Puh ... cop," I said and gestured each phonetic sound by tapping my fingers against my thumb. The interviewers *oohed* and *aahed*.

It all came down to the group interview. Present were several men and women from various walks of life, most of them, like me, soon to graduate from college. They came from colleges more esteemed than Fordham, and most of them were white and from backgrounds far more impressive than my own. I was the only person of color, something I'd grown used to as an English major at Fordham.

There I had gotten four years of practice not only of being the oddball but of owning this distinction and using it to my advantage. As a freshman, being the token black made me feel inadequate for the first time in my life. Luckily, I eventually found my way and realized that many of these white students were far more intimidated by me than I could ever be by them.

Many had never seen an educated sister from the 'hood. Some came from towns where there were no black people in sight. Some had black friends, but not *my* type of black. I was unforgivingly urban in both my choice of language as well as in my attire, meaning I said it like I meant it and had no qualms about using words like *dope* or *wack* while eloquently expressing my views about Plato's *Republic, laissez-faire* economics, or early feminist tropology in Victorian literature.

My wardrobe consisted of myriad Nike Air Max 95 sneakers; expensive designer jeans and T-shirts from Iceberg, Armani, Versace, and Dolce and Gabbana; Vanson motorcycle leathers, despite the fact that I had no license to drive either a motorcycle or a car; and the best urban accessory of all: a mean mug, as a result of which the typical pickup line that men created for us girls was, "Smile, shorty, you need some sunshine in your life?"

I must have been interesting to look at as I walked around the college's Rose Hill campus alongside white students with bed head, wearing Fordham hoodies, running shorts, and flip-flops. Rather than assimilate, I learned that my difference was my strength. And here I was once again being put to the test to show just how "special" I was.

Who would have thought that getting a public school education would be to my advantage? As I listened to the answers of many of my competitors, I had to keep from chuckling. Clearly they had no idea what they were getting into. (I'd one day eat these words because clearly I had no idea what I was getting into either.) But regardless of how ill equipped I may have been, I was leaps and bounds ahead of these blessed individuals who came from communities where dysfunction did not exist, where expectations were high and systems organized.

Growing up in public school and in public housing, a.k.a. the projects, I knew better. I knew I'd encounter difficult parents, indifferent children, and incompetent administrators. When the group was asked a "What would you do?" question about how we'd respond if the mentor assigned to us to help during our first year failed to show up for the first two weeks of class, my answer, the one that I'm sure got me the fellowship, was again different.

"Isn't it in the contract that we sign?" a white girl with ginger-colored hair had asked. "All teaching fellows are required by law to have a mentor that visits them and advises them on what needs to be done to improve student achievement, right? I mean, the law is the law. And if that mentor didn't report to me, I would get her fired and the fellowship would have to provide me with a new one, one who was professional and abided by rules."

"I agree," a young white man had chimed in, "I wouldn't take no for an answer. I'd call the teaching fellowship office, or tell the fellowship office at the college that I've been assigned to and report her. She couldn't do that, could she?"

These applicants clearly came from a world in which they were used to getting things their way and if things weren't just right, all they had to do was pull out the Constitution and, *voilà*, everything would fall into place. I'd be amazed how often white people used our nation's founding documents as proof of their unalienable rights.

Living in different circumstances, you learn a different lesson. You learn that you better make some damn lemonade. Hell, if my ancestors could figure out a way to make the small intestines of a pig—chitterlings—a delicacy, I could figure out how to run a class without the help of some fairy godmother who bestowed a few jewels of wisdom once a month.

Finally, I interjected: "Personally, I wouldn't waste time trying to locate this mentor who's been designated to help me in my first year when I have a class of children waiting on me to teach them. How could someone who just drops by every once in a while offer me advice, anyway? She won't know my kids. She won't be there enough to learn the quirks and peculiarities that my students possess. She won't be there enough to know their interests, their fears. She won't know about their home lives, who gets picked up on time and who doesn't.

"Aside from their own parents, I will know my kids better than any-one else," I continued. "The relationships built spending eight hours a day with those children I will use to my advantage so I know what they need to be taught academically and socially. I'll know who gets along with whom and whom I need to keep separated. I'll learn how to com-municate with each of them. And most of all I'll get them to trust me, to know they are loved. Because that's my job.

"I may have never taught before, but I'll put my all into trying to, like everything else I've ever done in my life. I'll know more than this mentor can gather from a few visits per month. The way that I look at it, children need me to get a job done, and I'm going to do it with or without her."

The interviewer tried to hide her smile, but it was clear that my an-swer was exactly what she was looking for. The other interviewees gave me a look I had seen often at Fordham. It was the look the hare gives the tortoise as the tortoise crosses the finish line, the look that speaks to the bewilderment of the observer who just watched this seemingly power-less creature, this tragic mulatto with a chip on her shoulder, steal their crown and their glory from right under their noses. I knew this look all too well. I was in.

———————

The letter made it official. As I opened the envelope, my mom and Trey both cried for me as if I had just announced to my parents that I was get-ting married. They were both aware of how such a position could change the trajectory of my life. For my mother, the letter meant stability, a steady income, and benefits. It meant a career, one I could probably have until I retired. It meant a strong union that would provide me with due process, that would fight for me and my employee rights. To come straight out of college and have a career, one in which I could move up vertically and with hard work maybe one day become an administrator and possibly open my own school, was a blessing. While most people view teaching as a job that pays less well than other equally time-consuming professions, my mother saw the glass as half-full. In her eyes, teaching represented security. It represented peace of mind.

Trey cried for his own reasons. As my mother left to call everyone in the family, Trey fought back his tears. At first I thought they were solely tears of elation until I noticed the pain behind his eyes. Having been raised by a single mother who'd taught me to be a go-getter, I'd never considered how my success would affect my personal relationships. I had no concept of male dominance, just sheer will power and determination. It never occurred to me that as I continued to move to the next rung in the ladder, I could be leaving someone behind. Trey, who was always much wiser than his years, had apparently thought of this already. Somewhere in this festive occasion meant to celebrate new beginnings, he knew, this letter also meant goodbye. Perhaps not at this very moment. But sooner rather than later, I'd be moving on.

Being a student in a four-year college with a boyfriend who hadn't finished high school wasn't a big deal to me at the time. Trey was far more knowledgeable than I on a number of things and read more books than even I did as an English major. His decision to drop out of school and receive his GED made sense to me, as his school experience as a young black man in an entirely different school district was far different from my own. It was a big deal, of course, to my mother. She had no issues with Trey when he was just her close friend's oldest son. It was when we became a couple that the trouble started. She was totally against the idea. Trey was good enough for "them *other* girls on the street," but not good enough for her Pam. I never thought I'd fall for a guy like him, but it was love at first sight—for me, anyway. Well, not exactly, because we had known each other since I was in my mother's womb. Then one day when he came to visit I saw him with new eyes. He showed up on my doorstep, looking needful of love, to say the least. He sought comfort from my mother, who was his godmother and a woman whose solid morals and strict parenting encouraged even the most wicked "thugs" on the block to do right.

Trey asked if he could spend a week or so at our place, running away from his troubles, whatever they might have been. I'd never thought about the idea of us as a couple, but something about that day was different. He was a beautiful disaster, with big, boyish brown eyes and thick lashes that told the vulnerability of his soul, hidden beneath his manly physique. We became an instant item, and I never felt more alive in my life.

After years of informal therapy through friends and *Oprah's Lifeclasses*, I learned that my infatuation with Trey was part of my attempt to fill the void left from being fatherless for half of my childhood, thanks to my parents' divorce and my father's being in prison. Unfortunately, my daddy issues were only heightened in my relationship with Trey, because he had his own issues that were in direct conflict with mine. Still, I loved him enough to look past these matters, past the times he'd abandon me for months without even a goodbye, past the lies, past everything. Hustling to survive and ashamed of our differences, he'd vanish, only to re-surface months later when he was ready to come back to reality, when he couldn't stand being away from me any longer.

During his disappearing acts, I had damn near failed an entire semester because the aching had gotten so bad. I was away from my mom, who had no idea that while tucked away in my dorm room I was going through a serious bout of depression over Trey's being missing in action for months. If she had known, she might have decided not to inform me of a woman's deliberate slip off of a building on the North Side.

Living in Edenwald Projects was dangerous, but death by suicide was never something that crossed my mind. I myself had just missed death by cross-fire on two separate occasions, one in which I literally stepped over the body of an unconscious, seemingly dead neighbor's body; homi-cide was always the way one died, and bullets were always the culprit. The story goes that she died of a broken heart, after learning of another woman, and could think of no other idea but to end her life. Her despair pained and frightened me; her man was obviously her world very much the way Trey had been mine. The news of her tragic death, and even more tragic lives of her children doomed to lead motherless existences, buried me even deeper in my depression. On my Faulknerian Literature final exam, instead of using the blue booklet to write an author study using two or more of his works, I wrote what I like to call an "academic suicide note."

Dear Dr. Kraus,

I cannot bring myself to complete this final. I cannot think. I am severely depressed and am on the verge of tears even as I write this. I just don't have the energy to do this right now. I know you don't care, but I don't either. Fail me.

Sincerely,
Pamela Lewis

Regardless of my suffering, my heart was always open to Trey when he returned. "How could you still love me after all this time?" he'd ask. I'd just hug him silently, letting him feel my response. Then the tears would pour out of his eyes, and we'd embrace for what seemed like hours. I knew he loved me as much as he could love anyone, given the fact that he had yet to learn to love himself. The only possible cure to escaping his own demons was a feeling of self-worth. I'd be his surrogate provider of love in the meantime. I was committed to being his ace, his rock, or what we called his "ride or die." But somehow, the day I received that letter, he knew we were on two different paths and that nothing would ever be the same.

Butterflies. That anxious feeling you get when you're starting something new. You're nervous because you're encountering unchartered territory, yet not nervous enough to want the feeling to go away. Adrenaline is pumping through your body, and your heart feels as if it's going to explode. Your hands are clammy, and you stammer when you speak. You know that every bat of an eye, every unbecoming idiosyncrasy, is being watched. You desperately want to make a good first impression. You want to be intriguing. No. You want approval.

I was used to this awkward dance for acceptance with boys. But I didn't expect to feel this way when getting ready to meet my students for the first time. Preparing for my first day in a real classroom, I ransacked my closet, struggling to find something to wear. *Just what does a teacher wear anyway*, I wondered.

I thought back to the dozens of movies, television shows, and commercials that had offered an image of what a teacher's wardrobe should be. They almost *always* seemed frumpy, which didn't appeal to me at twenty-one years old. I wanted to still feel pretty, and mom jeans with gawdy sweaters just didn't seem appropriate for a girl my age. Mrs. Zoldan, my third-grade teacher, was probably the best-dressed teacher I ever had; she floated around in silk caftans from Bergdorf Goodman while calling us *lovey* and *darling*; I simply adored her. Still, I couldn't afford even a knockoff version of her glamorous style. I had to think of someone closer to home, closer to what I could manage to pull off.

Then it came to me: *my mom!* She didn't dress like those dowdy old women on television who gave detention. She wore cute hip-hugger jeans topped in the fall with some pretty autumn-colored sweater that looked amazing with her sun-kissed skin. Her jet-black hair was pulled back in a long ponytail that hung down her back. Her arresting beauty didn't require much to turn heads.

I ran to my closet and pulled out a sleek pair of jeans, black pumps, and a long-sleeved, button-down white shirt, then brushed up one side of my hair and fastened it with a decorative comb. The effect seemed trendy but professional. Then I dug through my dresser drawer to find the pair of rimless glasses that I always seemed to forget to wear and put them on, along with my mom's dainty work watch. I stared at myself in the mirror, satisfied. *Ms. Lewis at your service.*

Ms. Lewis. Hmm. I wasn't used to being addressed as anything other than "Pam." "Ms. Lewis" was my mother. I would have to get used to this. Just then my phone rang. Snoop Dogg's "Beautiful" chimed through its speakers. *I'll have to change that,* I thought. Or would I? I decided to put my phone on vibrate until I figured that out.

The caller was Quincy, a teaching fellow whom I'd attended summer classes with and who would be attending master's classes with me for the next two years.

One perk of the fellowship program was that we'd all receive a free master's degree in education, something that was right up my alley, considering all the loans I'd be paying off for my undergraduate tuition. Because Quincy's last name was John, we had been pretty much forced to get to know each other ever since orientation because we had to stand next to each other in practically every line. After the fifth time of saying, "You again!" we decided to exchange numbers.

"Hey, you. Whatcha got on?"

"Ugh, Quincy, as if!" I retorted. Quincy always brought out the playfulness in me.

"Not like that, silly. For work."

That made more sense. Quincy would never hit on me. We had a true friendship, which was not the case with most men I knew, who were usually always waiting in the wings. Not that Quincy wasn't attractive. Like Trey, he was tall and muscular from running track in school, and his exquisitely manicured locks hung just below his shoulders. But his best feature was his smile. Mansour, our African classmate, swore that Quincy was a lost Senegalese brother.

"Are you sure you have no family from Senegal?" Mansour would ask suspiciously.

"Sorry, bro, maybe before the Middle Passage, but I'm from Bed-Stuy," Quincy would reply, flashing a toothy grin.

"I was about to say, 'Don't get fresh,'" I replied to Quincy. "Anyway, tell me if you think this looks good. Button-down shirt, jeans, pumps, and, get this, glasses. How's that for a trendy young teacher?"

"Well, I think I may win this battle, honey," he replied. "Wingtip shoes, blue jeans, white button-down, crimson tie, and a corduroy blazer, the kind with those brown suede patches by the elbow. Anyway, I just wanted to say good luck. Gotta run and catch this train. Call me when you get out so we can meet at the 2."

Quincy was what we sisters would call a good man, and it was reassuring to know that he'd be teaching our children. Many of them had never seen a man like him. He was sweet, mild-tempered, and well educated, and he actually had a career at the age of twenty-one. Feeling more confident, I kissed my mother goodbye after she performed her daily psalm of protection over me. When it came to prayer, the church elders who were called upon to cast Satan back into his fiery abyss had nothing on my mother. If they were God's prayer warriors, Mom was a scripture samurai.

"He who dwelleth in the secret place of the Most High shall abide under the shadow of the Almighty," she intoned. Then she added her usual conclusion: "Therefore, Father, I loose Your guardian angels to protect Pamela's comings and her goings, on her way to work, while at work, on her way to class and back home. In Jesus's name. Amen." If there were any destination in the world that the devil had to be rebuked from, Mom covered it. Covered it with the blood of Jesus.

The South Bronx was a bypassed stop on the train when I was growing up in the North Bronx. I rarely used public transportation anyway, as we didn't travel far beyond our own community very much. The only family member of mine who frequently traveled outside of the Bronx was my father. He drove through the Horseshoe, the driveway where we lived, to pick me up every other Saturday for our court-ordered visitations until one day he drove to Maryland to live. A few years later, he was accused of driving across state lines with an ankle bracelet and keys of coke in his trunk, parking him a space in a maximum-security prison for seventeen years. It wasn't the first time he'd been convicted. More than a decade before, he'd made headlines for the same thing, only then he had crossed international borders; the drug bust had been the largest in Canadian history. Surprisingly, he was sentenced to only nine months for that one, although he was never allowed in Canada again.

As for my mom, she didn't fly, drive, or take the train, but that hadn't mattered much given that despite our several moves, we never left the North Bronx. She liked the comfort of familiarity and knew our community like she knew the back of her hand, unashamed of its roughness yet in a never-ending quest to soften its touch. We spent a good deal of time living in Edenwald Projects, but Ma had her ways of making it seem as though we lived in a far more inviting place.

Yet as good as she was at covering up ugly, I don't know if she'd have been able to do so if we'd lived in a place like the South Bronx, home of the school I was heading toward. The South Bronx had been ignored for decades by the government and deliberately vandalized by slumlords. As I gazed out the window of the subway car, I realized that South Bronx poverty would take some getting used to.

———————

Burning. If someone were to describe what the South Bronx was like back in the '80s, this might have been one answer. "The Bronx is burning" was a phrase often used to describe the southern part of the borough, although I didn't hear it until I took an African American History class at Fordham. And although I'd lived in the Bronx my entire life, I hadn't seen evidence of its truth until this moment.

As new teaching fellows assigned to this high-need area, which had the tragic distinction of falling within a congressional district with one of the highest rates of poverty in the country, we were given copies of *Amazing Grace*, Jonathan Kozol's wrenching tale of life and death in the South Bronx, to prepare us for what we would encounter. But no book, however powerful, could prepare us for staring ignorance, neglect, and oppression directly in the face. Growing up in Edenwald Projects, I'd seen my share of all three, but I'd only scratched the surface of understanding ghetto life and its harsh realities.

The Bronx had long since stopped burning by the time I began teaching. But as I passed the stops on the Number 2 and 5 elevated lines south of East 180th Street, I realized that several abandoned buildings remained as enduring vestiges of these blazes. Burned out, vandalized, and beyond decrepit, these buildings were hideous eyesores. Edenwald Projects, a complex of forty red-brick buildings on either side of 229th Street that had been built in 1953 and was home to more than 5,000 people, differed little from most of the city's public housing projects, with garbage gracing the sidewalks, gang graffiti on the walls, and the pungent, musky aroma of urine in the stairwells. Yet something in its architecture was always beautiful to me. Was it beautiful to me only because it was home?

I wondered if the children I'd be teaching had found beauty in this government-forsaken land. Empty lots covered with nothing but waste and a sporadic patch of grass were everywhere. Bedbug-infested mattresses had been tossed in the middle of sidewalks along with dog feces, used sanitary napkins, discarded condoms, and dirty diapers.

And where were the trees? There was a lushness to many parts of the

North Bronx, but the South Bronx was the epitome of the concrete jungle. Not surprisingly, members of Grandmaster Flash and the Furious Five, the rap group whose song "The Message" chronicled troubles within the community, grew up here and said it best of all: "It's like a jungle sometimes, it makes me wonder how I keep from going under. Huh, huh, huh, huh, huh, huh." Sometimes you have to laugh to keep from crying.

The elementary school where I'd be teaching was a red-brick building that was home to about 500 children, all of them black and Hispanic and nearly all of them poor enough to qualify for the school lunch program. It had been fifty years since the *Brown v. Board of Education* decision to integrate all schools, yet New York schools were the most segregated they had ever been. When I arrived, the area was bustling with children and parents. Nearby, I saw a long line of people that wrapped around the corner waiting for a pantry to open.

As poor as many of the people in this neighborhood apparently were, many of the children were wearing expensive clothing. Retro Jordans and Nike Air Maxes, sneakers that I knew could run you a hundred dollars easily, were on several pairs of feet. Mothers had had their hair and nails professionally done, and Louis Vuitton, Gucci, and Coach bags were slung over shoulders (some real, some fake). I wasn't sure why this surprised me, having bought my share of too-costly items not too long ago. But looking at this sort of consumption now was unexpectedly troubling.

I had been assigned to teach special education. So, as I'd been instructed to do, I walked to the lunchroom where all the special education students were waiting to be picked up by their teachers. The buses would always come late, so special-education teachers would wait in the cafeteria for them to arrive. While the general-education students had already begun their lessons, my first half-hour of every day would involve standing over my students while they ate, making sure that no one threw milk across the table or punched anyone in the face.

My school was what is called a barrier-free school, which essentially means that it had more special-education students than the average public school, thanks to amenities like ramps and elevators that made the building more convenient for special-education students to use.

And speaking of special education: I would learn that having an IEP (an individualized education program) was like having a rental key to the city. It protected a child from all sorts of harm, consequences, and realities, but only for a short period of time. A child could beat up a teacher and nothing would be done about it if his IEP showed that he suffered from some emotional disturbance. This made sense, because children with any issue beyond their control should not be punished for such behavior. Problem was, by the time these children graduated from high school, *if* they graduated, these outbursts were no longer excusable, resulting in the arrest and imprisonment of many students of color who had early on been tagged with the label "emotionally disturbed." Similarly, special-education students were given modified promotion criteria, which allowed them to be promoted to the next grade based on a percentage of their grade's curriculum; therefore they would not be held over if they failed the state exam. This modification lasts only until the eighth grade, as all high schools in New York require special-education students to pass the same number of Regents exams as their general-education peers in order to graduate with a regular high school diploma. The slight advantage—which really boiled down to only a few points—was that special-education students could pass with a 55 percent, as opposed to the standard 65 percent, bar. Special-education students who could not score 55 percent on these exams would receive an IEP diploma, a form of recognition of goals achieved—however, not one accepted by employers, universities, or even the military.

Furthermore, there was a disproportionate placement of minority students in special education. That population included large numbers of black and brown boys who were labeled "disturbed" because of home life, who were angry and therefore hard to manage, or who in some cases were allowed to be disrespectful to authority because their parents had issues with authority. For many, that meant that all teachers were bad, all police officers were the devil, and all judges or anyone else who had the power to make or break them were evil; the remnants of slavery, Jim Crow, and police brutality left a clear, definitive divide in the minds of many, with poor, black, and brown people on one side and better-off white folks on the other. To many students, teachers, just like any other white person in their community, were oppressors.

Some special-education children suffered from chemical imbalances, but many of them suffered from "illness" that could have been prevented. Many of these children were victims of their own circumstances, the trauma they'd experienced in their environment and home lives that in many cases were generational. In many cases, while most would assume the community school building to be a symbol of freedom and opportunity, many children, and their parents alike, saw it as a symbol of oppression. (While it disturbs me to reveal this, one five-year-old special-education student told a colleague of mine that she was intentionally misbehaving because her mother told her to "give those bitches attitude.") Many children had no fear of getting "in trouble," as they were certain that their parents would defend any and all behavior if in fact the children felt they were being disrespected. The issue lay with what or how a child defined being "disrespected." "You're not my mother" is a phrase I'm sure many teachers could attest to hearing, especially those lacking the color, language, or culture of the student. Indeed, we did not look like their mothers, and that meant, for many children, that they shouldn't respect their teachers. Many parents agreed with this notion, particularly single mothers who were accustomed to raising their kids all alone, who hadn't received any help from anyone, and who could not delight in the idea that all of a sudden this power should be handed over to someone else, especially someone lily-white who drives in from the suburbs. I was too young to look like their mothers either, but I was lucky enough to look like a big sister or, at the very least, a cousin or someone on their block.

As a result, general-education teachers often grew tired of these children with authority issues disrupting their classrooms again and again. These teachers often requested evaluations, and many of these children were placed in special education and labeled "emotionally disturbed." Some would even be diagnosed by outside agencies with "oppositional defiance disorder."

Students who could not be controlled in community settings like a 12:1 classroom (twelve students to one teacher) or a 12:1:1 classroom (twelve students to one teacher and one paraprofessional, another adult qualified to help in a classroom but not to teach independently) were candidates for District 75, known as D75. Unlike school districts that cover designated geographical areas, District 75 contains schools around the city that are filled entirely with special-education students. These students cannot be part of the general population of students because a regular school isn't "restrictive" enough to accommodate students with these special needs.

In some cases children placed within D75 have extremely low cognitive abilities. They may suffer from severe Down syndrome, low-spectrum autism, or a serious mental illness like schizophrenia. I have had the displeasure of seeing a few students in schools leave for D75, the reality not being one that we community school teachers ever believed to be a good thing, based on what we heard. Students who frequently had outbursts were warned, "You don't want them to put you in D75, do you? There, a teacher has the right to put their hands on you, bring you to the ground, and put a knee in your back, just like the cops do!"

On the surface, the teachers of general-education classes might seem insensitive. But when teachers are rated on how well their classes perform on a test despite the fact that children under their care are two and three grade levels behind or have severe behavioral issues that prevent them and other children from learning, it's easy to see how a teacher could want those children removed.

Sending such children to special education isn't always the answer. Many parents don't want their children stigmatized with the label "special ed." But an equal number of parents fought to get their children special-education services because they believed in special education's ability to help their children. Some of the best parent advocates were former special-education students who recognized their own disabilities in their own children. Some parents did not see a stigma in "special education" at all and preferred having their children placed in special education to their having to repeat a year of school, a far more embarrassing placement to some. Some saw the option of a disability check that they might receive every month. These parents could easily be viewed as unfit, but it's difficult to judge a person who doesn't share your tax bracket.

I was assigned to teach a fifth-grade class of students classified as "learning disabled" in a 12:1 setting. Having only twelve students sounded like a breeze, especially because I knew that some general-education teachers had up to thirty students in their classrooms. I found the table in the cafeteria with my room number taped on the side and saw only three students sitting there. One boy had thick black-rimmed glasses and a bowl haircut, which gave him the appearance of being very brainy. The other boy was playing with action figures, crashing them into one another and laughing hysterically each time. The little girl was the quietest of them all. Her eyes were so small that I could barely see them, and she had acne, a sign of puberty or its approach. She wore her thick, gorgeous hair in sectioned braids held with little-girl barrettes. She ate her breakfast quietly and expressionlessly without attempting to socialize.

"Hi," I said cheerfully.

The brainy-looking kid looked up from his cereal, brushed his bangs from his forehead, and offered me his hand. "Hi, my name is Jesús," he said. "I guess you'll be our teacher. Pleased to meet you."

———————

By the time we had walked up the stairs, Jesús had talked my ear off about everything under the sun that a ten-year-old could possibly know about.

He seemed to be a kid who should have been placed in the "gifted and talented" class, not that we had one at that school. I wondered what on Earth he was doing in special education.

Just as the students were unpacking their book bags, there was a knock on the door. Standing outside were two black women, one of whom I recognized as Ms. Edwards, one of the assistant principals. The other was a stranger.

"This is Ms. Lake," Ms. Edwards said, introducing the woman beside her. "She'll be your paraprofessional this year. You've been blessed with one of our best paras in the school. I'm sure you two will get along just fine."

Ms. Lake, although old enough to be my mother, seemed very meek. She clearly understood that age had nothing to do with titles. As a para assigned to meet the specific needs of the learning disabled children in the class, she was under the supervision of the teacher and was responsible for following the teacher's instructions. For me, this would take some getting used to. I was only twenty-one and this was my first real job. It was hard to picture myself bossing around someone who was older and more experienced. But Ms. Lake smiled at me reassuringly. I realized that God had just provided me with a lifeline.

With Ms. Lake following quietly behind her, Ms. Edwards marched into the classroom and began to scrutinize my bulletin boards, which I had covered the previous week in preparation for the first day of classes in pink and yellow paper with colorful borders. She also examined the furniture—the desks, shelves, and cabinets.

"I like what you did with the place," she announced. "It looks very inviting. The only problem is the way you have these desks arranged."

She began rearranging the neat rows of desks into clusters of four while the kids were still sitting in them. They hooted and hollered, enjoying the ride. When she was finished, the children were sitting face to face rather than facing the board, as I had placed them.

I remembered sitting like this when I was in elementary school and never thought about why; all I knew was that the arrangement made it hard for me to fight the temptation to talk to my friends. I was always considered a goody-goody, and I always abided by my teacher's rules. If clustering desks encouraged me to break the rules, consider how such an arrangement affected students who didn't adhere to rules to begin with.

"This isn't Catholic school, Ms. Lewis," Ms. Edwards explained. "Children cannot sit in rows in public school, where our belief is that students should be engaged with each other at all times through accountable talk. In fact, you don't have your accountable talk stems up on the wall. Ms. Lake, please help her with that today." (Accountable talk stems, by the way, are a system of prompts designed to help students present arguments based on evidence.)

Ms. Lake began rummaging through cabinets, found the scissors, construction paper, and markers I had bought and began cutting and drawing what must have been what Ms. Edwards was referring to while I considered what she meant by "our belief."

Accountable talk stems were part of the so-called POEM, or "point of entry model," an arrangement in which teachers became facilitators and only briefly. Children were expected to spend most of their time doing everything themselves, with the teacher teaching only what was called a "mini-lesson" for ten minutes and then letting them work in groups or with a partner and finally independently.

When I was in middle school, I was accepted into a weekend and summer program for gifted children called the Fieldston Enrichment Program, the focus of which was less teaching and more student-to-student interaction. It was the best learning experience I ever had. My brain was challenged in a way it had never been challenged before, and learning was fun in ways I could have never imagined in public school. We ran our own debates, conducted our own research, and created our own projects.

However, we weren't struggling students. Our teachers didn't teach us how to think; they taught content. For example, we hadn't learned the structure of a traditional debate; we didn't know what a rebuttalist was, or at what point in the debate the rebuttalist could speak, or for how long, so they taught us those sorts of things. But when a topic for debate was chosen, they didn't have to teach us how to prove one's point. They simply posed a question for us to debate or form an opinion about and expected us to provide text-based evidence to support our point of view.

This was simple enough for us because we were all superb readers, meaning we were no longer learning to read but reading to learn. We also weren't taught how to be studious. We didn't have incentive charts with smiley faces, and we weren't rewarded for paying attention; that was expected of us. Being in the program was itself the reward for outstanding academic achievement, and we were expected to maintain high standards or risk being booted out.

Yet even with a mother who instilled in me the importance of education, along with teachers and classmates who echoed my mother's vision, it was easy for me to sometimes lose momentum because I lived in a community and attended a middle school whose culture did not encourage learning. Many of my special-education students and even general-education students were in serious trouble.

With only ten minutes to teach a concept, I found myself forced to send my students off to fly before they were ready. What would seem to be an easier setup for the teacher was actually much harder because instead of explaining a topic to my entire class, I'd have to let them work on that topic by themselves and run from student to student to explain things, their hands seeming to never go down.

Luckily, I had at least one other adult in the classroom with me, and luckily Ms. Lake had been well educated on the island of Montserrat, unlike some paraprofessionals who could help a teacher decorate but couldn't help them teach. (One year I had a paraprofessional who couldn't speak English. In her defense, she could have been a scholar in her own language. But she could not speak a lick of her intellect to me.) Ms. Edwards finally left us alone, and Ms. Lake, who had completed the accountable talk stems, began stapling them up on the wall. The prompts were "I agree with _____ because. . . ," "I disagree with _____ because . . . ," "I'd like to add . . . ," "My text-to-text connection with this information is . . . ," "My text-to-self connection with this information is . . . ," and "My text-to-world connection with this information is . . . ."

Accountable talk stems were supposed to encourage participation and thinking. This made no sense to me. I hadn't had to follow a script when I was a child. I hadn't had to have someone tell me how to think. I just did it. Was I really supposed to teach my fifth-grade students, most of whom were twelve and thirteen years old, how to have a conversation? Didn't they talk at home? Shouldn't they already know how to talk and share their opinions? I mean, every child had an opinion, right?

Again, I had to remind myself of my own childhood. I wasn't naturally talkative or confident; I was shy and easily intimidated, probably in part because I was an only child and my parents were divorced. Once on the train downtown to Manhattan, I had a chance to observe white children for the first time and was astounded by how opinionated they were. A pair of siblings, both somewhere around my age, were speaking to a stranger about a movie they had just seen, explaining in detail both its pros and cons, what made a particular part of the film epic and what should have been omitted. As I gawked in amazement, all I could think about was whether the stranger actually wanted to hear their opinions. But whether he did or not, the children clearly felt that they had the right to express themselves. I wondered if their whiteness had anything to do with their confidence. Whatever the reason, watching the interchange made me feel inadequate. If the stranger had turned to me and asked what I had thought about the movie, I would have been frozen with fear.

I eventually found my voice in the classroom because I realized that my answers were usually correct and my teachers seemed to like me. I wondered how much self-image played a part in my students' inability to find their own.

By the time Ms. Edwards left, a few more children had straggled in and taken seats, apparently late because their school bus had not arrived on time. I finally had time to introduce myself and officially start the day.

As I stood in front of the classroom and looked at my first class of students, I realized that these kids, kids of all shapes and sizes, different shades of browns and beige, boys and girls, though mostly boys, some young and some too old to still be in elementary school were—mine. An overwhelming sense of responsibility engulfed me. I was twenty-one, and I had become a maternal figure for twelve students in a heartbeat. The innocence in their eyes as they eagerly awaited an introduction of sorts prompted me to begin.

"H-hello, class," I stammered. "My name is Ms. Lewis, and I will be your teacher this year. Ms. Lake will also be with us this year. Now, I need to know all of your names, and I have a cool idea to help me remember them all. Are you ready?"

The kids looked at one another excitedly. I wrote the word *aim* on the board, along with the question "What is an adjective?" and asked the students to take out their writing notebooks. After explaining that an adjective describes a noun, I told them that their task was to select an adjective that described themselves. The challenge was to pick an adjective that started with the first letter of their first name. I wrote a list of adjectives on the board to provide some suggestions. Then I showed them how the exercise worked, using my own name.

"Since my first name is Pamela and I'm excited to teach all of you, I'll be Excited Pamela." I wrote this on the board. Then, as I had been instructed over the summer, I enacted a "Think Aloud," chronicling the order of thoughts in my head as I corrected my mistake.

"Hmmm," I said with excessive inflection. "I think I forgot the rules of the game!" Grabbing the eraser, I feverishly erased the word *excited*.

"I *am* excited to teach you," I said, "but I can't use that word because Pamela starts with the letter *P*." I slapped my forehead for my error, making the kids giggle.

"Now I want to pick an adjective that means the same thing as *excited*."

I began to pace back and forth while looking up at the ceiling for another word. Finally, I pretended to retrieve a *P* word.

"I'll be Passionate Pamela because, although *excited* would be a great adjective to describe myself, it starts with an *E* and since I need a *P* word and *passionate* kind of means the same thing . . . ?"

"It's perfect!" one kid screamed.

This was fun. I decided to get Ms. Lake involved.

"Ms. Lake, would you mind telling us your first name?"

"Not at all," she replied cheerfully. "It's Denise. Everyone says that I'm easy to get along with and a pleasure to be around, so I'm going to call myself Delightful Denise."

"Wonderful," I said as I put our two examples on the board. I underlined the *P* in both *passionate* and *Pamela* as well as the *D* in *Denise* and *delightful*. Then, since my ten minutes of fame were up, I set the kids up to "turn and talk" to their neighbors to brainstorm possible adjectives. Once they chose the adjectives they were going to use, they were supposed to stand next to their chairs. One by one, they'd tell me their adjectives, followed by their names. After they had all stood, I planned to go around the room and try to remember each child's name and adjective. The kids took off, excited at the challenge.

When I was in the fifth grade, I could have done this with my eyes closed. I probably would have come up with five more adjectives using the letter *P* to show off. I would have "turned and talked" to my best friend, Lillian, and probably made up an entire song about my passion (for the letter *P*) and her loveliness (for the letter *L*).

My skills along these lines were hardly surprising. Partly because my mom was a teacher, reading and writing were more exciting to me than playing with Barbies or video games. Even when she played with me, she always managed to incorporate education, including her own. When she had to take art classes at City College to receive her master's degree, she brought home her work, and we worked on it together, not simply as a game or arts and crafts but as an assignment that I was helping her to complete for school. She instilled in me a love for learning, which naturally made reading something enjoyable because I learned something new every time I read.

I also owe my love for reading in part to my second-grade teacher, Mrs. Bivona. Mrs. Bivona used her read-aloud time to read the world's greatest children's classics. She taught me to close my eyes and visualize the words that she read. *Charlotte's Web* was my absolute favorite, and I often found myself switching characters, empathizing with every one of them. I cried with Fern when she begged her father not to kill the runt pig with his axe. I felt pride when Wilbur won the blue ribbon for being "some pig." I felt determined when Charlotte laid her eggs. Thanks to this book, no one could have told this little projects girl that she couldn't handle the daily operations of a farm.

In addition to the new worlds we were exposed to through books, Mrs. Bivona also introduced us to such basic things as morning dew, which she allowed us to walk through and smell on school trips, and gardening, which she and her husband did together. She'd bring in "exotic" vegetables for us to sample, vegetables like cauliflower and radishes, which both frightened and intrigued us because we had never tasted them before. She talked about her husband, who had almost the same name she did. In my mind, Don and Donna Bivona were like Disney royalty, and her life was yet another story that I could try to visualize with my eyes closed.

The word *husband*, like the words *radiant* and *humble* from *Charlotte's Web*, was one that many of us were unfamiliar with at that age because we were growing up in homes with single mothers or unmarried parents. Mr. and Mrs. Bivona were a real husband and wife, like in the movies. I loved them for providing me with a marriage story that had a happy ending. I had a story for her too. I told her my daddy sold drugs.

Even though Mrs. Bivona and I came from two entirely different worlds, I was able to connect with her through her passion for reading. By the time I was in fourth grade, I'd spend lazy Sunday afternoons curled up with a book, sometimes appropriate, sometimes not. By fifth grade, I'd read every Judy Blume book ever written, along with several volumes of *The Baby-Sitters Club* and *Sweet Valley Twins*. Lillian and I would call each other on the phone and in our best imitation of an English accent—it seemed more intellectual to us—we'd read the synopses on the back of our most recently purchased books in the hopes of "selling" them. Pretending that these synopses had been written by us, we pretended to be two unspoken-for authors shopping around for an agent. Pretty geeky, but the moral of the story is that reading was the thrill of my prepubescent life.

Clearly, I was going to have to separate my own academic abilities and experiences from those of my students. I would have to look at learning through a new lens, one through which reading was a chore. As I circulated around the room, listening in on the discussions among my students and answering their questions, I looked down at their jotted ideas and was at a loss for words. Students who had shown the most excitement about completing the task were the most confused. I realized that I had to stop assuming things.

In my mind, the raised hand of a child eager to participate signified understanding. A healthy buzz of voices and smiles on faces meant proper execution of an assignment. But here, a raised hand simply meant a desire to be acknowledged. Engagement meant effort but not necessarily excellence. The idea that I was merely a "disseminator of information," as pedagogical theory would have it, became increasingly ridiculous.

I had assumed that the only reason I used to raise my hand in class was that I knew the answers. But watching my students' faces light up with excitement that day despite their wrong answers made me see just how much a teacher's love could inspire a child's desire to try. I realized that I had to give my own teachers more credit; I had raised my hand because I felt safe. It was Ms. Alexander, my first-grade teacher, who first recognized my intelligence through my shyness, who first helped me to lower my guarded feelings in the classroom. She made me feel adequate when I did not, as I knew I was the youngest in the class as a result of my mother's skipping me from pre-K to kindergarten in the middle of the year, and now I was in a public school with big kids that went all the way to fifth grade. My anxiety kicked in immediately, but Ms. Alexander worked on my being one of the more vocal students in the class. She gave me my voice in the classroom, something that I would ultimately use to assert myself for years to come.

My heart melted at the thought of these little ones who, although they had known me for only an hour, had entrusted me with their feelings. Even within this short period, they felt safe enough with me to get an answer wrong, knowing that I wouldn't make them feel ashamed.

I bent down to talk to one group that seemed to have the right idea. The adjective *playful* was written in a little boy's notebook. *Great*, I thought. *Someone's got it!* I wondered what the child's name was and looked for it in the front of his notebook, assuming that his name would be Pedro or Paul or Patrick. Instead, I found the name Andrew. He looked up at me for confirmation that he'd executed the task properly.

"That's a *great* try," I said to him, careful not to burst his bubble. "But remember, the adjective is supposed to start with the same letter as the first letter of your name."

He continued to stare at me, seemingly unaware that I was telling him that he hadn't followed the instructions.

"Sooo," I continued, "we need to find an adjective that starts with the letter *A* because Andrew starts with *A*." By this time, every hand was up and waving me down for help. I decided to write the letter *A* on his paper with a blank line next to it for him to fill out the rest of the word, then planned to get back to him after I'd given him time to think. Ten minutes later, the boy had a new adjective, one that still did not start with the letter *A*.

"No, sweetheart, remember it needs to start with the letter *A*. But, boy, do you work hard! High five!"

He jumped up in the air to give me a high five.

"In fact, I have a word for you! You are A-mmmm—"

"—azing!" he completed.

"Now we've got it. Now see if you can come up with another one. And remember, it has to start with the letter—"

"—*A*!"

"My man!"

I walked over to another boy who was on the verge of tears. He had to have been at least twelve, and the pressure of the activity was just too much for him. Several pieces of paper were crumpled on his desk.

"This is too freakin' hard, miss," he said staring miserably at the wads of paper in front of him.

"O.K. Well, what's your name?" I put a hand on his shoulder. He let it stay there.

"Steve."

"O.K., Steve. Tell me a bit about yourself."

"I don't know." Apparently he was frustrated because I hadn't just abandoned the idea of completing the task altogether.

"Well, what do you like to do?"

"Play video games."

"Great. So, you must be smart to do that, right?"

Steve gave me a look suggesting that the mere mention of his possible intelligence could be nothing more than a joke. Before I could reassure him, another boy in the cluster chimed in.

"Special . . . as in *special* ed!" he said, laughing hysterically.

So he's the wise guy, huh?

"Shut up!" Steve scoffed. "You in here too, so what that make you?"

"Not 'cause I'm stupid, though," the other child shot back. "I'm just bad. I passed both tests last year. You couldn't pass it if the teacher gave you all the answers."

Steve balled up his fist and was ready to let loose. He could do some damage if I didn't intervene.

"O.K., our first move of the day. Steve, please sit over there so that you won't be bothered by—what's his name, anyway?" I asked the class.

"Reggie," the troublemaker replied, clearly aware that my question wasn't directed toward him. "And my adjective is *Rebellious*."

By the time Quincy and I met up later that afternoon for master's class, I was both exhausted and energized. Having run up and down four flights of stairs countless times even before lunchtime, I had abandoned my black pumps and settled on more comfortable ballet flats. My once-soft curls had frizzed out. Still, I was ecstatic. I had learned so much about my students in just one day, and all I could think about was coming back the next day to learn more. Reggie was going to be a problem, but by the end of the day he was showing promise. Steve was emotional, but he could easily be talked down. His eyes lit up whenever I smiled his way, and his anger usually subsided with a stroke of his hair. I loved him immediately.

As I rambled on to Quincy about my twelve students, some of whom I had yet to meet but had heard about from their peers, passengers on the train just stared, apparently amazed that these two young people were real teachers.

The classroom was buzzing by the time Quincy and I arrived. As I surveyed the room, I saw my classmates telling animated stories about their day. Clearly, they'd all had as crazy a day as I'd had. If we had played my icebreaker game from earlier in the day, there would have been some Shocked Susans, Petrified Pauls, and Bewildered Belindas in the room.

Demographically, we were a mixed crowd of white, black, and Hispanic college grads, many of the people of color being men and women like me who could closely identify with the communities in which we'd be working despite having transcended many of their ills. Our instructor, Ashata, was just right. She was half white and half black, and she lived in the community where she taught.

Her passion for her community and its people was evident without being overkill. If she had omitted racial discussions from the class, she would have been doing a disservice to the children who would then have a WASPy, out-of-touch man or woman for a teacher. If she had been too militant, she would have scared off half of her class from ever teaching these poor black and Hispanic kids. She was just right. And we all found comfort in her like Goldilocks in Mama Bear's bed.

Eric, a young white guy from Orange County in upstate New York, sat in the back, less outwardly affected by his first school day. I assumed that was because he wasn't surprised by whatever he'd witnessed. During our orientation course over the summer, he'd announced that he didn't expect much from the parents or from the children we'd be teaching, a comment that nearly cost him his head. His exact words were, "We all know that parents in Orange County are much better than parents in the South Bronx."

Ashata, who taught in Harlem, stared at him in disbelief while his classmates began to berate him mercilessly. Alisa, who was Dominican, had grown up in the South Bronx; had taken part in Prep for Prep, a college preparatory program for gifted students; and had attended Harvard, was *the* most irate of all.

"How dare you sit there so smug and make such a broad generalization?" she demanded. "I grew up in the South Bronx, and my parents were stellar, hence the reason I was able to attend an Ivy League school. You've got some nerve."

"I didn't mean it like that. What I was trying to say was—"

But it was no use. Eric couldn't get a word in edgewise. But as we sat in class on the first day of school, he was probably thinking, "Told you so." This had just been our first day as teachers, and even the most liberal-minded of my classmates were probably thinking that maybe Eric was on to something after all.

Of course, I knew better than anyone that his words were untrue. My mother had been a wonderful parent, despite the fact that we lived in the projects. All my friends envied me, and a slumber party at Pam's house was something they'd eagerly attend. My mother smothered me with love and attention, cooked the best meals ever, bought me just as many books as she did toys, did homework with me, tucked me in every night, and told me she loved me more times than there were minutes in a day. I was considered lucky by everyone, even kids who lived in two-parent homes in better neighborhoods.

But many kids who grew up in the projects didn't have such wonderful home lives. Even my life, despite how much my mother loved me, was far from perfect. There was lots of love, lots of laughs in my grandmother's house, where my mother and I lived off and on for several years, but there was also lots of bickering, cursing, and hurtful words. There were tragedies, close calls, police officers, hospital visits, methadone clinics. . . . True, Eric had generalized, which was always frowned upon. Yet how could one expect all or even most kids from the projects to live lives comparable to those lived by kids in Orange County? Through teaching in the same South Bronx neighborhood over the course of a decade I would see many fine examples of parenting. But I'd be lying if I said that I didn't experience a considerable amount of family struggles that ultimately impeded a student's ability to progress: child-abuse cases, shelter living, gang affiliation, and incarceration, just to name the most prevalent issues.

Eric had failed to realize that, as a white man raised amid privilege, acknowledging these differences made him sound racist, whether he realized it or not. But there was a truth that he had tried to put into words. It would take someone who was black, who had been poor, and who had a pass to speak the truth about what has been termed "the response to oppression" or mental condition caused by urban poverty to articulate this truth. As I continued to teach in this community, I realized that that someone could be me.

These sessions, which allowed us to air our problems and anxieties about our experiences in the classroom, would prove to be the most valuable part of the program.

"A parent came in with alcohol on her breath first thing this morning," said Astonished Amy, a young white girl from out of state. "Should I call ACS?"—the city's Administration for Children's Services.

"The school I teach in frowns upon teachers' making direct calls to ACS," Reasonable Rita chimed in. "I think it's best to just inform the school counselor, and she will determine if the child is really in danger. We're not experts on child abuse."

"Bullshit," Brazen Bill interjected. "We're mandated reporters. Don't you remember the workshop we attended over the summer?"

When I think of my coursework toward my master's degree in education, what I remember more than the textbooks, the educational theories, and the methodologies were these therapeutic griping sessions. Looking back, I find that the decision to provide not only coursework but also a forum in which our professors served as both instructors and mentors was probably the best decision the New York City Teaching Fellowship ever made.

When someone who does not come from poverty enters that world for the first time, that person will invariably suffer culture shock of sorts, as many of the people they encounter will display a common mentality to which visitors are unaccustomed. Trying to deal with this mentality and the problems that arise from living in a poverty-stricken environment while doing one's job is strain enough for a teacher who desperately wants her students to succeed. Being asked to address these problems because those in control believe that teaching will always override the limitations of a child's home life is enough to make teachers lose their minds. This demand is what spawns the Irate Irenes, the Perturbed Penelopes, and the Crazy Christines of the teaching profession. This is what makes teachers indifferent. This is what makes us quit.

For teachers of color who identified so closely with their charges, the dilemma was especially great. It pained us to simply teach content as if we didn't see the real issues that made our kids fail. Imagine a doctor being told to continue to prescribe Tylenol to a patient with a compound fracture. Imagine that doctor watching his patient cry out while crawling away in pain. How would the doctor feel, knowing he had a better way to help heal the patient? Wouldn't the doctor feel responsible if the patient later bled to death?

Most of us are so committed to our students that rather than leave, we scream to have our voices heard. We yell out that the plan isn't working, that we need to stop ignoring the obvious. But no one hears our cries. Without these griping sessions, we'd lose our minds.

Of all the concerns expressed during these griping sessions, what was feared most of all was the dreaded "rubber room" or "teacher jail." To be honest, teachers receiving this punishment didn't actually have to sit in a padded room or a jail cell. They sat in an office, along with other teachers under investigation, awaiting hearings. But they weren't allowed inside the classroom until they could be proven not guilty of whatever they'd been accused of doing.

No one wanted to go there. But we all knew that any one of us could be the next victim. All that was needed was a false accusation from a parent looking for a lawsuit, or a spiteful child who was angry because he had been given lunch detention.

Who would do something that evil? Well, a child with displaced anger because his father hadn't visited him for months. Or a mother who hadn't received the child support she was expecting. Or a little girl who was being molested by her uncle's friend, or her uncle, or her own father, or a grandfather who was raising three kids because his daughter had overdosed on heroin. Or simply someone who had learned that life ain't easy and that nothing would be given so it had to be taken, regardless of who got hurt in the process. We fledgling teachers sought advice on these matters because our jobs were always at risk of being snatched away from us, especially because we didn't have tenure.

"So, should we or shouldn't we break up a fight?"

"Of course you should. What are you going to do? Let them beat the crap out of each other?"

"You're damn right I am. Let security deal with that. What if when I separate them I accidentally bruise or scratch someone? Not me! I'm not touching them."

"So you're just going to let them kill themselves? Wow! Teacher of the Year."

"Better them than my career."

It was clear. There were two kinds of teachers in the world: those who played by the rules and those who didn't, those who made sound and logical decisions affecting their employment and those who thought with their hearts, ignoring that voice of reason for the sake of what a child might need. Every day we were faced with questions that could make or break us.

Give out your phone number to parents and students, or don't? What if they begin stalking you and calling you at all hours of the night? I thought of all sorts of scenarios, like prank calls, threats, and angry voicemail messages cursing me out. Or fathers calling to "mack" rather than to find out about their sons' grades. One teacher told me that calls made from your cell phone could even be used to accuse you of having an inappropriate relationship with a student.

What if the child can't do his homework because his mother never had any formal education and he needs your step-by-step instruction? Maybe the parent doesn't speak English and can't help with her son's reading. Or maybe the parent was just never into school enough to be able to assist? I'd learn later that many parents didn't even believe it was their responsibility to do homework with their kids. School was for school, not for home.

To hug or not to hug? Kids need hugs and ask for them, sometimes because they don't get enough at home and sometimes because despite all the love a child receives at home, that child still has more to give. Still, does a teacher want to be accused of getting too close? Remember how easily something innocent can be turned into a rubber room case.

What about kids who are being abused and want to scream for help without telling on their momma or daddy or uncle so they lie and say it's someone else?

How about lice jumping from a child's head to yours? Don't forget about that bad case of ringworm little Karry had for two weeks.

To clean a cut or not in an era of HIV? Send him to the nurse. No, the blood's about to drip on the floor, and you must at least keep it from running down his leg. Latex gloves, anyone? Sure, make the kid feel like he has the cooties.

Walking home from the train station, I realized I'd have to make a decision. In the words of the late great singer and bandleader Louis Jordan, "Is you is, or is you ain't . . . ?" Was I going to commit to this thing or wasn't I? Was I going to do what it took to just get by, or was I going to truly teach the "whole child," as they like to say in the education world? Will you or will you not love the children you'll be teaching, despite all the baggage they may be carrying?

The boy who lives in a shelter and doesn't smell the greatest every day but wants to hug you anyway. The girl who didn't bring lunch for the class trip and could eat the school peanut butter and jelly sandwiches that you ordered but wants the same yummy turkey and cheese heros and a bag of chips that everyone else is eating. Will you still hug that boy? Buy the girl lunch? My answer, an emphatic yes. In fact, the boy gets more hugs than anyone else in the room, and the girl without lunch money gets pizza and fries even though they cost $25 at the Museum of Natural History. Could you tell I always rooted for the underdog?

2
The Honeymoon Song

In life, there will be people you meet and situations you encounter that you will plumb forget. I'm sure there are students I'll see in the street to whom I'll be forced to say, "Hey, honey!" instead of calling out their names because, frankly, I won't remember their names. But some people and experiences are forever seared into my memory. Certain people and experiences can make you lose and find yourself again.

I had been bitten by the love bug, struck by Cupid's arrow, made woozy from Love Potion No. 9. This is what I call the honeymoon phase of my teaching career. No matter how much drama there was, no matter the stress, I was in my own bubble and nothing could burst it.

One could argue that I was blinded by my love for my profession. I talked about my work constantly. The most trivial thought could conjure a smile: the way LaKeisha wrote her letters so bubbly, how Nick's nose was always running, the lime-green suit that my principal, Ms. Singletary, wore on Tuesdays with the "Can't tell me nothin'" face free of charge. Teaching was the hardest thing I ever did, but I believed in what I was doing and that was all that mattered.

Take bulletin boards. This is one of those things all teachers hate at times because they require so much work but adore because they let you tap into your inner Picasso. During this point in my career, when I was still head over heels in love, I didn't care if I stayed at school until seven at night, cutting out stencils and scaling and sketching and coloring marvelous works of art.

By now Trey and I had moved in together. Every morning he would drive me and my heavy teacher bags to work. The bags contained all of my teachers' guides, which I really didn't follow but used just to stay on pace with the content, along with my lesson plans, which he would sometimes write out for me when I came home too tired to do any work. I taught him the "point of entry model"—the lesson plan template we were expected to use—and given that Trey was just as creative and intelligent as I was, I felt confident that once he knew the formula he could write up my plans when I was too busy doing nine-page IEPs for my students, grading papers with extensive feedback, or making lovely bulletin boards. He was losing me to my work, but he tried to hold on to our love as much as he could by helping me with my tasks.

"Hey, babe," he'd say, "since you're teaching latitude and longitude, I'll come up with some coordinates from all seven continents for them to find with a partner. Then maybe you can supplement a short text about each city for them to read, then scale it down to fit your classroom and have them stand at the points."

"Dope idea, thanks, babe, that's why I love you."

Trey was in between jobs, and I was still earning (in 2003) a starting salary of only $39,000 a year with tons of taxes being taken out of every paycheck, so we pinched pennies. I was too in love with my kids to notice the crack in the glass that was our relationship. We loved hard, but love doesn't trump a faulty foundation.

When I did bulletin boards, when I created lessons, I spent entire evenings thinking and researching and Googling and reading and preparing. I considered my students' affinities, their strengths, their weaknesses; and, that word I must admit I hate sometimes, I differentiated instruction for each student. Again, a lovely idea. It's lovely to think of each student's having an individualized lesson for every subject of every day. But realistic? Not unless you have a teacher who's young and full of energy and doesn't do the things that most people her age do, and also has a few extra hands to help, in my case Trey's and of course Ms. Lake's.

What about teachers who had children of their own and a man who wasn't as understanding? What about general-education teachers who had thirty papers a night to grade instead of twelve and no para to help? What about teachers who did have paras but temperamental ones who refused to do paperwork or think creatively, who weren't well enough versed in content to even help out, thereby limiting their assistance to taking a physically disabled kid to the bathroom? Ms. Lake was agreeable and left-handed just like me. We were a match made in heaven.

Together, we were two inspired artists, and our children were our muses. When you're in love with what you do, every emotion is heightened, and when we felt empowered, we felt like Marvel comic book heroes. I cannot tell you how satisfying a completed bulletin board is to a committed teacher, especially the bulletin board outside the classroom. It's a chance to publish your students' hard work as well as your own, and you feel as though you've truly accomplished something. For the kids, it's a deep source of pride, and they're beyond enthusiastic about showing off how awesome their teacher is for taking the time to create such a display.

From time to time my outside bulletin boards would be vandalized by students from other classes who were jealous of how good they looked or had a beef with one of my students. Papers would be torn off, and an occasional "Fuck you" would be written on select students' work. Ms. Lake would simply take down the defaced material and start all over again. I would be angry, but that wouldn't keep me from creating more award-winning bulletin boards.

Being a school on the chancellor's radar—a school deemed low-performing on the basis of test scores and thus earning a place on the chancellor's watch list—meant having a swarm of regional administrators in our school all the time. They would pop in to try to "catch us in the act"—I guess to see if we were teaching. Maybe they assumed all the kids were failing because the teachers sat around playing Solitaire. Who knows? I didn't understand how a teacher was expected to teach normally with strangers breathing down her neck or how children, some of whom had attention issues that kept them distracted or yearning to be noticed, were expected to behave normally in the presence of these outsiders.

Usually my students would behave well because they loved me and didn't want me to get into trouble, but sometimes a child with emotional issues cannot help himself. Knowing this fact would keep me on edge the entire time the visitors were in my room, as an emotional outburst would surely delay a lesson, which, on a normal day, would be fine. If we lost five minutes because a child labeled "emotionally disturbed" as per his IEP had an outburst and I needed to dedicate five whole minutes to calming him down while Ms. Lake directed the rest of the children to continue their work, I was fine with that. But when being observed, we were not allowed to be human.

Teaching under a microscope took the magic out of teaching for most of us. Luckily for Ms. Singletary, the principal, the visitors would let her choose what classrooms they would visit.

"Room 303. Ms. Lewis speaking."

"Lewis, it's Singletary." She was whispering. "Listen, they'll be in your room in exactly fifteen minutes, so whatever your best lesson is for the day, have it ready and open just in case they ask for your plans. If it's not the one you're currently doing, stop mid-lesson and get back to it later. If you've done it already, start all over again and make sure the kids play along like it's their first time hearing about it. Tell the kids they'd better be on their best behavior. Gotta go!"

Before I could wonder whom she meant by "they," *they* came in, armed with stiff clipboards and equally stiff countenances. I'd already prepped my kids and told them to try to act as normal as possible. I didn't expect fifteen people to come in at one time, but still I began.

I wrote the word *aim* on the board and posed a question: "How do we use fact to formulate an opinion?" In an ELA (English language arts) curriculum, we always had to compare fact and opinion. By now I realized that the students didn't always necessarily understand the difference. I thought they might understand the difference better if I presented the information holistically, showing them that while fact and opinion are different, they could work in tandem for a greater purpose, and in this case, that greater purpose was writing a research paper.

Problem was, if they didn't quite get the concept the first time around, I would have witnesses. It was a constant struggle to maintain what was called "academic rigor" without being called out if students failed to understand what I was teaching. And what was rigorous? Although I had fifth-graders who were still struggling to add single-digit numbers, I was expected to teach them fifth-grade math, which included adding fractions with unlike denominators. This lesson was definitely up there on the rigor meter. But would my students be confused?

Why couldn't the observers have visited yesterday when we were sharing our folk tales about New York state geography? That was a lesson I definitely wouldn't have minded putting on display. We were currently up to the geography unit in our social studies curriculum, and because the genre of the month in our English curriculum was folk tales, I thought it would be cool to merge the two to show that while folk tales were fictitious, they explained in a silly or creative way something that was naturally occurring.

Yasheed and Lizette partnered up and wrote "Niagara, the Sky Giant, and the Water Barrel," a charming account of the creation of Niagara Falls. Sometimes I had to ask them questions to keep them on track, but in the end their story was their own and it was amazing.

Niagara the Giant stole all of New York state's water, leaving the people angry, thirsty, dirty, and suspicious as to the thief's identity. For some reason—that was not really explained, but who cares, they were only ten—the entire state blamed little Yasheed and Lizette, so the two of them went to the old wise man—nice touch, huh?—and asked him what to do.

He told them they had to climb the sky to steal the water back from Niagara, who kept it tucked away in a huge barrel guarded by a dragon. They did as they were told, but the dragon caught them in the act and roared to alert the giant, who grabbed the barrel and ran off. As he ran, water splashed and formed puddles on the floor. Niagara slipped on them and fell, sending the barrel flying over his head and dumping out all the water. And that is why we have Niagara Falls. I was beyond proud of these two youngsters' creativity.

Rebellious Reggie decided to work alone. This, I learned, was better than dealing with him as part of a group. Reggie was older than many of my students, who in some cases were as young as nine because self-contained classes could hold as many as three grades in one classroom. Little Eliana had a January birthday and wouldn't be turning nine until then; however, Reggie, because of his behavior, had been held over on multiple occasions and was in the fifth grade. At fourteen, he wanted nothing to do with the rest of my students. On top of the age difference, Reggie was troubled, and he sometimes came to school in a very depressed mood. He spoke to a counselor about his issues but never wanted to share them in the classroom. Instead, he enjoyed talking to me privately about other things and his schoolwork. Still, though he would talk to me, he wasn't always the most happy-go-lucky kid and didn't really want to be bothered with "turn and talks" with the rest of the students on these days. But not having control over how my classroom was run, I was forced to make him work in groups every day even though his doing so did not benefit anyone involved. When no outsiders were around, I let him stay in his corner all day, where he would complete his work quietly and diligently, but when someone was coming in, I made him sit in a group and begged him to be nice for fifteen minutes because I'd be in trouble if anyone saw him sitting by himself.

"But I do better working independently," he would whine. "Working with these kids slows me down. They have no idea what I'm talking about half the time. They're just babies."

He was right. Reggie's voice was already changing, and he had hair on his upper lip. He had surely already kissed a girl, if not done more, and had given me reason to believe that he may have already experimented with weed. He watched the same kinds of television shows that I watched and knew how to travel the city. Many of my other boys still thought girls had the cooties, watched *SpongeBob SquarePants*, and were picked up by their mothers after school.

"I know, sweetheart, but you know how these people are. Everything is about how you guys interact with each other. Sometimes in life we just have to play the game, give them what they want, even if we don't agree."

Reggie shook his head. "And they call *us* the retards."

"Just do me this solid and play nice when someone walks in, please?"

"I got you, miss."

"Thanks. Give me dap." We fist-bumped.

Luckily, Reggie was beginning to like me and was also all about deal-making. He hated writing—the physical action of it made his wrist hurt—but had a great imagination. There weren't enough computers to go around for him to be able to type all of his work all of the time, and typing took too long anyway because my students didn't know the keys. We were on a tight schedule to get work products on the bulletin board, and none of these realities would be considered a viable excuse. I made another deal with him: I'd be his scribe for one sentence, and the next sentence he had to write on his own.

He came up with this: A boy named Reggie lived with his mom deep in the forest. One unfortunate day his mother became sick and died, making him an orphan. Angry about his mom's passing, he decided to storm out of the forest. As he stomped past the trees, the leaves turned fiery red and orange, reflecting his rage. Zeus above noticed the change and immediately called his three sons, who were in charge of Winter, Spring, and Summer, to come and see what Reggie had done.

No human had ever possessed such powers. That's when Zeus realized who this angry boy was. He was his illegitimate son, conceived during one of the times Zeus had descended to Earth to find a young maiden to entertain him for the night. When the maiden learned she was pregnant, she decided to hide in the forest to raise the child alone.

Zeus had long forgotten about the maiden and was unaware of her pregnancy. As he watched this half-human, half-divine boy turn the leaves the color of fire, he realized that there was a new season, of which someone needed to be in charge. Zeus and his three sons, happy to see their new brother, came down to Earth and introduced themselves. They said the boy would be in charge of Autumn and there would be four seasons instead of three. Reggie cried because he finally had a family.

Rebellious Reggie had clearly been inspired by Greek mythology and maybe by *The Maury Povich Show*, but he'd come up with the story all on his own. His story also spoke to some of his own pain, needs, and desires hidden beneath his tough façade.

There were other lessons I wished my visitors could have observed, such as the one in which the students learned two-digit–by–two-digit multiplication by way of a popular new dance called the Thunder Clap. I'd been home grading math quizzes and watching MTV music videos when I noticed that the kids were having trouble remembering what numbers were to be multiplied and in what order. Usher's new hot song "Yeah" was blaring in my ears, so I stopped grading for a minute because I knew the dance break was about to start. I saw him and virtually everyone else doing the Thunder Clap, slapping their hands together and then sliding one hand into the air like a rocket to the moon.

I thought this would be a perfect way to get kids to remember to multiply both numbers in the one's place first, using the rocket hand as an arrow or guide: Clap, shoot straight up, then clap, shoot diagonally to the left. For repeating the process with the number in the ten's place, clap, shoot diagonally to the right, then clap and shoot straight up. The next day I played the song and did the dance. The kids not only loved it, the problem was solved. I can picture my students grown now and having to multiply when tipping a waiter and hearing that infectious beat in their heads.

But the visitors did not come during these triumphal moments. They came when I was ready to do one of my "Hmm, not sure if they'll be able to do this, but I'll give it a try" lessons. I crossed my fingers and said a prayer.

We talked about the word *perspective*. It was a concept I was passionate about teaching to students who were black and brown and, more important, poor. I asked them if they remembered hearing the word before, and Steve said he remembered our discussing the word the previous day when we read "The True Story of the Three Little Pigs!" by Jon Scieszka. Nice, Steve. Extra cookies for you during snack.

I then took a glass and filled it halfway with water. I asked the class if they agreed that the glass contained water. They all agreed. After they understood that this was a fact that could not be disputed, I asked them if they thought the glass was half-full or half-empty. "Show of hands for half-full." Most of the kids raised their hands. "Show of hands for half-empty." The remaining kids raised their hands. Finally LaKeisha raised her hand and said in her scratchy voice, "Hey! No one is right or wrong. It's how we choose to look at it. I say half-full because it makes me feel like I have more to drink!" Everyone laughed, including the visiting administrators.

Next I put a T-chart (showing information in tabular form) for fact and opinion up on the board and asked the students to tell me facts that could be found in both the traditional story of the Three Little Pigs and the one told from the wolf's perspective that we had read the previous day. They came up with the expected answers, like "The wolf eats pigs" and "One pig made his house of straw, the other of sticks and the third of bricks." Then I asked them to decide if they believed the wolf's story, which was that he didn't intend to eat the pigs when he came to their doors but rather to ask for a cup of sugar. I told them to use their list of facts to formulate an opinion. They all agreed that they believed the wolf was lying because, as one student pointed out, "If the wolf eat pigs, why would he go to they house for some sugar? They not even cool like that!" They got it.

Now it was time to connect this approach to our social studies curriculum. I told the students that they would be using facts to formulate an opinion on whether we should celebrate Columbus Day. They would be using primary sources written by Columbus himself as well as other sources of information about Columbus. I looked around at my students' engaged faces and at the faces of the visitors, which looked a bit more relaxed than they had when they'd first entered the room. I finally exhaled.

I don't want anyone to think that teaching at this particular point in my life was a rose garden. I had bouts of frustration, rage, panic, confusion; I thought that most of the policies had been written by individuals who were out of touch with my community. Did I like the idea that I couldn't dash out to the bathroom because my forty-six-year-old paraprofessional who had two children of her own and was old enough to be my mother could not legally be in the classroom alone with twelve students? Of course not. Did I understand why we had to spend hours upon hours of preparation putting up bulletin boards just to have to start all over again every month? Sure didn't. Did I feel that professional development was a joke, that it did not help develop our craft as teachers but instead assessed us on the same skills on which we tested our students? Absolutely. I kid you not when I say that we were pulled away from our work to sit in meetings where we had to read paragraphs and highlight the main idea and write a summary of what we'd just read.

Did Ms. Singletary have her ways about her, like her door being closed more often than not? Could I count on one hand how many times she had replied to a question of mine by asking, "Did you talk to your immediate supervisor first?" And as for Ms. Edwards, my immediate supervisor, sure, she was a maniacal micromanager who would criticize me for being a minute and a half over during a reading workshop or complain that I didn't circulate in the room—something teachers do when students are working independently—during the five minutes she observed me during a read-aloud session on the carpet. This portion of the lesson didn't require me to move around, as my students were seated cross-legged in front of me for story time. Instead of using common sense and writing "N/A" ("not applicable"), Ms. Edwards decided to add it into the pile of duties I *should* have been doing. As for my being a minute and a half over, as punishment I was told to observe a master teacher during her reading workshop. During her workshop, because there were no administrators observing her, she went over ten minutes. It was a great lesson, but it might not have been if she'd followed the rules. I realized that teachers didn't believe in anything we were being told to do. We closed our doors and did what made sense and played their stupid game only when we were being watched.

My students weren't always engaged. I had to nudge a few awake when they should have been paying attention. I broke up more than a few fights. Some parents could never be reached. Home numbers turned out to be the numbers of local stores and restaurants. At first I thought maybe they were parents' work numbers, until being told more than once that I had the wrong number by a disgruntled Korean nail technician or Eddie, who takes orders at Domino's Pizza. After that happened a few times, I realized some parents just didn't want to be contacted. Some were irate. There was even a time that my colleague Sylvia and I were threatened in the middle of the street by a parent who was upset that the Administration for Children's Services had been called about him.

The previous day we had bumped into his daughter after school and discovered that she had a black eye. She admitted that her father had hit her in the face with a wooden brush. Because this man had already been reported to ACS, he was furious when he got yet another visit. He waited for Sylvia the next day, and when he saw her he proceeded to curse her out.

"Let me tell you something, bitch! If you ever even *think* about calling ACS on me again, I'm gonna fuck you up!"

Scared Sylvia picked up her pace as we headed to the entrance of the school. I had other plans.

"Who you calling a bitch?"

Somehow the girl from Edenwald Projects entered this delightful conversation, Queen Latifah's "U.N.I.T.Y." playing in my head all the while.

"Mind your business, bitch!" he shot back. He waved his finger in my face.

"You have 0.2 seconds to get that finger out of my face before I—"

By now Ms. Edwards, who had apparently been running toward us from down the block the entire time, caught up to us and dragged me away in the nick of time. She ordered Sylvia and me to continue to the school entrance, clock in as if nothing had happened, and retrieve our students. Thankfully, I was never written up for this and I never concluded the altercation the way Queen did in her song: While she punched her adversary "dead in the eye," I reluctantly walked away. I expected scenarios like this, but wasn't prepared for the feeling of rage that consumed me.

When Ms. Singletary heard about the altercation, she leaned in and whispered to me, "I heard you were about to beat a brother down." She chuckled.

I was taken off-guard at her playfulness. She never joked around with her staff.

"Ummm," I stuttered, "I was. I mean, I wanted to, but then Ms. Edwards came and—"

"As much as that bastard may have deserved it, you can't let him bring you to blows, you understand me?"

She walked away before I could even respond.

No, teaching was not a walk in the park. But despite the issues I faced from day to day, they weren't enough to make me give up, and that had a great deal to do with my kids and the relationships I built with them. Some children defy the odds against them, making you wonder how on Earth they could be so sweet and seemingly unfazed by the realities they faced every day. They make you feel obligated to stay despite everything that makes you want to run as far away from teaching as possible. They can survive all that life has thrown at them and still smile. These children make it all worthwhile.

Then there are children who make you feel as if you're losing your mind, who frustrate you in ways that no adult could because as children they often lack reason or are horribly inconsiderate and without motivation, making you have to beg them to do so much as pick up a pencil. Take the problems of an average American child and multiply them by a hundred. That, my friend, suggests the frustration level of a teacher trying to educate many inner-city children. Next, try to picture that same child, who has sent you to bed with anxiety, who has put you in a bad mood for a week, who you're convinced was sent by Satan himself to make your life hell on Earth, turning into the best, most polite, most thoughtful, hard-working young man or young woman you've ever known.

I've been fortunate enough to have experienced this time and again. Some children I have taught I will remember for the rest of my life. It is their faces I picture whenever I am in doubt.

Jennifer, a beautiful eleven-year-old with hazel eyes and a dirty-blonde ponytail that fell down to her waist, had cerebral palsy. So did her twin sister, Jessica, who had a more severe case, requiring her to have a home attendant. Jennifer could walk, but she mostly used a wheelchair to get around. Her leg muscles were extremely weak, forcing her to hold on to people or objects at each step when she tried to walk on her own. She and her health para had to leave ahead of the class for lunch to give her time to get downstairs on the days she used her walker rather than her wheelchair. Her single father raised the two girls alone and, though Jennifer would complain that he was overprotective, did a damn good job.

Jennifer was one of those students God placed in my class to remind me that my life really wasn't as tough as I thought it was. If she could face so many obstacles and come to school all smiles, why couldn't I?

What Jennifer lacked in physical ability she made up for in mental strength. She was the most articulate student I ever taught. Her leg muscles may have been weak, but her brain was stronger than those of most adults.

Until Jennifer's arrival in my class, I hadn't known anyone with a physical disability. When I was growing up, there weren't any students in my school with wheelchairs or crutches. I never thought about this, although now I knew why. Jennifer was my student because my school was "barrier-free." We had elevators to transport students with physical disabilities as well as ramps and wheelchair-accessible bathrooms. Schools without these accommodations could never enroll a child with a physical disability.

Jennifer will forever be one of my all-time favorite kids in the universe because of the life lesson she taught me on our fifth-grade senior trip. I had grown accustomed to having a physically disabled student in my class-room and treated her no differently from the way I would have treated anyone else. Jennifer didn't get special treatment. She was punished along with the rest of the class when they deserved it, and she participated in all trips and out-of-classroom activities. I didn't consider the possibility of problems on our senior trip to Camp Freedom in Connecticut.

The children had been waiting for the trip all year. It would be their first time traveling as a class out of the state. By the time we boarded our buses and were on our way, the kids were beside themselves with anticipation. There would be hiking, gladiator jousting, trampolines, and human foosball. Every sport under the sun would be available, from tennis and volleyball to baseball and basketball. There would even be an ice cream sundae party. But what the kids were most excited about was rock climbing.

"What if I fall, Ms. Lewis?" LaKeisha was quite the rational one.

"Well, you'll be hooked up to a harness so that if your foot slips, you won't."

"Oh! Just checking. Well, if that's the case, I'm going to climb higher than everyone else."

"Not me," Jennifer chimed in. "I'm beating everyone!"

A look of confusion crossed LaKeisha's face as she pondered Jennifer's words. I could tell that we were both thinking the same thing.

For the rest of the trip Jennifer and the other girls chatted about what they planned to do once we arrived, what color their prom dresses were, and how often they'd visit me after they graduated. I smiled and nodded, but I wasn't really there. I was preparing myself for the possibility that Jennifer's senior trip might go down as one of the most devastating days in her young life. What was she supposed to do? Watch everyone else have fun? I was certain that my status as "favorite teacher ever" was about to change drastically to "the teacher who had destroyed my senior year of elementary school."

When we arrived, we were met by camp staff members who described the activities available. Each of the teachers, paras, and parent chaperones were given up to ten children to supervise. Jennifer's health para, Ms. Fay, was assigned to the half-dozen physically disabled fifth-graders in attendance, including Jennifer and Angela, my other physically disabled student. Camp staff members assured us that these students would have just as much fun as the other students and would participate in some exciting arts-and-crafts activities. While the rest of the physically disabled students seemed O.K. with this, Jennifer definitely was not.

"But that's not fair! First of all, I want to be in Ms. Lewis's group!"

"No problem," I replied quickly. "Ms. Fay can take my group, and I can sit with you guys." The other kids in the group I had originally been assigned to supervise exploded.

"Chill, Jennifer!" one child called out. "She's our teacher too! What about us?"

"I never said you guys should be punished," Jennifer replied. "What I said was that I want to be in Ms. Lewis's group too, with you guys!"

We suddenly realized what Jennifer was suggesting. She didn't want an adult swap. She wanted to be in the group that would be outdoors doing physical activities. The kids looked to me for an answer.

"But Jennifer, sweetheart, you can't do all of those things," I told her patiently. "What did you plan on doing—watching on the sidelines while you cheered everyone else on?"

"Some things don't require me to walk or stand. Like the zip line. All I have to do is hold on and zip on by to the other side!"

This was true. I agreed that she could be a part of the group, but if there was something she could not do, she had to promise not to complain about having to sit out. We shook on it.

Everything seemed to be running smoothly. Jennifer went on the zip line, the trampoline, and a few more activities. When the kids wanted to play kickball, she sat out and cheered. Maybe this would turn out fine after all.

Then came the next activity, rock climbing. Uh-oh.

The kids were waiting for this one. They were already fighting over who would go first. I looked over at Jennifer, who was still all smiles. I knew how badly she wanted to do this. But maybe she was satisfied with what she had been able to participate in and wouldn't be too bummed sitting this one out.

One by one, the kids were harnessed and began to climb. LaKeisha made good time but stopped midway after she looked down. Another student moved even faster but didn't make it all the way up because his arms began to hurt. Eventually, everyone who tried seemed to be comfortable about not reaching the top. The wall was pretty high after all, and they *were* only ten and eleven years old. As each child got a chance, I continued to eye Jennifer. She seemed as chipper as ever.

"O.K., guys, on to the next activity," I finally announced. The kids lined up single file, and I began to walk to the next point.

"Aren't you forgetting someone?" Jennifer said defiantly. I turned around. Her hazel eyes had turned dark greenish gray. She was clearly pissed.

"Jennifer, you promised," I said. "We shook on it. You said you wouldn't get huffy when we got to the activities that you couldn't do. Now let's move on to the next one."

"What I *said* was that I wouldn't try the things that required me to stand without support. Who said I couldn't climb?"

A camp staffer chimed in. "Sweetie, rock climbing involves both the muscles in your legs as well as your arms. You have to use both to hoist yourself up. In fact, much of the stress rests in one's ability to push off of one rock with a foot."

Jennifer considered this information for a moment. Then she said, "Well, I don't have to use my leg strength. I can just use my arm strength."

This was breaking my heart. But I had to be realistic.

"I'm sorry, Jennifer. You heard the woman. You need both your legs and your arms to climb. Didn't you see how tired everyone was after the climb? If they were able to use both their arms and legs and were still exhausted, how could you manage with just your arms? Come on, Jennifer. You promised to be rational."

Jennifer's eyes began to tear up. And there you had it. I had just ruined her senior trip.

"But—you won't even let me try," she wailed.

I didn't know what to do. If I didn't let her try, she would think I was the most horrible teacher ever. But if I did, she would be even further embarrassed. I heard in my mind something that I had often heard parents say: "Sometimes you have to let them get hurt so that they learn from it and become stronger."

I made my decision.

"Jennifer, you have to promise me that if I let you do it, you won't get mad at me if you can't. And I can't protect you from getting your feelings hurt if you can't do it. I will do everything in my power to make sure that doesn't happen. I will make sure no one laughs at you. If they do, they will be forced to sit out for the rest of the trip. Do you guys understand?" I shot my eyes at the rest of the kids with the look my mother gave me when she meant business.

"Yessssss, Ms. Lewis." Flat, but a promise.

"I'm trying to protect you from further embarrassment, but if you insist, I'll let you go. Promise me you won't be upset with me if things don't go as planned."

Jennifer's eyes lit up. "I promise."

I said a little prayer as the harness was put around her body. *Please Lord, keep these kids from laughing or saying "I told you so." And please keep Jennifer from being too embarrassed when she can't do it.*

Jennifer turned around to face us before she mounted the wall. "Can I get a little motivation here? Sheesh!"

The kids started screaming, "Go, Jennifer! It's your birthday! We go'n party like it's your birthday!" It wasn't, but 50 Cent's "In Da Club" was still relevant. This *was* a birthday of sorts, a rebirth, a day on which she was adamant about creating a new Jennifer, one who would never be told No ever again. The kids continued their chant. I looked away while the rest of them looked on. Then I noticed the cheers were getting louder. I looked up. This little girl was halfway up the damn wall.

"Whoo-hoo! Go, Jennifer! You *go*, girl!" I yelled. Jennifer climbed higher and higher, her legs dangling beneath her the entire time. She was lifting her entire body weight using only her arms. I'd never thought about it before, but she must have had really strong arms from pushing herself every day in her wheelchair.

By now we were making such a commotion that everyone within a fifty-foot radius had their eyes on Jennifer. I couldn't see her face, but I could tell she was grinning. At this point, she had climbed higher than everyone else, her dirty blonde ponytail flying in the wind. And then it hit me. She wasn't going to stop. She was going to go all the way, something no child in the group had been able to do.

When she finally reached the top, she turned around with a grin wider than the Cheshire Cat's. I felt like crying. I had never felt so overjoyed and lousy at the same time. I took out my cell phone as they were about to lower her back down. The picture I took sits in my living room today.

On Jennifer's graduation day, she cried harder than any child in the fifth grade. She sat at the end of the row, and when her name was called, she walked with her forearm crutches until she got to the bottom of the stage. There she removed them, and the nearest fifth-grade teacher ran off the stage to meet her and help her up the steps. The entire fifth-grade teacher team, along with the guests and administrators on stage, gave her a standing ovation. There wasn't a dry eye in the room.

As Jennifer began to walk across the stage toward Ms. Singletary and her diploma, she held on to the hand of a teacher in the front row. One by one, she was passed into the hands of another crying teacher until she finally reached me at the end of the row. She fell into my arms and we embraced, both in tears. I then walked her the couple of steps to the lectern where even Ms. Singletary was crying. With one hand she offered Jennifer her diploma, and with the other a sturdy handshake.

I made sure to see Jennifer walk across a similar stage when she graduated from high school a few years ago. That time, she got a standing ovation from the entire auditorium.

Jennifer is one of those students I will always keep in touch with. I will be there when she graduates from college, when she gets married, when she has children of her own.

I'll leave you with the letter that I wrote her at the end of fifth grade, back when I wrote all of my students farewell letters. She framed it, and it hangs in her home today.

Dear Jennifer,

I first want to begin by saying that you have made me so proud to be the teacher of Class _____ this year. You and all of your hard work, determination, and courage have helped make this class one of the most talked-about classes this year. Do you remember our discussion earlier this year when we were preparing for our play? You said something remarkable that has stuck with me to this very day. You said, "This is our chance to prove to everyone that we are just as intelligent as the rest of them!" Jennifer, sweetie, you have definitely proven how capable, intelligent, and wonderful you are to everyone who meets you.

Though I hope this is not goodbye, and I want you to remember that you can always stay in touch with me and that I'll always be there for you, I've prepared some things to write to you that I would like you to read and hold onto for many years to come.

I want you to always remember how blessed you are. You have many qualities that most do not have. Yes, we already know that you are a very, very beautiful girl. Yes, we all know how very bright you are. But you aren't just book smart. You are clever, witty, and you have lots of charisma and leadership ability. As you continue to approach adulthood, you'll be thinking more and more about what kind of profession you'd be most successful in. I want you to keep these gifts in mind as well as how magnificent you are at public speaking. Who knows? You could be a famous orator one day!

Please keep this letter in a safe place and review it whenever you are feeling down and out. I'm serious now! I'm hoping that whenever you're feeling unsure of yourself—because teenagers do that a lot—after reading this letter, your common sense will pop back into your head and you'll say to yourself, "Self, what's wrong with you?! You are amazing, and don't you forget it!" I don't care who tells you otherwise, O.K.? You will come across people in life who will try to break you down. If you stay true to yourself, you won't be able to be knocked down by anyone!

You're going to go far, Jennifer. Just being who you are guarantees success. Your only job is to make sure you don't allow anything to change who you are. Push through life's challenges as you have done so far and conquer them, just as you did when you climbed to the top of that rock wall. Continue to be an inspiration to us all. It was an honor to have you in my class and I shall always remember you.

Love,
Ms. Lewis

———————

Sydney was absolutely stunning. Her skin was the last shade of brown on the color palette, her eyes the shape of almonds. But she hated the color of her skin and did her damnedest to hide her body from sight, mostly with those ankle-length bubble coats that were popular around this time. Sydney wore hers all day long, using it more as a security blanket than for warmth. She put up the hood and often zippered the coat up to her chin, as if hoping to become invisible.

As disturbing as this image may be, it was the other ways in which Sydney tried to hide that were the most devastating to watch. She created an armor of hate. She spewed obscenities that were unfathomable for a girl her age. At age eleven, she fought like a grown man. She intimidated every person she encountered, bullied her peers and her teachers, and had adopted a persona that basically said, "Fuck with me. Go ahead. I dare you." She even insulted herself, figuring that if she had already done the job, there'd be no ammunition left for anyone else.

"I'm pitch black and ugly," she'd say, almost laughing. "I wish I could scrub my skin light." I never found it funny.

"Your skin is beautiful, Sydney," I constantly reminded her.

"You have to say that," she scoffed. "You're my teacher."

"That's not true. I keep it real, and I wouldn't say you were beautiful if I didn't believe it was true."

"You wouldn't want this skin."

"That's not true."

"That's easy for you to say. Ninety-nine problems, but your skin ain't one." This was her nod to a Jay Z song from his Black Album. She was right. I couldn't relate. My life had been filled with complexion compliments and tress tributes. My "prettiness" was always in relation to long hair and lighter skin; it had little to do with my facial features. Skin and hair were all that mattered in my black community, and I was considered lucky by those who coveted my color and my curls.

Being fortunate enough to have grown up without such a devastating blow to my self-esteem allowed me to see beauty without a distorted sense of reality. But Sydney, like so many little black girls, suffered from a warped perception of beauty. Just as girls who struggled with bulimia and anorexia could not look in the mirror without seeing themselves as fat no matter how thin they were, Sydney and millions of other little girls in America and elsewhere in the world were doomed to see ugly staring back at them in the mirror, regardless of how beautiful they were.

As Sydney began to trust me, our relationship eventually became a good one, despite her attempt to ruin it from the very beginning. By the first day of school, she had already decided that she would be the boss of the class.

"I'm not sitting there," she announced in reference to her seat assignment.

"I'm not turning and talking to that nigga," she spat when I asked her to Think, Pair, Share. "He gets on my fucking nerves."

On another occasion: "Easy, breezy, lemon squeezy. You ain't the boss of me!"

It was never-ending. Because of Sydney, I did a lot of soulful humming under my breath the first few months of school—anything to keep calm. Like the parent who called me a bitch, Sydney was a constant reminder of how close I was to letting my "ignant" or ignorant side out—that is, the side a person develops unconsciously when growing up in a hostile environment. Sometimes I had to abandon all the educational theories I'd read about, the ones that asked the students to stop inappropriate behavior rather than simply order them to do so, the ones that asked for strategies and behavioral charts and plans. Those may have worked for some, but not Sydney. Sydney couldn't have cared less if I had moved her from a blue card to a green one because of her behavior. Many teachers of color who were held in such high regard for their excellent behavior-management skills usually ignored the stuff that white people kept feeding us and took matters into our own hands. I wasn't asking Sydney anything.

Once I reintroduced myself as boss, Sydney had a new-found respect for me, one that allowed me to get results from her that many others could not. What I discovered was that she was brilliant. Her use of imagery was outstanding, and she could write poems that would have impressed Nikki

Giovanni herself. She was a voracious reader, often choosing books from her own collection rather than the ones I suggested from our classroom library. She read books not suited for children's eyes, like *Dutch* by Teri Woods and *The Coldest Winter Ever* by Sister Souljah, books that were vivid and captured the reader but were full of things that little girls should not read about, like oral sex and flipping cocaine.

I asked Sydney's mother if she knew that her daughter was digging into her own reading material, only to discover that these books were indeed Sydney's property and her mother had bought them for her because they kept Sydney's interest. "As long as my baby is reading, you know what I'm saying, Ms. Lewis?"

Hey, it worked. Sydney's ability to decode multisyllabic words was just as great as her ability to analyze a character's thoughts and actions.

As much as I understood what her mother meant, however, I still tried to turn Sydney on to books that were age-appropriate, and in the process we developed a strong bond. I realized that her ability to understand concepts beyond her years was astounding. But she didn't need to read about pimps and crack houses to be stimulated; America had plenty of jaw-dropping history that was mature in substance. Sydney was ready to get the real, unadulterated truth about this country. She could learn about issues that would normally go right over the head of someone her age. If Sydney wanted raw, she was going to get it.

"Today, boys and girls, we're going to begin watching excerpts of a miniseries of videos called *Roots* in conjunction with our slavery unit for social studies," I announced one day. "It aired in the late 1970s as a television adaptation of a book by a man by the name of Alex Haley, who claimed to have traced his family lineage all the way back to Africa and a man named Kunta Kinte."

The class giggled at the idea of watching anything to do with people from Africa. But we had some takers. And as I'd anticipated, my Number One sponge was soaking up every word.

"Shhh, ya'll. This sounds interesting."

I played *Roots* for days, weeks even. Even after our unit on slavery was over, I found ways to continue playing the videos for other subjects, like writing. When we discussed supporting details, proving a thesis statement, even literal versus figurative language, I played my *Roots* tapes, giving writing activities like, "Explain how Kunta was enslaved yet still free." I asked thought-provoking questions to prompt their critical thinking, like, "Why is Kunta the only slave with shackles still on his feet?"

For many, the answer was very superficial.

"'Cause he kept trying to run away," Steve yelled out.

"Yes, but go deeper. Why was he the only one trying to run away? Weren't they all forced to work against their will?"

Sydney sucked at her teeth and rolled her eyes, disgusted by her classmates' inability to see the symbolism in Kunta's shackles.

"Duh!" she snapped. "He wasn't a slave in his mind like the rest of them fools."

I wasn't as disappointed in the other students as she was. I knew they were only ten and eleven, that they were special-education students and had been raised in a culture that didn't always encourage children to think critically. For most of them, *Roots* would serve as a story no different from that of Cinderella. I would still teach the things their young minds needed to know, like plot, character, and sequence. I would still use *Roots* as a vehicle to test their reading comprehension, such as finding the main idea, comparing and contrasting, and using context clues. But for my precious Sydney, *Roots* was intended to set her free.

And it happened just like that, as quickly and easily as a key opening a lock. Sydney had finally freed herself from her own mental prison. The burden she'd been carrying because of her color dropped to the ground and shattered to shards of glass.

We were watching the episode in which Kunta becomes smitten with a fellow slave named Belle. In an effort to compliment her, he says that a light-skinned mulatto girl isn't attractive to him and he likes a different kind of face. Belle begins to blush, but when he compares her face to the face of his Mandinka people, she becomes highly offended.

"I ain't no African!" she says. "I'm American! My daddy's American and my daddy's daddy was American."

I glanced over to Sydney, whose eyes hadn't moved from the screen. I stopped the tape. Discussion time.

Immediately, Sydney's hand shot up. "Why she bug out like that? Like, Kunta had to be saying, 'Damn, girl, I was just trying to pay yo' ass a compliment!'"

I didn't even bother to acknowledge her foul language. I let her continue.

"I mean, I know we make fun of Africans still even now, but shit. She sounded like calling her African was like spittin' in her face!"

"To her it was," I replied. "But where was she born, Sydney?"

"In America. She just said it. She was, and her daddy, and her grand-daddy and back and back and back."

"And where was Kunta born?"

"Duh. In Africa."

"And does Kunta feel uncomfortable admitting to being African?"

"Of course not! He loves it."

"So if someone told Kunta that his face looked African, what do you think he would say?" Come on, Syd. I know you got this.

"He'd probably say, 'No shit,'" she cackled. "No, for real, he would probably say, 'Thank you' 'cause he was proud. Kinda like if someone called him handsome. He took it as a compliment."

I waited for her to put it all together. I could almost see the wheels churning.

"So, Sydney, why do you think Belle isn't proud to look African?"

"'Cause in America, if you was black, you was a slave! Ain't nothing proud about that!"

She paused. "So, you mean to tell me that I think my skin is ugly be-cause I live in America and black people didn't like being black 'cause in this country black meant you was a slave?"

I nodded.

"You mean to tell me that I think I'm ugly not 'cause I really *am* ugly but because of what this country did to my ancestors? That they were ashamed and then that passed on all the way up to me?"

"That's exactly what I'm saying, Sydney."

"So if I lived in Africa, I probably would've never thought black was ugly, right?"

"Nope."

She banged her fist on her desk. "Ooh! This stupid country!"

I knew of Africans who used bleaching creams, but I wasn't going to share that detail just now. They too were victims of imperialism.

"So I'm sitting here believing the same thing these slaves believed about themselves?"

Sydney wanted to laugh and cry at the same time. She was mulling over all of this with a look on her face as if Ashton Kutcher had just run into the classroom in a trucker hat, followed by MTV cameramen, screaming, "You've been punk'd!"

Hoodwinked. Bamboozled. Led astray. Yes, Sydney had drunk the Kool-Aid. We all had. "Yes, sweetheart, you've been deceived." I chuck-led a bit despite the seriousness of the mood, hoping to quell some of her anger.

"All this time I been thinking something that was never really even my own thoughts! I hate bein' told what to do!"

I didn't know if Sydney was going to punch someone or jump for joy. I didn't even know how to respond. But finally it came. I looked her straight in the eyes. At that moment there was no one else in the room but her and me.

"So then stop listening."

Sydney never took her eyes off my face. For a few seconds she just sat there, her eyes locked with mine as though in a trance. She then proceeded to the coat closet, hung up both her bubble coat and her shame, and never wore either one inside our classroom again.

3

Love Don't Live Here Anymore

By now I'd been teaching for two years and was pretty much un scathed. Obstacles came and went. Problems arose and were solved. The ones that were here to stay I'd learned to deal with. Certain things you just learned and moved on from, like knowing to lock up anything of value whenever someone other than your own paraprofessional was around. When Antwan and his crisis para Rosetta had to spend a day in my classroom because his teacher was absent and a hundred dollars was stolen from my pocketbook, I learned that Rosetta was the school thief and that I'd better pack up my stuff when she was around.

I learned that although so-called teacher's choice money—funds we received each year for teaching supplies—was only about $250 for general-education teachers and even less for special-education teachers, teachers would spend at least a thousand dollars of their own money throughout the year. Much of the stuff we bought wasn't even something we could keep, like the bulletin board paper and borders we'd be asked to change every month and the school supplies we'd buy for our students because many parents wouldn't or couldn't buy these items themselves.

Schools often offered their own bulletin board paper, but it was cheap and tacky-looking. My students deserved classrooms that looked just as pretty and inviting as those in white neighborhoods, so I would buy the good stuff elsewhere. Some items, such as sets of books and pricy furniture that could be used in any classroom, were good investments that lasted for years. But I learned to write my name in black marker on everything I bought and hope that nothing got "lost" over the summer and landed in another teacher's classroom.

I learned to stay out of Ms. Singletary's way and not be even thirty seconds late for work to prevent being potentially embarrassed in front of others or getting a letter in my file. I learned that I'd be staying after school from one to four hours a day just to write long comments on the kids' work that most of them struggled to read and many didn't even bother to read. The days of writing "100 percent" with a smiley face, something teachers did in the old days, were long gone and the days of writing detailed "glows and grows" comments for each piece of work that went up on the bulletin board were here to stay. That meant twelve math pieces, twelve writing pieces, twelve science pieces, and twelve social studies pieces every month. It was such an odd feeling to share seemingly personal, potentially embarrassing commentary for everyone to read. I wondered if white children were embarrassed like this.

It would have been easier simply to tell each child what he or she had done well and what needed work, because my students couldn't just read a long list of instructions and understand it anyway. I would have to verbally explain my written directions to practically every child. But verbal conferences didn't leave the required paper trail, and as a result long, time-consuming paragraphs had to be written for each child for each task and be replaced every month. This never-ending busywork had less to do with student achievement and more to do with making the bulletin boards look good. It wasn't a draft for them to improve on but something that would go straight into their portfolios after they were taken down.

What was worse is that students had to have their scores posted regardless of what score they'd received, this coming down the pike as a result of Big Data and the new business model that was gradually being forced upon us. Even students who failed a task had to see big 1's on their papers posted on a bulletin board where everyone else could see them. I worried that the kids would make fun of one another, but they never paid enough attention to their scores to even bother looking at them. Many had already felt defeated, and so a 1 was just that . . . a number.

Each piece of written work required a critique that would then be critiqued by my administrator.

Attempt Number One: "Jesús, I love the bold beginning that you used in your introduction, and you did a good job with your body paragraphs, providing a strong topic sentence for each. Your essay, however, didn't contain a conclusion and left me feeling as if there was more that had to be explained. Overall, this was a solid essay and I'm very proud of you. You earned a score of 3 out of 4."

The critique of my critique was also given a 3 out of 4. According to Ms. Edwards, I shouldn't be negative at all, even if the student did something wrong. "Have the child look at their work again and ask them if they think they should do whatever it is that they need to do to improve," she advised. This didn't make sense, given that the kid wasn't going to revise the essay. This was the piece that would go up on the bulletin board and then be taken down and put in the child's portfolio.

Students were also supposed to be asked hypothetical questions. None of my children talked that way, and none of their parents did either. Heck, neither did I. If anyone were to ask me, "Do you think your aim was effective?" I would have been more insulted than if a consultant had simply said to me, "Your aim needs to be more effective." It's not as if saying "no" would have sufficed, even if I had backed it up with evidence. It was their way or the highway, so if my aim was not to an administrator's liking, I would have had to change it. Anything less was patronizing as far as I was concerned. Just the same, Jesús would need a conclusion whether he thought his essay was complete or not, so why ask him? I think he would've appreciated my "keeping it real" over a trick question.

Attempt Number Two: "Jesús, I love the bold beginning that you used in your introduction, and you did a good job with your body paragraphs as well, providing a strong topic sentence for each. Please take a look at your last paragraph provided. Do you think that you concluded your essay?" Would Jesús really have jumped out a window if he had heard a declarative statement about his lack of a conclusion?

The longer I taught, I realized that my evaluations, and any professional development I would be receiving, would be more about how I asked questions than about strengthening my content areas. Someone up top had gotten the memo that schools were too teacher-led, and like all new pedagogical approaches, a horrible game of Telephone would result in completely idiotic suggestions by administrators. Jesús could not be *told* that he lacked an introduction; he had to discover it himself. This was perplexing, as it would make sense to believe that he did not know this on his own, and if he did, he either did not care to include it or had too many issues with creating one. Still, rather than receive help on how to make the writing of a conclusion easier for Jesús, I would continue to receive input about the way I asked a freaking question. I wondered if such a focus existed in white schools across the country. Did teachers of white children receive assistance on actually developing their strength in their content areas, or were their professional development workshops and evaluations a means to micromanage them?

Every time I turned around, there were new consultants who had been hired to provide professional development to teachers. These consultants had generally never taught in the 'hood, never taught black and Latino children, and in some cases never taught at all. One particular group of consultants, Aussies, as they were called, were Australians who had been brought in to instruct us how to teach poor kids from the Bronx. The Aussies knew about literacy because Australians allegedly read more books than Americans and their country was ranked Number 4 in the world in PISA (Program for International Student Assessment) at the time. No one considered the fact that Australia's culture was very different from ours and maybe that culture, rather than the approach, had something to do with the rankings.

Despite these problems, at this stage I would have given the profession a 3 out of 4 as well. It wasn't perfect, but the kids made up for it. I was an official teacher, and a pretty damn good one.

But at a certain point, taking it all in stride was no longer an option. Things were becoming too overbearing, and fast. We teachers swallowed tension thick like arsenic-spiked milkshakes, working in a school culture that threatened the demise of our already fading spirits. I hadn't truly been on the receiving end of the abuse, but even the younger sibling who watches big brother get beat before bedtime has nightmares.

I couldn't tell you exactly what Ms. Singletary's issue with her staff was other than the fact that she managed us while under a lot of stress. A black woman in her early thirties with penetrating black eyes, bright nails, and a high-pitched voice, she had come from a community similar to the one in which she was now a figure of leadership and was the epitome of the phrase "You can take the girl out of the 'hood, but you can't take the 'hood out of the girl." That rings a bit true for me too. Not that I could ever be compared to Singletary, but there's a grit, a toughness, a chip on the shoulder typical of someone who comes from where we come from. It's a blessing and a curse, that grit. It can propel someone toward greatness or help them descend into their own hell.

Again and again I watched Singletary's relationships with teachers deteriorate. She would ream them out for seemingly trivial infractions and in the process destroy their self-confidence. I watched her give a teacher who was assigned to my reading block a failing evaluation despite his seemingly flawless lesson. She would argue that I did not have principal eyes, that there were pieces of his lesson that I overlooked as a non-administrator. I had to agree with her. She was no dummy. Maybe he did make mistakes that I was unaware of. Still, she seemed a bit harsh. He insisted that he could have walked on water and it wouldn't have mattered. She was tough for sure and offered no mercy, except with me.

You can imagine how nerve-wracking this was for me. I was glad that I was among those who had an amicable relationship with her; however, it was uncomfortable to see so many around me cower when she walked by. Her explanation for treating me with mercy might have been that I was a relatively new teacher, and good to be so young. At the age of twenty-one, with absolutely no teaching experience, I managed to discipline a bunch of boys with hair on their upper lips and bass in their voices. I managed to teach children with severe learning disabilities to like school. Kids who had previously put their heads on their desks the entire day and gone to sleep actually wrote essays for me. But was I the best teacher in the school? I would imagine that to be impossible. Maybe Singletary saw a bit of herself in me. Takes one to know one, right? Could she have known that I was from the same kind of neighborhood as she was just based on looking at me? Speaking to me?

Was it possible that she saw the connection I had with my kids, a connection that could never be truly the same with someone who was different from them? This isn't to say that teachers from other economic or ethnic backgrounds can't connect with children of the ghetto; good teachers who love children will find a way to connect with their charges even if all they have in common is love. Still, I must admit that my kids "got me" more than they got their other teachers because I *was* them—them in ten years, that is, if they didn't get caught up in the realities of 'hood living. Maybe Singletary saw this connection and celebrated me for reaching the hardest-to-reach kids because of it.

However, even though she didn't hate me, she still made sure that I viewed her as strong and emotionless. It was her armor, and she never took it off. Except once. She probably wouldn't want this revealed, but I am going to share a secret. Ms. Singletary *could* show compassion. Let me rewind a bit.

I'd been living with Trey for quite some time, and things were getting a little rocky. As with my teaching career, I was originally excited by the novelty of a new life with my beau, but also as with teaching, I learned that everything wasn't what it was cracked up to be. I started to resent him for so many things: all the times he'd left me when I was in college, for example. Trey was actually moving in the right direction and was doing everything he was supposed to at that point. I just held a serious grudge, something I didn't foresee happening at all. We both held on to our own demons and couldn't let go. The rage would manifest in our arguments, and we argued often, and hard.

Finally we called it quits, and it was an ugly breakup. Over the past few months, he'd punched holes in walls and in our car windshield. Girls whose names I didn't know began calling him. I once ran out of the house in my pajamas because I wanted to see if he'd chase me. Worst of all, I cheated. Not with my body, but with my heart. And before I could even digest my feelings, Trey picked up on them and went ballistic.

The feeling of loving another man was so foreign to me that I didn't know what to do with it. I kept my feelings to myself, but Trey knew me well enough to know that something was up, and one night he confronted me. The truth sent him into a whirlwind of emotions. After years of having my heart broken by Trey, I had finally broken his.

Regardless of how much someone might deserve it, there are no words to describe how it feels to know you've hurt someone you love. I sobbed the entire night, finally falling asleep around dawn from sheer exhaustion despite a pounding headache. Only problem was, I had to go to work the next day. The sensible thing would have been to take a mental health day. But I had just called in sick a few days earlier because of the flu. And so I staggered in with my eyes swollen from crying and a migraine that would not let up.

As soon as the payroll secretary saw me, her eyes popped. "Why didn't you stay home?" she demanded. "You look like shit."

"I didn't want to get written up for missing another day," I replied. It was true. Being absent more than one day a month was something we all dreaded. The absolute rule of thumb was to never, and I mean never, take off more than once a month unless you were on your deathbed.

"Well, let me see if I can get Ms. Singletary out of her office," the secretary said. "You really shouldn't go into your classroom looking and feeling as horrible as you do."

When she gently knocked on the principal's door, an annoyed Singletary poked her head out, then summoned me inside. "What's the problem?" she demanded as I sat down.

"I'm just having a really bad morning," I replied weakly.

"Evidently. Why did you come in? You clearly aren't in a space to teach right now."

"I know, but I had the flu last week because there's been a bug going around in my classroom, and I just didn't want to take off another day because I didn't want to get written up and—"

I couldn't hold it in any longer. I began bawling right there and then. And you won't believe what happened next. Singletary walked over to me and stared at me for a moment as if she could find written on my face the answer to a question she had. The question must have been, "What should I do?" because she hugged me tightly, the way a mother would hug her stupid "think she grown" child. I sat there in her arms and sobbed, partly relieved to have someone hold me, partly bewildered as to where on Earth this random act of kindness had come from, and mostly embarrassed because as the secretary had accurately said, I really did look like shit and now my nose was running to boot.

After we finally pulled apart, I opened up to her about everything, and for a moment she became my surrogate mother. (I had stopped talking to my mother, who had become increasingly concerned about my rela tionship with Trey.) I told her that I had broken up with my boyfriend of five years. She nodded as if to say she understood, being a woman from the 'hood herself, one who had probably shed her share of tears when she was young. She probably knew how I could cry so hard over a breakup because she understood that young love of any persuasion had its drama and that drama could only intensify in communities like ours. Singletary was a survivor, just as I was. As I sat in her office, I wondered what pain she was hiding behind those intimidating dark eyes.

As much as I had a new-found respect for Singletary's stoicism, the truth remained that working under her was literally making me sick. I was consumed with anxiety, fear, and nausea. I felt as if I were developing an ulcer. I already had a habit of biting my nails, but since working for Singletary my fingers had become sore and bleeding. I complained about work to everyone from my friends to former professors. One of those professors would ultimately be responsible for my leaving.

Mark Naison had been my favorite professor at Fordham because despite our obvious differences I felt that he understood me more than any of the others. A white Jewish man in his early sixties, he taught African American studies, and I quickly discovered that he knew our culture better than some black people did. This knowledge grew in part from the fact that he had grown up in the '60s, had been deeply involved in the civil rights movement, and had been welcomed into the family of his black girlfriend after his own family turned their backs on him.

We met my senior year after several students advised me to interview him for my journalism class. My assignment had been to explore in depth an issue affecting the college. I chose an easy one: racism on campus. Dr. Naison's name came up when I was interviewing some students of color for the assignment. They said he was the most honest and fearless professor on campus and would give me all the information I needed.

I was surprised to find out that he was a white guy. I'd expected to see a mellow Rastafarian with unkempt dreadlocks that fell to his ankles once released from a black, green, yellow, and red crocheted Rasta tam, or possibly a militant brother in all-black, maybe sporting a leather jacket and a T-shirt with a clenched black fist. I expected his office to be lined with posters of King Selassie I, the Rastas' messiah and former emperor of Ethiopia, or pictures of Marcus Garvey in his memorable feathered hat.

Instead, his office was full of books about urban studies, black studies, and education. From classic black literature like W. E. B. Du Bois's *The Souls of Black Folk* and Booker T. Washington's *Up from Slavery* to *Yo' Mama's Dysfunktional* by Robin Kelley, he left no corner of the urban experience untouched. Even his musical selections were broad. When I arrived, "Sweet Home Chicago" by Robert Johnson was playing on his boom box stereo.

I was surprised to see that his disposition was very much that of an old Jewish man: his speech pattern and the like. There was nothing about him that was phony; he wasn't a "wigga"—a wannabe black man—he was a historian, a historian on black history. I learned through our meeting that unlike what I had seen in the American public school system, Dr. Naison wasn't afraid to unmask certain truths about our people's achievements, nor was he afraid to dig up pieces of history that many white Americans would prefer stayed buried, stories that went against the narrative that we had been told about ourselves and our ambitions or lack thereof. In short, he wasn't afraid to admit the truth, regardless of how fucked-up white people may have looked, or felt.

I explained my assignment to him. We had to submit a few personal logs about our topic prior to writing the article, and in response, my professor wrote some baffling comments. In one log, I complained about being invisible to some of my white classmates and fellow Fordham students. I noted a time in which I had just unlocked the lobby door to my dorm's building and decided to wait for the two girls who were a few feet behind me. This was me being exceptionally considerate, because they were far enough away that I could have let the door close behind me without it slamming in their faces. Still, I decided to hold the door, and instead of taking the door from me or even saying 'Thank you,' the two girls continued to walk through the threshold of the door, talking to each other as though they had not seen me, while I just stood there with the door in my hand and an extremely puzzled look on my face. It wasn't long before I called out to them, "You're welcome, bitches!" To this, they turned around with the same puzzled look I'd had on my face a few moments before. In my commentary about this event, I explained that it bothered me that they treated me as if I were "a doorman," to which my professor wrote, "What's wrong with being a doorman?" This professor had always given me "A" papers, and I actually really liked her, but it was as if she did not appreciate my truth. Instead of her placing the "ism" on race, she affixed it to class, placing the shame on me rather than on the two girls. I didn't think I was better than a doorman, but I'd be damned if I were treated as such when I was there to get an education just the same as everyone else.

"What you experienced with that professor was aversive racism," Naison informed me very bluntly. He didn't make an excuse for my professor's intentional gloss over the obvious. Her ambivalence was unacceptable in his eyes. For once, I hadn't been made to feel as though I had to apologize for my feelings. That day, I discovered that racism wasn't always blatant and that I could actually label certain situations as aversively racist, that it wasn't me just being extra sensitive. In America, if a white person had treated you badly but hadn't called you a nigger to your face or hadn't burned a cross on your lawn, the bad treatment wasn't racist but, rather, a figment of your imagination. As I thought of this new term that Dr. Naison had given me, I realized that the entire public school system was an aversively racist institution. We were no longer shunned from white restrooms and water fountains, but our students were being robbed of the same resources found in public schools in New York City known for being predominantly white because of "property tax." It wasn't racial, it was economic; however, let's not pretend we don't know who the poor folk in New York City are. To date, of all my years of teaching in the 'hood, I have never had a white student in my class.

Even less obvious to many was the lack of cultural connections provided in typical school curricula. Many educators saw education as consisting merely of textual facts and figures; they did not think race or culture was relevant to what their students needed to learn. Many did not consider the fact that education was never meant for our students, as black slaves were not even allowed to read and Hispanics had not even arrived in our country. The education model, like every other institution in our nation, was created for the improvement of white people. Our learning styles and affinities were never considered, and our history was considered only in February. And this history included only the years since our enslavement, excluding our history before the Middle Passage. Our years in slavery were never taught to students for the purpose of overcoming mental slavery, as I had with Sydney. Our curriculum never taught about Mansa Musa, king of the thirteenth-century Malian empire, ranked as the richest man to ever live, above Sam Walton, Warren Buffett, and Bill Gates's combined net worth. Most students would never learn that Africa is the richest continent in natural resources. There was so much to learn about their people that our school system in America would never deem important to teach. There were some teachers like me, who made attempts to teach them what they needed to know, but it wasn't mandatory, which meant that if a teacher decided not to, her children would remain ignorant to the greatness of their people. I hadn't learned of Tulsa, Oklahoma's Black Wall Street and how white rioters had burned it down until I sat in Dr. Naison's class. Public school students never learned of this affluent, self-sufficient black community composed of twenty-one churches, twenty-one restaurants, thirty grocery stores, two movie theaters, banks, post offices, and transportation systems. They would never learn about black excellence at its best.

Back in the 1940s, psychologists Kenneth and Mamie Clark helped to prove that segregation created feelings of inferiority in black children through the use of what has been colloquially termed "the Doll Test," an experiment in which black children were asked to assign characteristics to an identical set of dolls, different only in race. The majority of these black children preferred the white doll to play with over the black doll and assigned positive characteristics to the white doll. These findings ultimately contributed to the *Brown v. Board of Education* court decision to integrate schools.

Since then, however, the Doll Test had been re-created several times, including the most recently aired instance on CNN's *AC360* with Anderson Cooper and Soledad O'Brien in 2010, and the findings were almost identical to the results of the Doll Tests conducted in the 1940s. Even in the new millennium, black children were still assigning positive characteristics only to white faces. The integration ruling could not stand alone in combating these feelings of inferiority because we were still racially segregated among economic lines. Furthermore, even schools that were more diverse contained black and brown children who lacked self-love. It was clear to me that findings of doll tests would remain the same until black children were taught their own greatness. Only then would black children choose the black doll. In the meantime, I felt it was my responsibility to not allow my black students the choice, but to choose for them.

After my meeting with Dr. Naison, I knew immediately that I would take his class my final semester. I knew there would be no holding my tongue. Dr. Naison was a lifelong activist and refused to stand for injustice. It was no surprise that I remained in touch with him long after graduation.

When I told Naison about how Singletary ran her school, he found the situation deplorable. More times than I could count, he tried to persuade me to leave. I couldn't help but be reminded of the white candidates I had competed against when applying for the teaching fellowship. Once again the "white guy" was talking about what was and wasn't acceptable. As he spoke, I reflected back on the answer to the question that had won over my interviewers during the admissions process, the question in which we were asked what we'd do if our mentor didn't show up. I thought of the answers the white kids had given. Dr. Naison, like my former rivals, had grown up in a world in which certain things simply weren't tolerated. He would rock the boat in a heartbeat.

"Pam, this is nonsensical," he said to me again and again. "To let yourself remain in an organization where you're abused just doesn't make sense. I have friends who are principals and assistant principals and who would love to have a jewel like you on their team."

"But I wouldn't necessarily call it *abuse*, just very rigid," I replied in Singletary's defense.

I knew she had to have a tough shell being both black and female. I was sure she felt that if she showed tolerance of any kind people would walk all over her. I was sure she even had to fight against those who were angry that she was in a superior position. The truth of the matter was, many white people hate the idea of having a black man or woman as a boss. I was also positive in the fact that I wanted to make excuses for her, that in some weird way I loved her, just because. I knew she was under pressure, and it bothered me to see a bunch of white people coming in to check in on her and her school every day. I wanted her to win, I wanted her to be victorious. Still, I also wanted to kick this nervous condition that had begun to develop since I'd been working there.

He was right. Why was I worried about hurting Singletary's feelings? I could be working somewhere where I was happier.

As I complained to my former professor about my problems, I couldn't help but wonder why blacks were so quick to accept wrongs being done to us. What would it have taken for me to finally say, "Enough is enough"? Was it our history of slavery that allowed us to just grin and bear it? Did we feel we weren't good enough to have the very best life had to offer?

I was probably only one of few teachers who did, but I cared about Ms. Singletary. She was tough, and I knew that toughness had come from somewhere. She was also suspicious of everyone, and I had no idea what she could have encountered before and during her principalship. Being a black woman principal was a big deal. I could only imagine what kind of haters, both whites and people of color, had tried to bring her down.

We black folks had a saying about ourselves. Unlike other races that stuck together, we often displayed the behavior typical of crabs in a barrel. Snatched from their freedom, crabs held captive in a barrel will climb on top of one another to try to get out of the barrel. Because it would be impossible for all the crabs to climb to the top and escape, the ones that were close to escaping were usually pulled down by the other crabs. The spots for black leadership within education and every other field were slim to none. So it was in the real world. As a result, we as a people will often identify with stories regarding this kind of behavior. And if you still have not realized where this conduct originated, let's say it together: *SLAVERY.*

In the meantime, I threw myself into my work. Aside from the mindless paperwork, I had the job of actually trying to get students, many of whom were two to three grade levels behind and seemingly uninterested in much of what school had to offer, to pass an exam. While my colleagues walked around reciting sing-songy words of encouragement like "Super!" and "Great job!" I relied on my hipness and youth to relate to the kids in different ways. "That's dope!" I'd say to my boys already going through puberty. And when they got too rambunctious: "Chill! You're wildin' out!"

Being from the inner city can definitely win you some cool points, and being young didn't hurt either. Many of the little boys in my class had crushes on me at first, but these crushes developed into a son's love for his mother or at the very least for an aunt or big sister. As young as I was,

I was tall and I was tough. Despite how rough some of my boys were, I developed enough classroom-management skills to make sure they never fought in front of me. The minute I thought one was even *thinking* about turning violent, I'd demand in my deepest voice, "We got a problem?"

I had no problem letting a boy know that he couldn't intimidate me. So many of the boys who would be wrongfully labeled emotionally disturbed and put on medication simply needed someone strong enough to deal with them and their issues. While therapy was definitely something these boys benefited from, respect was something that we teachers of color definitely required. Many teachers of color I knew could defuse a potentially aggressive situation with something as simple as a look, a look that said, "Don't you dare bring that foolishness into my classroom." We were more than their teachers; we were family, and we demanded the same level of respect, which they often gave.

Some parents even playfully suggested that I could hit their children for misbehavior, something they knew I would *never* consider, nor did I truly believe they would have been fine. Often, these parents came from other countries, or had attended Catholic school during a time when being paddled was accepted. It was their way of sharing their authority with me, as spanking a child was acceptable only by parents or in institutions where teachers were revered and feared. Even more often, parents would offer to beat their children for me, those who knew what the consequences would be of my actually doing something so outrageous. These parents were ready and willing to come to the classroom and beat their children in front of the entire class, as a way to humiliate their children into good behavior. I of course declined all such offers; however, I understood that this was a cultural normality and a remnant of slavery. Violence was passed down from generation to generation and had not originated only from the master's crack of the whip but out of slave mothers' fears that their children would be sold away if the children partook in mischief as children sometimes do. Beating their children was better than a beating from the master, and definitely better than being sent away. I didn't agree with their methods, but I understood where they were coming from. Of course, in other places in the country, such treatment was looked down upon even if performed by a child's parent, but in the 'hood, I can guarantee the lack of judgment that never came for one's beating of his or her child.

My boys proved to be protective of me as well, although their feelings sometimes manifested themselves in unexpected ways, as was the case with Alfonso. Alfonso had issues with reality, although he could read you the *Wall Street Journal*. The only problem was, once asked what he had just read, he would tell you "Superman." In fact, he thought he *was* Superman and would blow on kids with his icy breath to freeze them whenever they made him angry or burn them with heat vision that he shot out of his eyes. Alfonso was also fond of me. He'd confess his love for me in the middle of a lesson and sing me love ballads in Spanish. He also had issues with personal space and would stroke my hand or pet me like a dog.

"Get off of my teacher!" my other boys would scream at him.

"Leave her alone!"

"Stop petting her head. She look like a dog to you?"

Alfonso would always respond in one of two ways.

"She's my teacher too." Or, what truly made my heart melt, "But I love her."

He did, and he didn't know any better. I'd tell him that I loved him too and so did his classmates, to which he'd then chortle, "Yeah, right!" or some other skeptical response. Usually, one of my sweeter boys would chime in at this point and say something encouraging that would make him smile. As for his petting, I would simply remove his hand from my head and hold it in mine for a few seconds before handing him a pencil. Ms. Lake would take the cue and immediately walk over and sit with him for the remainder of the period.

———

Trip days were the worst. I always hoped we'd take the school bus rather than walk or take the train because those trips meant having to deal with the men on the street. One would think that the cat-calling typically accepted in communities like the South Bronx would stop in the presence of children. For some reason, I imagined that a woman walking with an entire class of elementary school students would get a pass for that one day. Having grown up in Edenwald Projects and heard men objectify my mother as we walked down the street, I should have known better. To be silent would have been to be ashamed of one's objectification of the woman's body. Doing so was in fact not only acceptable but expected. Men and teenage boys performed this ritualistic mating call despite the frequency of rejections. Their intent was not so much to "bag a shorty" as much as it was to assert pseudo-power, of which they usually had none. In fact, it was the men who had nothing going for themselves who demanded the most attention to be seen. They might as well have been screaming, "Pay attention to me, please!" or "I'm not insecure!"

Those who did have money—through whatever means that might have been—still struggled with their esteem so much that all the money, cars, and attention they received was not enough to keep them silent. They still needed more.

"Damn, Ma, your ass is fat!" a man on the sidewalk screamed one day as I walked past with my class. Usually I'd flip the bird to someone so uncouth, but given that I was surrounded by impressionable children, I chose to ignore the statement. *Just keep walking, Pam. You'll be up the block and away from that creep in a minute.* Problem was, there was another creep on the block up ahead. Then another and another.

Usually during these walks my students would merely snicker. However, sometimes a few of my boys would retaliate, by telling the guys to shut up or eyeballing them from a distance, as if their spindly little bodies could ever match up to the physique of a grown man. The boys in my class had grown up around these types of men and were all too familiar with the way they objectified women, some of whom had already probably begun this rite of passage themselves when in the presence of older boys.

Even during lunchtime, when my boys were allowed to gather in the cafeteria, I'd worry about the well-being of the few girls in our class. I felt the need to protect them, remembering back to when I was a young girl. I would remember the fear I felt whenever I had to use the restroom in middle school, alone in a hallway filled with lurking boys who were waiting to pounce on fresh prey. Several times I would be met by a gang of boys who would circle me like hungry piranha and trap me. One would hold me down while the others groped and "copped feels," as they called it. I was too afraid to scream and too afraid to even admit to being afraid, saying no more to my molesters than, "Chill. Ya'll play too much." These boys were as bold to even attempt touching me while my entire class of tracked honor students walked together to our next class. A couple of my friends who were considered unpopular and nerds but were still athletic and able to kick some ass would push them off me as we continued to walk the halls. As a result of these experiences, I paid close attention to the whereabouts of my girls when they left my supervision. I knew what many little boys were being taught to think about women of their own kind and I knew the power it would bring boys who felt as if they had none.

Black feminist scholar Moya Bailey even created a term for our experiences as black women. *Misogynoir* examines how race and gender often intertwine to create a deeper level of typical sexism already inflicted on white women. We see it rear its repulsive head in many instances, in shameful acts committed by various groups, including our own brothers. My male students were learning at an early age to question the value of women of color; I had to demand respect and present myself as Teacher Momma in order to shift my experience from no respect to ultimate respect.

In turn, my boys proved to be more protectors than aggressors. My boys were seemingly torn between what their environment taught them was expected of a man and their respect for me. But respecting me posed a problem as well. *Do I respect Ms. Lewis by defending her honor or do I respect her demands to keep my mouth shut and keep walking?* It took a kid who decided to defend my honor while simultaneously ignoring my authority to cause some real ruckus.

———————

Now is as good a time as any to introduce you to Lorenzo. I actually wanted to take Lorenzo home, change his last name to Lewis, and pass him off as my son. Of course, not at first. At first, as with Sydney, I thought he would be the death of me.

I first laid eyes on Lorenzo the day Ms. Edwards came to the door of my classroom with him by the arm and an explanation.

"Lorenzo and Mr. Capella aren't meshing well at all," she announced. "We think it would be best if we kept Lorenzo with you."

Mr. Capella was the other fifth-grade special-education teacher. He taught the students who were labeled emotionally disturbed, and I taught the students who were labeled learning-disabled, not that the line was always clear.

"But I have twelve kids already," I protested. "I thought—"

"You thought right," Ms. Edwards replied. "But considering the situation, it'll be counted as a variance." She nudged Lorenzo inside and vanished.

Lorenzo had big, brilliant eyes that were deceiving. He looked like a sweet little boy who could do no wrong.

"So what did you do?" I wondered aloud.

"I told Mr. Capella to suck my dick and called him a motherfucking faggot." He spoke these words to me as calmly as if he had been broadcasting the weather.

Ah.

Lorenzo ran past me and crawled under the first desk he could find. He should have had a 1:1, a paraprofessional just for him. I always managed to keep one paraprofessional because each year I'd end up with a student in need of a 1:1. However, because of budget cuts, the only 1:1's provided by this time were health paras. A health para might have to take to the bathroom children who are physically disabled or escort them to the nurse for daily medication. A 1:1 could also be a crisis para who had to supervise an emotionally disturbed child. Lorenzo would have been the ideal candidate for a crisis para. But though these paras are still found in District 75 schools, the chance of finding them in regular schools today is slim to none.

Lorenzo simply didn't adhere to rules. Lorenzo did his assignments and followed class rules, at least most of the time. But if he chose to ignore me, there wasn't a thing I could do about it. But our relationship grew strong not so much because he respected me more than he respected Mr. Capella but because he liked me as a person. He decided to make my life as easy as possible and therefore didn't usually add stress to an already stressful situation. In his ten-year-old brain, he believed that his decisions to not listen to me were decisions that would not hurt me.

For example, when I didn't get a chance to finish the Chinese food I was eating at my desk during lunch, Lorenzo didn't think twice about walking to the back of the classroom, grabbing my fork, and helping himself to a heaping mouthful of broccoli with garlic sauce. As far as he was concerned, I was his Teacher Momma and such intimate acts normally exclusive to family applied to us as well. He didn't think of how badly something so innocent could go. He didn't know that all it took was one kid going home and saying Ms. Lewis and Lorenzo did something as inappropriate as share an eating utensil to put me in the rubber room. Luckily no one mentioned it, and, just in case, I threw out the rest of my lunch.

Then there were his outbursts.

"Would y'all shut the fuck up and let her teach? Y'all niggar talk too goddamn much!"

As often as I'd asked Lorenzo to stop calling out without raising his hand, intimidating his peers, and using profanity, he continued to do all three. When Lorenzo cursed out his peers, he sincerely thought he was doing me a favor. I knew this because he would always turn to me afterward and smile.

"Suck a dick, you fucking faggot." This Lorenzo said to the man who apparently felt the need to alert the entire block to my plump rump.

The man appeared to be amused by Lorenzo's defense. It only prompted him to continue.

"You wanna keep all that goodness to yourself, little nigga? I feel you. I would too. Ya'll some lucky ass kids. I *wish* I had *that* for a teacher when I was your age. Mighta paid more attention." The man licked his lips. I was no longer a person but a *that*.

My few girls—as special education was usually dominated by black and brown boys—were now on the verge of vomiting. They just looked at me in disbelief. I felt for them the most; they too would soon have to deal with this. Princess was indifferent. I looked her over and realized she was already accustomed to it. She reminded me so much of myself at her age—a little girl in a grown woman's body. She had already begun menstruating. Her mother had informed me of this after she had been absent from school for two days and I called to find out what was wrong. Her mother said she couldn't afford any more Maxi-Pads that month and their family of women had run out.

"We're all sync'd up in here! We 'bout to kill each other, Ma!" *Ma* was me.

"Okay, well you know there's . . . err, umm, sanitary napkins in the nurse's station. Princess can come in and will be fine! They may even give you some to take home."

"Nah, we're good. Please, you don't wanna deal with Princess and her pissy attitude right now, trust me! Just give me some work for her to do at home. She'll catch up."

Again, an intimate conversation for an intimate relationship between mother and teacher.

Nyasia, who was but a pipsqueak and innocent as a dove, just continued to stare at me with "Why" eyes.

"Because they can, honey. Get used to it." That's what I wanted to tell her. Instead, I just smoothed her hair down and smiled.

The silence was deafening as we continued our walk of shame, shame on society for creating men like this, shame on those men who could not care less that children were present, shame on me for not knowing anything better to do than to be quiet. Lorenzo fixed that.

"Like she'd ever fuck with a bum-ass nigga like you. Pussy." For good measure, Lorenzo grabbed his testicles and shook them in the man's direction, then spat on the ground. Again, he turned to me and smiled, as if to say, "You're welcome."

Somehow when signing over your life to this job, you don't ever think of these scenarios.

It was one month before our class's turn for assembly. When I was growing up, the mere idea of an assembly elicited pure excitement. An assembly offered was a chance to get out of the seat you'd been sitting in every day for the entire year to look at something different. Whether it was an assembly on fire safety, an awards assembly, or, best of all, some kind of musical show didn't matter. The prospect of an assembly was enough to make me jittery all day as I anticipated being able to watch something that I could learn from, receive praise for, or be entertained by.

Holiday shows and musical performances had been an especially big deal at my elementary school. My music teacher, Mr. Graff, always co-ordinated one show for the kids and an evening show for the parents. My name would usually be typed all over the program because I was in several choruses, including the elite Choral Ensemble, for which I had needed to audition. As a member of that group, I was one of twelve girls who got to sing in three-part harmony and wear black skirts and white button-down shirts to all of our performances. We even left the building to sing for dignitaries like Governor Mario Cuomo.

But one thing I'd learned since my employment as a teacher was that each school had its own way of doing things, and the assemblies I had witnessed in the school where I taught were downright depressing. Some shows were so pathetic that kids literally fell asleep in their seats. Teachers were simply too tired to be creative. We had to spend most of our time doing silly "busy" work that administrators made us do to prove we were teaching, paperwork that did not assist in a child's learning at all. Luckily for me, I had Ms. Lake—and the Internet.

I also had one of my bright ideas. Dr. Naison had just began a project to trace the otherwise unknown history of African Americans in the Bronx. While seeking information about this population, he was shocked to discover that virtually all of the information on the Bronx and its culture, other than the borough's being the birthplace of rap, had to do with Hispanics. An entire generation of blacks seemed to have been left out of Bronx history, notably blacks who had migrated from Harlem and had contributed immensely to the borough's culture. Determined to have this information recorded, Naison went to the streets and began conducting oral history interviews of old-timers whose heyday was the 1950s and '60s.

As I began to read the information he collected, I learned a great deal about the Bronx and specifically the South Bronx, the neighborhood where I was teaching. Naison's analysis of what had gone wrong in a one-time cultural hub like the South Bronx was nothing short of amazing.

For most people, the South Bronx was simply a symbol of urban decay. When outsiders pictured the neighborhood, they invariably thought about drugs, violence, and run-down tenements. They thought of an abandoned community. They thought of poverty.

After reading Naison's interviews describing what the neighborhood used to be like, recounting how even after the community declined as a result of a major ongoing fiscal crisis, rappers created a genre of music despite hardly any resources and introduced the world to a style that produced some of the biggest-selling records in music history, I had a new-found respect for my community. Being a Bronxite myself, I knew much of the history about rap and innovation, but I had never seen it articulated so well. Three decades earlier, the talents and artistry had been stripped from what was once a thriving community through various budget cuts across the city that resulted in shuttered after-school and music programs.

I wanted my students to have the same sense of pride about where they came from. So I taught them a watered-down version of what I learned through my professor's interviews. These lessons eventually became a chronological story of our community's history through music that my kids would perform for their assembly.

I wanted my kids to know that the styles of music that came from the community had been spawned by the resources and mindsets of the people who had lived there over several generations, and that the music changed when the environment changed. Starting in the 1950s, the decade when doo-wop reigned, artists emerged from the South Bronx who had an amazing talent for singing. Kids sang in the choir because back then many of them still went to church, or they took part in after-school programs in their schools, programs that taught the arts and gave them musical skills that would stay with them forever. The South Bronx was also a major cultural hub for legendary jazz and Latin jazz artists.

I wanted my kids to know that their neighborhood had a rich culture. They needed something to be proud of. When the drug epidemic hit hard, things had begun to decline. The Bronx literally began to burn from fires caused by arson that could be seen on the train as people passed through crumbling neighborhoods. As the landscape changed, family dynamics and the culture began to change as well. Educational and social service programs lost their funding. Though gangs had hardly been unknown in the borough, by the late '70s and the '80s kids had more opportunities to buy illegal guns. The scourge of drugs—first heroin, then cocaine—began devastating families and making the streets terrifying. Increasingly, the South Bronx was a part of the city ignored by the government and by everyone else who could have helped to address its myriad problems.

Hip-hop was born out of a lack of resources and genius innovation.

While for the most part kids were no longer learning how to sing and play instruments, they learned to make an instrument out of a record player and rap to the beat. In the early '80s, Grandmaster Flash and the Furious Five created "The Message," a song that chronicled the devastation taking place before their eyes. A new street culture was born.

I taught my kids the story of their community, and they oohed and aahed as I played music and showed them dances and videos. I made the story even more real by telling them where these musicians lived—block, building number, and all. "My cousin lives in that building!" Steve shouted when I told him Grandmaster Flash used to live on Fox Street.

But I wanted to do more. I wanted to bring this culture back, to let my students see it first-hand as if they were living it. The only way I could think to do so was to get them to *be* the artists, to learn their songs, learn their moves, and perform their songs. Call it a stereotype, but my people *danced*, my people *sang*. Sure, not every black and Latino child has rhythm, but seriously, folks, it's in our veins. W. E. B. Du Bois discusses our inherent artistic impulse in *The Souls of Black Folk*. There's nothing wrong with admitting that we're artistically inclined people, and this was a great way to showcase that. Furthermore, I never encountered a child who didn't like music. I realized what I wanted to do for my class assembly.

My kids were going to dance through the decades and in the process teach a story of their community through the different genres popular during those years. They would be a living, breathing history lesson and have fun in the process. We'd start in the 1950s and work our way forward. Not to mention, my students would be paying homage to the forefathers of rap by having a schoolyard jam outside rather than in a stuffy auditorium. Unlike the original rappers, however, we wouldn't steal electricity from the streetlights to power our deejay equipment. I planned to get an extension cord long enough to run from inside the school to the deejay equipment in the yard so that we'd be totally legit. It was tempting to do as the rappers had done, but I needed my job.

The event would also include two Spanish songs. One reflected the Latin jazz presence in the South Bronx, and for that number I chose several girls to dance to a choreographed salsa number in tropical floral print dresses and flowers in their hair. That was easy, because many of the Puerto Rican girls in my class were accustomed to dancing at home with their parents and extended families. The other number was a *bachata* song that was more current as a result of the Dominican population's having grown exponentially since the '90s. I had seen it first-hand when I attended John F. Kennedy High School in the northwest Bronx, a school with an overwhelming Dominican population. Going to a school where more than half of the population was Dominican, a girl learns to love some *bachata*.

"One, two, three, pop! Two, two, three, pop!" I screamed my counts at the kids, who were surprised to see that I knew how to dance "Spanish."

For the doo-wop song my students would perform to, I decided to teach them a swing dance. I found a guy who knew how to ballroom dance and had posted pictures of himself in classes and competitions and invited him to our school. He taught my kids the basic step and even incorporated some fancy moves. Little Eliana, who was my only third-grader—although mine was officially a fifth-grade class, a special-education class like mine could, as noted earlier, have up to three grades in one classroom—was chosen to be Mathew's partner because she was small enough and light enough to be tossed into the air. Eliana did very well for her first try. She sat on the floor behind Mathew, who reached for her hand from between his legs. She let him snatch her from behind and jerk her into the air like a kettle bell. While in mid-air, she had to balance herself enough to land on both feet in front of him. She was amazing.

I also planned to wow the audience with the dancers' wardrobes. I put the boys in their school uniform vests and pasted big varsity letters on their chests to suggest the collegiate look of the doo-wop performers they would be impersonating. Eliana and the girls also did a number in which they would be wearing fluffy pink chiffon dresses, bob-cut wigs, and elbow-length white satin gloves to perform a song by a group that also came from our school's neighborhood.

The wardrobes of the rappers who flourished from the late '70s through the '90s were just as spectacular. My boys would be portraying Grandmaster Flash and the Furious Five, one of the first rap groups to emerge on the scene, and they had been a dramatic-looking group. Unlike the rappers we see on stage today, who wear jeans and hoodies, the first rappers were as done up as the glam rockers late '70s and '80s. Rappers wore headdresses, spikes, feathers, leather, heeled boots, and colorful outfits. They were show-stoppers, and being costume-y was part of their persona. My boys had the shades, the hats, the cut-off gloves, and denim vests. One even wore a spiked wristband.

My last group, being representative of early '90s hip-hop and beyond, wore Yankee visors, pin-striped Yankee jerseys, shorts, and knee pads in typical "fly girl" attire. The "Fly Girls," choreographed by Rosie Perez and of whom Jennifer Lopez was once a member, was a dance troupe part of the skit comedy show *In Living Color*, created by Keenen Ivory Wayans. The group opened and closed the show and sometimes danced during the breaks between commercials. Dance troupes were huge in the '90s and popular additions to all modes of entertainment, but especially rap and new-school rhythm and blues. By the time I put the last door-knocker earring on, they looked as if they were straight off the set of a Mary J. Blige "Real Love" music video.

When I told Dr. Naison what I was doing, he was ecstatic. Press releases were sent to the local TV stations. This was getting bigger than I had anticipated. What was supposed to be a simple assembly had become a schoolyard jam with a real deejay whom I had recruited for the occasion, real dance moves taught by a trained ballroom professional, elaborate costumes, and press that would be reporting on the event. Ms. Singletary was going to be thrilled.

"Since it's going to be outside, why don't we have a barbecue for the kids?" she suggested one day.

"Sure," I agreed. "Let's do it." Not only would my kids have a great time, but all the kids in the upper grades would be able to watch the show and eat some hot dogs and burgers too.

Ms. Singletary had the payroll secretary give me $100 from petty cash. I just looked at her.

"This won't cover the entire third, fourth, and fifth grades," I said.

"I don't know, girl," she replied. "Stretch it out as best as you can."

Clearly, I was also going to be the one to shop for this barbecue. My colleague Sylvia agreed to drive me to the supermarket, because I still didn't have a license. There we bought hamburgers, hot dogs, buns, containers of ketchup and mustard, and bottles of soda. Altogether, we spent more than $300. I wondered if I should have even bothered getting a receipt.

The day finally arrived. My kids were dressed to the nines. The deejay had set up his equipment. The food was on the grill. A TV reporter came with his cameraman and asked to speak with me. I talked to him for a while, explaining what the performance was going to be about. He also interviewed some of my kids.

Dr. Naison came too, of course. After all, it was his research that I had used to teach my students about their neighborhood. And he brought someone with him, a jovial African American woman in her fifties.

"This, Pam, is Mrs. Regina Giles," Dr. Naison said, introducing us. "She's the principal of an elementary school up the block."

"Hello, Mrs. Giles," I replied, holding out my hand. Naison was up to something.

"Why, hello, Ms. Lewis. It appears that you have put a lot of preparation into this. Did you do this all by yourself?"

"Pretty much."

"Now that's impressive."

The two of them found seats in the audience. It was time to begin.

Group by group, my students performed as the crowd went berserk. It was clear that they had never seen anything like this, a history lesson in the form of music, dance, and elaborate costumes. And, most important, the kids were having the time of their lives.

There were a few minor glitches. When Mathew snatched Eliana from underneath his leg, he pulled a bit too hard and sent her flying farther than expected. She landed on her behind instead of on her feet, and her cute little bob-cut wig fell off her head. *Note to self: Leave the acrobatic stunts to the experts.*

But overall the event was a huge success. Even my boys who were too cool to dance did their thing. They performed to Grandmaster Flash and the Furious Five's "The Message," lip-sync'ing about "people pissing on the stairs" and "stickup kids" doing "eight-year bids." I had the deejay scratch over the word *piss* to avoid complaints from parents, but I didn't mind. These kids knew all too well the horrors of the ghetto.

After a student named Ricky wowed us with his hops, flares, and finally a freeze in the air, feats I didn't believe he could accomplish until he told me about his subway breakdance crew that earned him a minimum of $50 a week, it was official: My kids had made South Bronx history. As hard as I had worked, it was worth it. The smiles on their faces were priceless. The smiles on the faces of the audience were priceless. Everyone congratulated us. Everyone, that is, except Ms. Singletary. She headed back into the school without even a thank you.

Let's be clear. I didn't put together this program for praise. I did it because I wanted to give my kids an opportunity to do something they enjoyed. I wanted to give them something they'd remember for the rest of their lives. I did it because I loved music, I loved my culture, and I knew that my kids, like me, had music in their souls.

I had another goal. To succeed in life, my students needed a means of escaping their present mindset without abandoning their communities. The performing arts offered one such means. These roles gave my students a sense of who they were, an appreciation of who they are now, and ambition for who they might someday become. I wanted to give them different eyes to see with, eyes that would let them look past the realities of their neighborhood to see that life there wasn't always so dismal.

And when you give your all for something, you expect at the very least a "Good job." Was Ms. Singletary angry because I hadn't acknowledged her to the reporters? Was she upset because Eliana had fallen, even though she hadn't hurt herself? Was it Mrs. Giles's presence? Did she think the whole performance had been a setup so that she would hire me? Was she simply jealous of all the attention I had received that day? I never knew and I never asked. You didn't ask Ms. Singletary questions.

But before I could feel guilty for expecting some kind of acknowledgment, Dr. Naison's expression helped me realize that my feelings were completely justified. As Ms. Singletary marched off in silence, his eyes followed her with a hatred that could be rivaled only by the look of a parent furious that his child had been passed over for the lead in the school play. Dr. Naison may not have been my dad, but as my mentor and as someone who had watched me mature from a student to a teacher of students, from someone who needed help and support to someone who devoted her life to supporting others, I could understand his contempt.

"Hello?"

"Pam. It's me. I need to see you."

Trey still had my heart, and he knew it. We hadn't spoken since I'd moved back in with my mother. Although I had given her the silent treatment the entire time I had lived with him, when we called it quits she was of course, the first one I called. And of course, she let me move back in. I decided to let him come over one day when my mother wasn't home. Dumb.

He looked beautiful as usual when he showed up at my front door. I had been so busy working that I hadn't thought about him much, but when I saw him standing there, I remembered just how in love with him I had once been.

"I need to tell you something," Trey announced. His voice trailed off as if he were trying to rationalize something in his head.

I took his hand and stroked it. He smiled as he let me lead him into the apartment.

For a while, we just stared at each other, not knowing what to say but comforted in each other's presence. It was a familiar feeling. I was used to spending time away from him and our finding our way back to each other eventually. We had so much history.

"Remember that summer when your mom asked me to take you to that Fieldston program every day because she didn't want you to take the bus all the way to Riverdale by yourself?" He shook his head, thinking about how overly protective my mother was.

"Yeah," I replied, a bit embarrassed. "I was thirteen, but she still treated me like a baby."

"And remember when you kept me company that summer, and I stole your Wu-Tang CD because I told you it was too explicit for you to listen to?"

He pulled me even closer. I felt myself getting weak. Trey had seen me grow up. We were like Omar Epps and Sanaa Lathan in *Love & Basketball*, only I didn't play ball and we didn't live in a nice black suburban neighborhood.

"Yeah." I giggled like a five-year-old.

"And remember when I asked you if the bodega had loosies, and you said you didn't know, trying to front like you even knew what loosies were?" He was laughing by now, thinking back to old times. He had been only fourteen but chain-smoked Newports, while I didn't even know that cigarettes could be bought individually.

"The point I'm making, Pam, is that you were innocent before me. I took your innocence, and I hate myself every day for it. I have to be honest. You fell fast. I was still a dumb kid with problems. I thought you were gorgeous and always secretly had a thing for you, but I didn't think I was good enough for you. And because I didn't know what to do with your love, I threw your heart away. And I am just so damn sorry, baby."

He said those last three words in slow motion as if he were flashing back to every dumb moment over the years, every time he'd acted inconsiderately, every time I reacted immaturely to his actions. We misconstrued love for readiness, and the tragic reality was that all the love in the world wouldn't have made us ready for the commitment needed in a serious relationship. As he tried to compose himself, I rubbed his back. I knew he was sorry. I was too.

"Pam, I know it looked like I didn't love you," he continued. "But I'm a broken man. We all are. A bunch of broken brothers. But you know what? This broken brother was slowly changing for good, and it's all because of you. By the time we moved in together, I know it took some time, but I was madly in love with you. Just seeing how you stuck it out for me despite how much I had hurt you. I truly thought we were going to make it. The problem was, I didn't factor in something that was detrimental to our growth. You had grown to resent me and for good fucking reason."

He was right. I had become so resentful of Trey that even his laugh had begun to annoy me.

"I don't want you to walk around here feeling like you're the worst person on Earth. I had it coming to me, baby. And between your innocence and me breaking your heart, I just want you to know that you were the victim in this. Not me."

By now I was crying uncontrollably. Trey had lifted a burden I had been carrying on my shoulders for months. I was a good girl who didn't hurt other people's feelings. I was someone who always accomplished her goals and her dreams. *Failure* and *giving up* weren't in my vocabulary. Not being able to make our relationship run successfully made me feel guilty. The guilt had gnawed at my soul every day, although I was so immersed in work that no one would have known. He took me in his arms. As he started kissing me the same way I remembered, it seemed we were going to pick up where we had left off. But then he held my face one last time as if he wanted to say something and instead turned to walk away. (I know, this was beginning to sound like one of those melodramatic Spanish *telenovelas*, right?)

"Baby, what's wrong? Did I do something wrong?"

"No, you didn't," he replied. "I just wanted to come here and kiss you one last time. I curse myself for not being patient and waiting longer before we made us happen. We could've had something that would last forever, but I let things start when we were too young to handle it. It'll never be right again. You deserve someone who knew what he had from the beginning. I want you to find happiness without the resentment attached."

And just like that, he proceeded to walk out of my life—again. In my heart I knew he was telling the truth, but I couldn't stand to see him walk away. I loved him. I also had developed anxiety over the idea of abandonment. This anxiety had begun in middle school and worsened when Trey repeatedly left back in college, but the problem was never addressed. At the time, I didn't know what a panic attack was. All I knew was that any time I was left alone with my thoughts about his whereabouts, I couldn't breathe. Afraid to tell my mother the truth, I held my tears for my pillow every night for six months until he finally called. Then the cycle would begin again. Trey would end up leaving three times, each more painful than the last.

As a result of his leaving so many times, I would lose my mind at the sight of a door closing in my face, even if the closing of the door was temporary. When we argued, Trey couldn't even go out for some fresh air without my panicking. I'd throw myself in front of the door, trying to keep him and my anxiety inside as he attempted to pry me off his body. My determination to keep him gave me superhuman strength, or so I thought. On this occasion I found myself doing this Wonder Woman move before I could even think.

In the past, Trey usually grew tired of wrestling and eventually retired to an empty room to cool off. This time was different.

"Pam, I don't want to hurt you! Let me leave, please?" Trey hated confronting his feelings, whereas I could never turn them off.

"No! Sit down and let's talk about it. Just don't walk out the door." I was crying and having trouble breathing. I grabbed his arm and began pulling and pushing him away from the door. He'd wriggle his arm loose and head for the door again. This went on for a while until finally he had had enough.

"Pam, get off of me," he said like he meant it.

"No!" We were both out of breath and panting by now. "I won't."

I held on with all of my strength as he continued to try to get away, but he couldn't pry me off this time, not gently anyway.

Gritting his teeth and using more of his strength this time, Trey curled his arm inward to gain the proper momentum.

"Get—

"—off!" He jerked his hand away, and wriggled loose, the motion flicking me off him as a dog would a flea. I lost my balance, feeling as helpless as little Eliana must have felt when Mathew flung her into the air.

Unfortunately, I did not land as safely as she had. As I stumbled backward, I slipped on our freshly waxed wooden floors and fell with my foot underneath me. A pain like nothing I had ever felt before shot up my leg and throughout my entire body. A howl that must have been mine echoed throughout the living room as beads of sweat broke out over me from head to toe. I realized that I had just broken my ankle.

I told myself not to panic. My mom would have had a fit if she knew Trey was in the apartment, so I told him to leave.

"You want me to leave?" he demanded. "Are you crazy? I can't leave you here alone!"

"Please, just go!" I moaned, wincing. Trey had maneuvered me into my bed. The pain was bearable so long as I kept my leg elevated and didn't move it.

"She'll go ballistic."

"I'm so sorry," he cried. "I didn't mean——"

"It's not your fault. You were just trying to get away. I should have never——"

I never in a million years thought I would ever ask Trey to leave me, but this time I was actually scared for his safety if he stayed. He agreed to let me call my mother and tell her to come home immediately; fortunately, she worked only fifteen minutes away by cab. He stayed for ten minutes, then lingered in the stairwell of the apartment building to make sure she had arrived. When he eventually left the building, he was more broken than my ankle could ever have been.

I told my mom that I had fallen. She cried as we rushed to the emergency room in a cab, a journey that had occurred more frequently than her heart could handle. We had visited emergency rooms more often than the average kid. Once because my throat was closing after an allergic reaction, another time because of a mysterious swelling of my calf that led to a week of prodding and poking and tests to see if I had cancer or a blood clot or some other unknown disease, something particularly frightening for her because her sister Pamela, for whom I was named, had died of leukemia when she was close to my age at that time. My mom also had to rush me to the emergency room several times for asthma, something I was predisposed to—not surprisingly, considering that our neighborhood was infested with roaches and my entire family smoked.

My mom and I have been rushing to the emergency room together ever since I was five, the first time involving a messy visitation scuffle. My mom wanted me home at the court-ordered time and was, let's face it, being a bitch about my father's keeping me a few extra hours. Rather than wait, my mother went to his place, and I ended up being a human rope in a very real game of tug of war, each of them holding one of my hands in a firm grip. I don't remember his punching her, but nothing else could have made my mother's eye close shut and turn black. She was also throwing up blood, and so an ambulance was called. She was still holding my hand so firmly that the medical technicians could not pry it away. I guess we both kept firm grips on the ones we loved. I boarded the rear of the ambulance with her and lay on top of her body as she lay on the gurney.

After this latest visit to the hospital, I came home sporting a brand-new cast up to my knee. The doctors told me it had been a clean break and that things could have been much worse. I would be fine as long as I kept off my foot for two months. *Two months.* I'd be fine, I kept telling myself. I had several students who maneuvered their way around our barrier-free school without any problems. *I could do this.*

Then I began to panic at another thought. Ms. DeSousa, one of my fellow teachers, had just come back from work after breaking her leg. She had been jogging in the park when a man came out of nowhere and tried to assault her. Running faster, she fell and broke her leg in two places. I assumed she had called in sick for two months because she had needed to, not because the administration had forced her to. After all, they got upset if we called in sick for one day and even made us postpone jury duty to avoid absences.

The idea of potentially being out of the classroom for more than a week was scary even for administrators. An absence required hiring substitutes, who lacked relationships with the kids and therefore had to brace themselves for all sorts of issues. The biggest fights always broke out when there was a sub, which goes to show that students respect teachers only because of their relationship with them.

That being the case, when I was called to jury duty, Singletary was highly concerned. So when I reported to the courthouse on 161st Street for the *voir dire* process, I decided to tell the truth about how I felt about this country, in hopes that my truth would keep me from being selected.

"Ma'am, have you ever been stopped by the police?" the prosecutor asked.

"Yes, I have, and it's because I'm black!" I said in my best Angry Black Girl voice.

"Do you have any relatives in prison right now?"

"Yes, my father is serving a seventeen-year bid right now for drugs."

"Do you think his punishment was just?"

"No, I do not."

"So you think he's innocent?" At this point, one of the defense attorneys perked up.

"No. I believe he did it, all right."

"I'm confused. So you think he should have gotten less time?"

"No, I don't think he should've served any time for the crime."

The lawyers looked at one another in confusion.

"We don't understand," the prosecutor said. "I thought you said he was guilty."

"I said I believe he may have committed the crime, not that I believe he's guilty. Who's really guilty when you live in a community where people sell drugs on every corner and are getting money, *good* money, for it? I mean, what would you expect little black and brown boys to aspire to?"

With that, I was dismissed.

If Singletary had a problem with my being out for a couple of weeks for jury duty, I was certain she would be begging me to come in, despite my broken ankle. I was wrong.

At this point, along with teaching my class I was one of three special education teachers who joined forces to teach reading in our respective classes; the others were Mr. Walsh and Ms. DeSousa. The plan was to have two teachers present for each reading workshop. Mr. Walsh would be with me during my reading block in the morning, and with Ms. DeSousa during her reading block in the afternoon. But because Ms. DeSousa had broken her leg, he became the sub for her class the entire two months she was out. I had to run my reading workshop alone, which was definitely harder than having two teachers in the class. Ms. DeSousa was scheduled to come back that coming Monday. This was Sunday.

I called Ms. Edwards's cell phone to tell her about the accident. I had "slipped" in my apartment, I explained.

"You're joking, right?" Ms. Edwards asked, not sounding amused.

"I really wish I was, Ms. Edwards."

"DeSousa is coming back tomorrow!"

"I know. What are the chances, right? But listen, I think we can still make this work, if you just change my room to the vacant room on the first floor so I don't have to hobble up three flights of steps. I should be fine."

"No way." She cut me off. "You can't come in here with that leg." Ms. Edwards wasn't having anything I was serving.

"But—we have ramps."

"And? I'm not trying to have a lawsuit on my hands. How long did they give you for the cast?"

"Two months." I was officially panicking now.

"O.K., well, I'll have Mr. Walsh take over for two months."

"Mr. Walsh? Wait, Ms. Edwards, I won't sue. I promise. Even if I do slip and fall in the building, I wouldn't dare file a suit. Besides, I'll be careful." I was whining now.

"No, no. That won't work. Mr. Walsh will fill in and continue the curriculum as scheduled. I'll give him your number so you can help him plan."

I was now on the verge of tears. My students would go ballistic come Monday when they didn't see me. Mr. Walsh would be devoured. My rules, the ones they had all learned to follow, would go out of the window. I had whipped into shape some of the most difficult students I had ever had, Lorenzo being my Number One makeover. He had become an entirely different human being. When he came to me he was only a grade level behind in his studies, and I was certain that he was behind only because he was too busy misbehaving to pay attention. Lorenzo had been placed in special education because of behavioral issues, and those issues had diminished over the year. He was now as sweet as country tea and academically the top student in my class. I had already begun the paperwork to shuttle him back into general education.

"Ms. Edwards, I'm in the process of transitioning Lorenzo back into general education. This will set him back. *Please* let me come in. I'm begging you."

"If he wants to be sent back to general education, I suggest he continue to progress as he's been doing. If the secret to the magic formula for Lorenzo is you, Ms. Lewis, then we can't move him anywhere. What about his next year's teacher?"

What about his next year's teacher? There wasn't really much to it. All Lorenzo needed was love and respect, a little praise here and there. I hadn't cracked any codes. He was a boy who needed some attention, some compassion, and some structure. Next year's teacher didn't need to be a savior, she just needed to be humane. Unfortunately, that couldn't be guaranteed.

Lorenzo would be pissed. Worse, he had this thing against white men, and as far as he was concerned, Mr. Walsh, like his former teacher Mr. Capella, was the devil. This was not good.

"But—but, Ms. Edwards . . ."

"Goodbye, Ms. Lewis. Please rest up. I'll be in touch." She hung up in my ear. I couldn't believe that she was more concerned about a lawsuit, a lawsuit that I had given her my word would never be filed, than about a child's well-being. She *knew* me. I wasn't the type to make waves. Sitting in bed, all I could think of was Monday morning and my students' shock upon hearing that Ms. Lewis would be gone for a long time. Two months for a child must feel like eternity. I knew first-hand what abandonment felt like, and I was sure that the lives of many of my students were far more complicated than my own had been. Their reaction to my absence would be far more severe than any panic attack I had ever experienced because of Trey. In some cases, I was the only maternal figure in their lives. Feeling more helpless than I had ever felt in my life, I just cried.

Mr. Walsh called me every week to plan and to update me on my students' decline. Lorenzo had been terrible, as I had suspected he would be, and had had to be removed. They put him back in his old class, the 12:1:1 class for emotionally disturbed children, because it was a more restrictive environment. Within a few weeks, the administration determined that even a 12:1:1 setting wasn't restrictive enough.

Eventually, it was decided that Lorenzo would go to a District 75 school the following year. A snap of the fingers, and he would be gone. I wasn't his parent, but I damn sure felt as if I had just lost my child.

When I finally came back to my classroom, I couldn't shake the sadness. I was glad to see the rest of my students alive and well and relieved that they had not killed one another while I was gone, but there was a hole in my heart in the shape of Lorenzo. I'd see him in the school hallway, playing basketball alone outside of his classroom. His teacher apparently allowed it, so long as he wasn't in the room. Before I escorted him back inside, I would talk to him about his behavior. He'd smile and look up at me with those same bright eyes the way he always had, but he didn't hear my words. Lorenzo always chose when he would listen to me, and, being gone for two months, I had lost the privilege to be heard. I had broken his heart. My heart was broken too, by the decision to force me to stay home away from him and the rest of my students. I would never forgive them for that. And I doubt he will ever forgive me. It's funny how heartbreak works. When someone or something breaks your heart, you can try to forgive that person as much as you want, but that love is forever tainted. Trey was right about that. I knew that I couldn't bounce back from this one.

———————

"Call her, Pam. She's waiting."

Naison and I rarely talked by phone. When we communicated, it was usually via e-mail. For Doc to call me, it was serious.

"Who?"

"Giles, who else?"

I had met her for about four seconds and already forgotten who she was. But Naison hadn't let the idea go.

"She is? She's waiting for my phone call?"

"Yes, she's in the office right now. She wants to interview you. Call her."

I couldn't believe his persistence.

"What's the number? I don't even have her number."

"Yes, you do. She gave it to you at the schoolyard jam. You put it in your phone."

The day had been such a whirlwind, I didn't even recall doing that. I checked my contacts, and sure enough it was there.

"O.K., I'll call," I replied, feeling pressured but sensing the urgency in his voice. Naison knew about all my issues with the school where I was teaching and wanted me out of there. Apparently Mrs. Giles's school wasn't under as much scrutiny, and therefore the pressure was not as extreme.

As frustrated as I was at the job, I really had no intention of actually trying to leave, at least not right away. Until recently, to leave your current employment you had to get permission from your principal. And of course no one would have dared walk up to Ms. Singletary and say, "Hey, can you sign this letter to release me? I'm kind of unhappy and would like to pursue my career elsewhere, in a place where my knees don't quiver."

But a new plan had been put in place that allowed teachers to leave their schools behind their administrations' backs. Before a principal could be the wiser, a school could have twenty vacancies and the principal wouldn't know until the other school officially accepted the teacher who had interviewed. Technically, if all twenty teachers didn't get hired until August, a principal could remain clueless with only weeks left before the beginning of the school year. Although I didn't know it at the time, I would be part of a mass exodus. The year I left, so did at least half of all of Singletary's staff. The pressure to perform thanks to low test scores and having an endless parade of consultants and administrators making pop visits had made Singletary a very uptight employer. Ironically, had I known that so many teachers were leaving her school, I might have stayed out of guilt.

Dear Ms. Singletary,

I am writing this letter to inform you of my decision to take a teaching position offered to me from another school. I was asked to teach my favorite subject, social studies, to grades K–5 and I am beyond excited to do so.

Though I am anxious to move on to new things, I will never forget this school or you. Teaching here has been an eye-opening experience, one that has strengthened my craft as well as my love for children. I would like to thank you for providing me with my first teaching experience and entrusting me with the lives of the children of this community. I also want to just say thank you for being there for me when you did not have to.

Respectfully,
Pamela Lewis

Dear Ms. Lewis,

While I am sad to hear of your leaving, I am happy that you have been assigned the position of your dreams. Continue to be the star that I always knew you were and please keep me up to speed as you continue to take over the world. You are an amazing teacher and I am very proud of you. I only wish I had more teachers like you. Most of my teachers are incompetent and even though many of them have been in the profession as long as you've been alive, you taught circles around them.

Wishing you luck on your future endeavors,
Ms. Singletary

4

I'm Looking for a New Love, Baby

As I entered my new school building on the first day of classes the following September, the weight I had carried with me constantly began to feel lighter with each step. The burden of test scores and micromanagement seemed to drift away as I walked through the doors of the Old School, my affectionate name for this institution because of its emphasis on tradition.

Huge murals of Nickelodeon characters lined the pre-kindergarten hallway, while the hallways through which the upper-grade students passed were decorated with images of real people—people of color from the Bronx who had made it. Their faces were a reminder that no matter how grim one's realities, it was possible to be successful. Some of the people depicted were musicians, some politicians, some athletes. Images of a very special president and a U.S. Supreme Court justice would eventually make their way to the wall, something that previously could have happened only in our dreams. I felt that something special could be brewing here.

Even though this school was just blocks away from my previous school and from the outside the two buildings looked similar, the culture of this school was entirely different. On my way to the principal's office that first day, I passed several children, all wearing uniforms, smiling, well mannered, and ready to greet me and hold open doors. The children seemed genuinely happy. A peace filled the halls, one that would let you breathe deeply and enjoy the bit of time between periods as you walked from your classroom to the bathroom, or to the lunchroom to pick up your kids, or to the gym to drop off your class for your prep period.

During these times I would stop and read the bulletin boards, which were always beautifully done and, more to the point, never vandalized, as in Ms. Singletary's school.

One day I mentioned this difference to Mrs. Giles. I couldn't believe how different the students were. Students who came from the same housing projects and were growing up in the same environment as the students from Singletary's school were so much better behaved. The children had a respect for the school that I hadn't seen in many of the students at Singletary's school, and it wasn't as a result of fear but of love.

"Ms. Singletary?" Giles offered a sardonic laugh when I mentioned her name. "She's . . . interesting." She pointed a finger to her temple and cranked it in a circular motion. "Seriously, consider yourself lucky you got out now because that ship is sinking fast."

I never thought about the possibility of a school's actually closing, even Ms. Singletary's. When I was a student, schools never closed no matter how "bad" they were. At most, they just earned a reputation for being bad schools.

But closing schools? Never heard of it, I mean aside from the movie *Lean on Me*. I guessed that that sort of thing happened elsewhere, with really terrible schools, like "drug dealing in stairwells" terrible or "kids smoking crack on the roof" terrible. But not the standard "bad" school. A school in a crime-ridden neighborhood was expected to be bad, and the teachers seemed to do the best they could. If there was pressure, I didn't notice any, and I damn sure didn't worry about my school's being closed. In my mind, it simply didn't make sense to blame a school for the problems of the neighborhood without doing something about the neighborhood first.

At the Old School I was assigned to teach social studies. I was ecstatic because that meant I could teach the subject I loved most, which was history. I would get excited teaching about the past and having students interpret what it meant. In my previous school, where I had to teach all subjects, I would cringe every time I opened a science textbook. Not that science didn't have its share of thrills, but in public schools in the South Bronx those thrills were hard to come by. For starters, there was no equipment for science experiments; at best we would be given some rocks and some soil and told to "make it work."

Pretty soon I was teaching my new students not only the

grade-appropriate curriculum but also their Bronx history, something that wasn't included in any of the "scope and sequences" section of the official curriculum but material I thought they should know. There was also an emphasis on oral history at the Old School, and I had my students conduct oral history interviews with their parents and relatives so they could learn about how things used to be. I played Jay Z's "December 4th," which begins with his mother's account of his childhood. I played Nas's "Bridging the Gap," in which his dad sings a blues narrative about raising a son who he predicted would be the "greatest man alive." My students *felt* me. In me they saw another projects kid who had grown up and become someone.

Social studies is often neglected in public elementary schools because of the emphasis on instruction in English and math, which are the focus because tests in those subjects are weighed more heavily. Only scores in English and math determine if a child is promoted, not to mention the fact that a school's rating is also heavily influenced by test scores in those subjects. But Giles used the fact that fifth-graders had to take a social studies exam as a reason to hire a social studies cluster teacher, who would teach the same subject to different groups of students in different grades during each day.

To gauge my students' knowledge, I passed out a sheet with questions like "What country do I live in?" "What continent?" "What state?" and "What borough?" Walking around and glancing at their work, I noticed that the kids knew they lived in New York, in the United States, and in the Bronx, but they didn't have a clue as to what was what. For borough, some answers were "the United States" and "New York." For country, "the Bronx."

Teaching special education, I had assumed that moments like this occurred only in 12:1 classrooms. It dawned on me that some general-education children in these neighborhoods were not doing much better than their special-ed counterparts. Lack of exposure was lack of exposure, and living in the projects often meant that mommy didn't have time to teach you something as irrelevant as the continent you live in. This led me to ask another question.

"Who can tell me your address?" In this class of about twenty fifth-graders, only ten children raised their hands.

"I know what street I live on," one boy said. "I just don't know the building number."

"Are you new to the building?" I asked.

"Nah. I lived there my whole life."

"I see," I said.

Then I asked the class, "Can you tell me your phone number?"

A few children raised their hands, but still only about half the class. Brian, who was thirteen, did not. Some of them flipped to the front of their notebooks and pointed to the number their parents had written down in case of an emergency.

I thought back to when I was five. I could have told you my address, phone number, mother's name, father's name. I knew to call 911 in case of an emergency. I even knew the secret code that anyone who came to pick me up from school would also have to know. Brownie, the name of my first cat, was the word they had to provide. If they didn't, I knew that my mother hadn't given them permission to get me in an emergency. Because my parents were going through an ugly custody battle, my mother was afraid—though unnecessarily—that my dad would try to kidnap me after school one day. She was overly paranoid, so much so that she'd even question me about drug paraphernalia.

"You see any crack vials in his apartment?"

"What's that?" I was probably eight.

She tried to explain the best way she could. Clearly not good enough, as I was soon certain that I had found one. It was a thumb tack.

My students, again, were not me. I constantly had to tell myself this. Just as many of them had not been exposed to many of my positive memories growing up, some of my focus, seriousness, and attention to detail, all great characteristics to have, were traits they had not developed because unlike me, they weren't growing up in survivor mode. Living in the projects didn't guarantee dysfunction. Others may have been born in the dysfunction, so much so that it was normalized. Daddies' selling drugs may not have triggered an alarm in some mommies' heads. There would be no scavenger hunts confusing thumb tacks with crack vials.

I continued with my questioning.

"O.K., last question. It's a two-part question. How many of you have parents who were born somewhere else?"

Again, half the class raised their hands.

Most of the students in this neighborhood had parents who were from Puerto Rico, the Dominican Republic, or West Africa.

"Where is your mother from?" I asked one of the African children.

"Gambia," she said.

The African American students looked at this child in amazement.

None of them could imagine a black person from outside the United States being able to be so specific in reference to a place she called home.

I asked a boy where his parents were from.

"Africa," the child replied. Giggles from the class erupted. Unlike the country of Gambia, they knew and had heard of the continent of Africa, but they treated it more like a country, a country whose name somehow connoted humor.

I silenced the children and continued. "I know that. But where in Africa?"

"Mali," he answered.

Again the class giggled. The boy didn't respond, but I wasn't surprised by his sense of control. Immigrant students were usually better behaved than students who had grown up in New York City and made more of an effort to learn. They typically had more respect for their teachers, and education was usually taken seriously. When students didn't behave, their parents often threatened to send them back to their country. This usually straightened them out. And when it didn't, off they went, as in the case of the son of the parent who playfully had given me permission to beat him. She had gone through all lengths to get him to take school seriously, even showing up at the school one day with a police officer to scare him straight. When I called to check up on him after he had graduated, she told me he was in the Dominican Republic.

"On vacation?"

"No *mija*, for good!" *Mija* was short for *mi hija*, or "my daughter." We were very close.

"I told you I wasn't playing," she reminded me. "And neither do they. At this school, they hit the kids that don't act right! *Papi* is a new child! Like day and night."

Finally one kid asked me a question. "Is it true that you grew up over here in these projects, Ms. Lewis?"

"No, I'm not from this section of the Bronx," I replied. "But I am from the Bronx, and I am from the projects."

The kids began to murmur among themselves, apparently in awe. Many teachers in the New York City school system lived upstate or in Yonkers, White Plains, Mount Vernon, or New Rochelle. Some lived outside New York state, making the long and grueling commute to the inner city from New Jersey, Connecticut, even Pennsylvania. Some of the black and Hispanic teachers lived in Harlem, but my being from the Bronx made my students feel more connected to me. And while some of the teachers had originally come from the Bronx, many had long since left, and those who hadn't usually lived in neighborhoods such as Throggs Neck or Pelham Bay, the safest parts of the borough.

"So, what projects did you come from?" one student asked.

I pulled up a map of the Bronx on my cell phone and showed them Edenwald and Co-op City. On the map, our two communities looked like hallway neighbors. They smiled.

Life as a social studies teacher was sweet. I had so much freedom; there was nothing or no one holding me back on how I wanted to teach and what content I decided to include. Of course, I followed the scope and sequence, but I supplemented with my own information.

One particular year was a perfect year to be teaching history. A black man ran for president and won. I did my best to try to convey the magnitude of what this meant to children who had been born after the year 2000. It was no use. My students were excited, but they would never understand the importance of what had taken place. Then Mrs. Giles had an idea.

"Lewis, I want you to spearhead a visit to the senior center as we approach Obama's inauguration," she proposed. "Get a group of kids together and have them conduct oral history interviews. I think it would be an eye-opening experience for them to hear first-hand what life was like decades ago. Then I want those seniors to come to our school on the day of the inauguration. Gonna have the upper-grade students watch the inauguration on the projector. I think it would be nice to bring the seniors there to watch it with them. What do you think?"

It was an excellent idea. I immediately began considering which kids should be included on the trip. I wanted kids who spoke well and who were never behavioral issues so as not to embarrass our school with some elderly woman scolding a child for lacking manners or using improper grammar. I decided on ten, a mix of the very highest-achieving and some who could use such an opportunity.

The senior center was more bustling than I'd expected. Elderly men and women walked around with far more pep in their step than the average grandmother or grandfather I was accustomed to, the ones stuck raising their grandchildren because their own children were unable to. I guess being a parent of a toddler at the age of sixty can wear one down. Seeing these seniors made me wonder if my own grandmother might have lived even longer if she had been able to socialize with fellow seniors instead of having to take care of our entire family for so many years. Her husband, who had worked in the coal mines of Appalachia, died of lung cancer at the age of forty-five. My grandmother, who never remarried, continued to smoke her Salems until she was also diagnosed with lung cancer, in her seventies.

The folks in the senior center had someone taking care of them; that was the difference. Life should be cyclical in that respect. Simple enough, or so it seems. But in communities like the one I grew up in, something had changed this cycle of life.

Almost an entire generation seemed to have never grown up, and their old mothers were often left still raising them and their children. Of course, I am generalizing. My mother, like many single mothers in her generation, raised me, but she still needed Nana to watch me when she went back to school for her degree, because she had no husband to help out. My mother also had siblings who needed their mother. Nana took care of everyone in our large extended family—made sure all had a roof over their heads and food in their bellies, of which she primarily cooked. She did so until she got sick, then moved in with us. She finally had her own room, but she hated the seclusion.

"Y'all live strange, Dodie," she said shaking her head to my mom.

Back in Edenwald, Nana liked sleeping on the pull-out sofa at night while we all slept in beds. She had her own room, she'd probably say if you asked: the kitchen, where she sat and played Solitaire, read the "funny papers," looked out the window (being nosy), cooked and baked from scratch, and smoked her lungs to death.

———————

At the center, each child was assigned to a senior to conduct an interview. The kids all came prepared with questions to ask and had been taught to improvise with follow-up questions, doing their best to truly capture the memories.

The day of the inauguration, I wore an Obama sweatshirt to school. I definitely got more than a few nasty looks from some of the white and Hispanic teachers. It was clear that in my school there was a serious divide, which surprised me, New York being such a liberal city. The black teachers were so proud of our president-elect. He was not just black but arguably one of the most eloquent speakers to become president in a long time. We loved him instantly. Many of the white teachers scoffed at the sheer ridiculousness of his electoral votes. When asked why, they *never* once confessed their true reasons for their disgust. It was always something else, something they always had a difficult time explaining. When Mrs. Giles announced over the loudspeaker that all the third-, fourth-, and fifth-grade teachers should report to the auditorium with their classes to watch the inauguration, the grumbling began.

"This is against our UFT contract and against school policy," I overheard one Hispanic teacher mutter. (UFT stands for United Federation of Teachers.)

Still, there were mixed emotions from nonblack teachers, symbolizing the sentiments of the entire nation. As I passed Ms. Salazar, a Filipino substitute, she smiled, her happiness obviously prompted by my sweatshirt. We had never really spoken before, but this moment brought together many people who normally didn't have much in common. Ms. Salazar leaned in to whisper to me, as if she knew our feelings weren't popular with everyone.

"You know what I told this guy on the train the day after he won?"

"What?"

"'Get over it.' He looked so angry. And I knew why. These white people haven't been this angry since the Civil War."

She was right. No one wanted to admit it, but the level of hatred on the faces of many people on the streets that day was personal. You would have thought they all knew President Obama personally, that he was the man who had stolen their purses, raped their little sister, shot and killed their husband for his cell phone. In their minds, they did know him, and he was that man. But because no one wanted to be called a bigot, they blamed their disgust on their hatred for the Democratic Party.

———

Within minutes, a van of seniors from the senior center arrived at the school to watch the inauguration. Everyone took their seats. Mrs. Giles began.

"Good morning, teachers, students, and invited guests. For those of you who are unaware, I would like you to look over your shoulders to the back of the auditorium and wave hello to our seniors from the senior center in the community. They have come to watch this moment in history with the youth." Giles playfully bowed deeply to her guests, suggesting that royalty was among us.

Then she continued.

"Boys and girls, what you are about to witness is something that many of us, especially our invited guests, thought we would never see."

"I know that's right!" one of the seniors yelled.

"That's right," Giles said. "You see, boys and girls, many of them have seen a time that was just plain unfair, a time when people were not treated equally. So we all are here today to bear witness as a community. This is a sign of good things to come. You children are the first generation that can truly say that when you grow up, you can be anything you want to be, even president of the United States. This is a new day for us all. Today is not about political parties. This is history."

As our new president recited the oath, the seniors stared at the screen with amazement. Many cried. Some hugged one another. But for me the most memorable sight of the day was Yakim, one of my students, crying harder than all the seniors combined. I wondered how on Earth at just ten years old he could feel the weight of a prejudiced world that had existed since before his birth. Either he was a reincarnated freedom fighter, or his parents were instrumental in giving him "knowledge of self." I told myself not to be surprised if one day we would be calling him President Yakim Moore.

––––––––––

I should have seen the storm clouds approaching. My life as a teacher was just too fulfilling. I had a great assignment as a social studies teacher, which meant less paperwork and responsibility overall, and more fun. What made it worse was that I was only in my twenties.

The truth was, several of the best and brightest teachers in schools were young. I didn't think twice when I was offered opportunities by Mrs. Giles, or even Ms. Singletary back when I taught at her school. One year she had asked me to teach after school—an assignment that came with extra money attached—when I hadn't even applied for the position, bumping me ahead of senior teachers who wanted the job badly and had already completed the necessary paperwork. I figured that Giles and Singletary simply recognized that I was intelligent, passionate, and hardworking.

In the world of education, seniority was the rule administrators were supposed to live by, and violating that rule inevitably produced tension. At the same time, young teachers like me who could actually teach and had classroom-management skills right from the start were often more sought after because we were the ones who had been indoctrinated with the newest educational theories.

Every few years something new came down the pike. Some of these changes, such as adding discussion and group work, were great components that had been added prior to my employment and are still valued today. But then some things that worked would be removed, and veteran teachers would become angry. Schools had no solution to the real problem in the schools, which was poverty, so they continued to experiment with the ways we taught the children. When a great new idea was rolled out, new teachers like me were more hopeful because we didn't know how many great new ideas had been rolled out in the past and then abandoned. Many veteran teachers in turn hissed and blew air.

This is not to say that there weren't some terrific veteran teachers, men and women who had been born to teach. As a child who attended public school, I'd had several teachers whom I'll forever remember, thanks to their phenomenal abilities. These teachers were never newly appointed teachers, and none of them fit into a mold but were unique in style and temperament.

I had been blessed with some amazing history teachers in my lifetime—Mr. Ryan, who taught eighth-grade history and was a comedian both in the classroom and at a local nightclub; and Mr. Thoman, a white guy with a patch of blond hair and a passion for American history who still doesn't look a day over twenty-five. He delivered his instruction with the calmness of a Buddhist monk and headed the environmental club but nonetheless would not hesitate to chase a bee around the room, spritzing it with the closest cleaning agent he could find. We adored his unintentional humor just as much as we adored the zany quirkiness of Ms. Santoro, our petite global-history teacher, with her beautiful mane of auburn curls. Ms. Santoro was beyond sweet and almost wept with us the day we told her that someone had just died.

School had just started and our favorite rapper, Tupac Shakur, was in critical condition, fighting for his life. An upperclassman who was able to go outside for lunch stopped home and had apparently heard on the news that Tupac had stopped breathing. While we were in class, she tapped on the back classroom door's window to get our attention—because we always sat in the back—and mouthed to us: "Tupac's dead!"

"*What?*" we mouthed back.

"Dead! He's gone!" her mouthing elevated to a whisper.

As she walked away, we all began to murmur in the back of the room over the details—if he'd had any last words, who had killed him . . . Ms. Santoro was rightfully annoyed.

"Excuse me, ladies, but do you mind telling me what is more important than you passing this Global Regents at the end of the year?"

"We're sorry," one of my friends tried to explain through her weeping. "It's just that someone very close to our hearts has just passed on."

Immediately, poor Ms. Santoro felt guilty for reprimanding us.

"Oh, dear! Who?"

"Tupac."

"I'm so sorry to hear! Did he attend this school?"

"Uhhh, no."

"Well, did you know him well?" Her hands were clasped tightly, her eyes sad with empathy.

Needless to say, she was caught off-guard when we confessed to not only his being a celebrity but also our having never met him, loving him only from afar. Still, she tried her best to understand while still insisting that we focus on the Fertile Crescent rather than whether or not the culprits to Pac's murder were some South Side Crips from Compton.

One teacher stood out most of all. Mr. Altschuler inspired me to become a writer. Our honors English class delighted in reading great works of literature like *In Cold Blood* by Truman Capote and *Native Son* and *Black Boy* by Richard Wright. The historical context for each novel was always provided to give us an even greater appreciation for the work itself. My life as a writer began in that classroom. Though learning had always been fun for me, in this class it took on an entirely new meaning.

Mr. Altschuler let us have conversations about race in class and was candid about the harsh realities of our lives. My brain soaked up his words like a plant in dire need of watering, thirsty for a new kind of knowledge that had never before been offered to me. While traditional in many ways, Mr. Altschuler was flexible in his approach, always seeing the bigger picture. When my friend Natyla was afraid to present her work in front of the class, for example, he asked her to write a stand-up comedy routine instead of a report. (Natyla is, to date, the funniest friend I ever had, and so giving her the opportunity to showcase her comedic talent was pure genius.) Natyla still had to create an introduction, a body with lots of details, appropriate transitions, and a conclusion. She also had to engage her audience and speak clearly. She earned an A for her efforts, and we all left the classroom having laughed so hard our stomachs hurt.

Unfortunately, not all of my teachers were so terrific. Too few people wanted to teach in low-income neighborhoods, where the challenges were so great, and as a result teachers who should never have been hired to teach inner-city kids presided over classrooms in the city's most dangerous communities because they could not find jobs elsewhere. Between not wanting to teach children with the issues urban children faced and not wanting to learn new rules, many veteran teachers were simply miserable.

As a student in the public school system and at my previous school, I had seen my share of those teachers. There was Ms. Lapinsky, a substitute in my elementary school, who wore a large-brimmed crocheted hat and a nightgown to work every day. She would choose a page out of a textbook to copy onto the board and order us to copy it in our notebooks, an activity that took the entire period. The next day she would choose another page and do exactly the same thing. Looking back, I realize that she must have suffered from some sort of mental illness. Still, she was allowed to be alone with us poor black and brown students.

By the time I entered high school, I realized that another ingredient could be added to the already toxic potion that brewed teachers from Hell. That was racism.

Teacher assignments involved politics that I hadn't understood as a child. It was harder to be assigned to a white school in a good neighborhood than to a black school in a bad neighborhood. For one thing, the white schools in better neighborhoods were choosier, and, more important, they experienced very little turnover. Teachers whose students are better behaved and have fewer academic issues tend to stick around. Anyone vying for a spot in such a school, especially because those jobs often paid more, would probably have to wait for teachers to retire or die even to be considered.

Mr. Todd, my sophomore English teacher, was typical of those who seemed to hate their jobs. He was old and crabby. He didn't smile at anyone, not even his colleagues, and generally looked as if he would rather shoot himself in the ear than teach. I didn't suspect he was racist. I thought he was just miserable. Then one day, my opinion of him took a turn into oncoming traffic. The crash that ensued left a few innocent bystanders a bit shaken up, a classic case of being at the wrong place at the wrong time.

My friend Rasheeda was part of my eight-deep clique within my gifted and talented program. We were all smart girls, but many of us, coming from inner-city schools and dysfunctional families, could not cope as well with someone like Mr. Todd. For other ethnic groups from different socioeconomic backgrounds, respect was key, regardless of whether our teachers were deserving or not. For us, respect was earned, and in Rasheeda's eyes, Mr. Todd did not warrant her respect.

Though lively, opinionated, and full of life in our other classes, Rasheeda refused to entertain the idea of communicating anything to Mr. Todd. This was actually very respectful, considering that she, like most of us, probably wanted to throw something at him half the time. Instead, she remained quiet, keeping in mind the adage "If you don't have anything nice to say, say nothing at all." This unfortunately meant that her participation grade in this class was much lower than in her other classes. All of ours were, really.

For the first time in my life, I wasn't the teacher's pet. The dynamic brother-and-sister duo Adeel and Shanzey Azizi, Angela Silverstein, Annie Kim, Mila Stapos, and Sarah Foster were. Their work ethic was far beyond anything I had ever seen, even in crabby old Mr. Todd's class.

One day in Mr. Todd's class, Rasheeda actually decided to participate, a first for her in this particular classroom. The fact that she had even decided to raise her hand meant she was showing tremendous effort to work against her feelings toward him. He called on her to read, but as she read, I realized how anxious she seemed. She stumbled over words that I *knew* she knew. This was a gifted program, after all, and we were high school sophomores. She was just nervous.

But before she could continue, Mr. Todd hissed, "I think that's enough, Rasheeda. I need a new volunteer." Sarah's hand shot up at the opportunity.

"Fuck it," Rasheeda said, slinking down in her seat and putting her head on her desk. She was embarrassed, but of course she wouldn't admit that. Instead, she became her usual indifferent self in Mr. Todd's class.

I was only in high school, but seeing a teacher destroy a student like that enraged me. And Mr. Todd's next action made it even harder for me to keep my mouth shut. After Sarah read a passage and her recitation was riddled with mistakes, Mr. Todd, instead of expressing frustration as he had when Rasheeda had read, was encouraging, offering the very responses Rasheeda had needed most.

"It's O.K., Sarah." "You're doing swell, Sarah." "Keep going, Sarah." Finally, I couldn't take it any longer.

"Why didn't you say all those things when Rasheeda was reading?" I demanded. Everyone turned to look at me, even Rasheeda, surprised by my boldness, and my concern, because it had nothing to do with me. It wasn't the first and wouldn't be the last time that one of us made a scene in class; the rest of the class had gotten accustomed to the ghetto black girls and their problems I'm sure by now and never stepped out of bounds to complain, even if they had a right to be annoyed. In this case, I always wondered if anyone else noticed the difference Mr. Todd made between Sarah and Rasheeda that day. Was I being overly sensitive or were they all just scared to speak up? In the end, my rant now left Sarah slunk down in her seat too, though it hadn't been my aim to embarrass her. She may have been wondering, "What did I do?" I'm sure this is what many white girls ask themselves when they are victims of our lashing out. Maybe if Sarah had never raised her hand, if we all had stood in solidarity against the evil man who might as well have spit at Rasheeda that day, maybe I would've cared more about her feelings. Maybe if she didn't use the belittling of one student as her own opportunity to shine, I would've considered her own embarrassment. Maybe it wouldn't have mattered at all. Still, it was a learning opportunity for us all. As much as I despised that man, I have to thank him for being the sparkplug that began my lifelong position as an activist and speaker against injustice. Sometimes one just needs to be angry enough to even speak up at all. And though Rasheeda didn't need or ask me to speak for her, I will always be thankful that she didn't tell me to mind my own business. As for Mr. Todd, he never even looked my way.

My activism didn't stop there. When Mrs. Smith gave Felicia her fourth F in a row on a revision of a paper that she had secretly copied from a student named Melody who had gotten a B+, I realized that Mr. Todd wasn't the only teacher with an agenda. Apparently, Mrs. Smith was so old that she hadn't even realized that Felicia's paper was an exact copy of Melody's. If she had had any scruples, she would have read Felicia's paper and said, "Hmm, this sounds so familiar." Luckily for Felicia, she didn't remember it at all.

When Felicia asked Melody if she could see her paper, Melody had no idea what she planned to do. Felicia knew that Mrs. Smith didn't like her and gave her grades that didn't always reflect her ability. Felicia had told Melody she wanted to see her paper just to read it and to try to improve her own work. She copied it word for word, assuming that Mrs. Smith wouldn't remember Melody's original essay, as it had been handed in several weeks prior. She assumed right. Mrs. Smith had no idea that she was grading Melody's paper for a second time.

Not only did Mrs. Smith give Felicia a failing grade on a better-than-average paper, she made different comments on the same sentences. On Melody's paper, she wrote, "Excellent thesis statement" in reference to a sentence that was "not a thesis statement" on Felicia's. Things that were "well-stated" on Melody's paper were "unclear" on Felicia's paper. If it had been my paper, I would have had some kind of media attention, and perhaps an investigation and Mrs. Smith's job. But Felicia simply demanded that she be assigned to a new teacher, something she had been refused in the past because Mrs. Smith was the only junior English teacher assigned to our gifted program. There was no way that a student in our program could be assigned to the other core classes in Kennedy ... until Mrs. Smith made her hatred for Felicia visible in red ink. Felicia was taken out of Mrs. Smith's class and placed in another junior English class the following week. We couldn't argue that Mrs. Smith was racist; Melody was a black girl too. But her disdain for Felicia made us consider other options. Could Melody have been "acceptably" black by closet racist standards? Considering that Melody had light skin and long hair, it was possible. There was also the "good nigger" approach to blackness that many white people were guilty of, which basically allowed them the right to demonize problematic black people without being considered racist, so long as they were accepting of non-problematic black folk. Melody was a quiet girl who did her work and was extremely well behaved. Felicia was a well-behaved student as well but had her issues, as most of us in our crew did. She didn't always hand her work in on time, and she may have rolled an eye here or there on a few occasions. We were well aware of the fact that many white people were accepting of black people so long as they didn't get uppity, so long as they didn't rock the boat, so long as they complied with the rules and did so with a smile. We knew that many white people were often much more forgiving of other white people. We also knew that if a black person made a mistake, no matter how slight, many whites would use it to justify excessiveness: academic penalties of all sorts, firing from one's job, incarceration, homicide. They truly believed in their hearts that their excessiveness was appropriate, no matter how illogical it was. We would hear that black unarmed men deserved to die because they didn't comply with a police officer's command, even though white people mouthed off to police officers about their rights all the time. We would hear that black women were difficult employees who deserved to be fired because they complained, even though many white women felt entitled to certain realities in their places of employment as well. We knew that students like us who gave attitude were threatening and thuggish, while white students who acted out in class were "troubled." Felicia wasn't a stellar student, but she wasn't an F student either. We couldn't prove it, but whatever Felicia's transgressions were, we were sure Mrs. Smith would have been more understanding if she were white ... at least, in our own minds.

In Ms. Singletary's school I encountered a teacher who hated black people without question. Even more surprising, she was black.

Ms. Jenkins was a fifty-something woman from the South. She wore denim overalls and a red bandana to school, looking more as if she were off to work in the fields than teaching children in a classroom.

I can only assume that growing up in the Jim Crow South had made her what she was. But what was the most depressing was the idea that a woman who had clearly grown up hating people like herself was teaching young black children. I could only imagine what messages she was feeding them about their self-worth. I wondered if my Sydney had ever been her student.

I especially remember one incident. We had been broken up into groups for our weekly professional development session, and I was in the group assigned to Ms. Jenkins's classroom. While waiting for the session to begin, we chatted about things that had nothing to do with our job.

One of the teachers had a copy of *Essence* magazine with a picture of Jamie Foxx in it.

"Oh, my God, he is so sexy!" Ms. Audrine said. "I'd give anything to have him for just one night."

Her vulgarity prompted a few responses. "Wow, Mildred, I never knew you were so freaky," Ms. Santiago said. I stayed quiet. I was too young to get into such a conversation with women fifteen years my senior.

"He's too black," another teacher chimed in. "Nobody would want to run their hands through those peasy naps!"

Everyone turned in shock. The speaker was Ms. Jenkins, who was at least a shade darker than Mr. Foxx.

I couldn't quite see the hair on her head given the fact that she wore a bandana over it, but I could see some hairs escaping what we call "the kitchen," near the nape of the neck, and they definitely looked coarser than any strand of hair Jamie Foxx could have had on any part of his body.

"Y'all wanna see beautiful?" Ms. Jenkins demanded. She got up, walked over to her social studies area, and pointed to a poster that many teachers had in their classrooms, a poster that was sold at many of the city's teacher supply stores and often came with borders and sometimes even a lesson on diversity on the back. It depicted boys and girls of all colors, dressed in their traditional ethnic outfits. The group included an Eskimo boy wearing a fur-lined hood, an Indian girl in a sari with a *bindi* (red dot) in the middle of her forehead, and an African boy wearing a *kufi* cap.

The lineup also included a little girl who looked as if she were from Sweden or Iceland and had platinum blonde hair and eyes the color of glaciers. She was cute. But so were the Eskimo and African boys and the Indian girl.

"You see that girl right there with them blue eyes?" Ms. Jenkins demanded. "That's the epitome of beauty. That hair, those pretty eyes!"

Her words were right out of my favorite Toni Morrison novel. I knew I was in the South Bronx, but I felt that I must have folded my arms, blinked, and landed somewhere in rural America where black folks lived on the poor side of town and read books about Dick and Jane, envying their seemingly picture-perfect lives. Jenkins was Pecola Breedlove all grown up, still wishing to God for them purty blue eyes.

We were all too stunned to say a word.

———

Giles loved committees. She had a committee for everything under the sun. I was on several committees that helped to make decisions about the running of the school, and, looking back, I can see how much my being chosen for these committees may have pissed off some of the older teachers.

"Hey, Beyoncé!" Ms. Cora said as I walked into the school's lobby. "Looking good, girl!" Ms. Cora always knew how to make someone smile.

"Uh oh, uh oh, uh oh, oh, no, no!" Ms. Tina sang as she twerked her derriere.

"What do you think this is, a 'Crazy in Love' video?" I laughed. The Beyoncé joke was getting out of hand. Ever since I had been persuaded to dye my hair lighter, people were calling me Beyoncé even though I looked nothing like her. I just had light brown skin, long straight hair, and a large gluteus maximus.

When I arrived in the meeting room, a group of older white and white Latina teachers who shared a penchant for vicious gossip and malicious rumor-mongering were already there. I knew to watch out for them after several teachers told me they were saying nasty things about me. This you would never know from the way they spoke to me face to face. When we were in the same room, it was as if we all were the best of friends. Behind my back? That was another story.

Every time any of them stared at me, all I could think of was Europeans' historical obsession with black anatomy. Sarah Baartman, an African woman known as the Hottentot Venus, had toured Europe so people could gape at her huge ass and enlarged labia. When she died, her vagina was cut from her body and put on display for more than a century at the Museum of Man in Paris. White people even gave her type of physique a name, steatopygia, which *Webster's New World College Dictionary* defines as "the condition of having a heavy deposit of fat in the buttocks or thighs, as in some Hottentot women."

A condition? African women have big posteriors. Somehow, that had become a crime, especially when you were supposed to be a sweet, wholesome teacher; having curves automatically sexualized a woman, despite how asexual she might actually be. Large bottoms should not exist in a classroom, as far as many were concerned, and at the very least, they should be contained. I wore snug pants not only because they looked good, but because wearing looser pants and dresses only accentuated this part of the anatomy and its tendency to jiggle. Spanx had become my best friend, especially after I had developed anxiety from writing on the board; not only was I giving my students a front and center view, but writing quickly and vigorously meant shaking my rump like in a Das EFX music video. Still, I was young and could not see myself wearing frumpy clothes. Was I supposed to wear a smock down to my knees? It wasn't like I was showing skin. In fact, though some teachers dressed very conservatively, many wore the same kinds of clothes I did but were never chastised for it because they weren't curvy.

Though blacks and Hispanics lived side by side in the community and often hung out together, one could find many incidents of racial tension between the two groups, with Hispanics often believing that they were superior to blacks and blacks resenting them for that opinion. Whether she said it or not, it was easy to make her treatment of me a race thing.

"Fuck her!" Ms. Reed, a fellow African American teacher, said one day. "She's just mad that you look good." Reed always said it like she meant it and was unapologetic in her delivery when it came to such things. She had already had plenty of run-ins with the crew, and her closest friend had already left the school in part because of their treatment.

We assumed they were racist. According to another African American teacher, one of the teachers in the Mean Girls crew once mentioned how unfortunate it was that a little girl in her class was what she described as "too black." When the African American teacher took offense, she allegedly responded, "No, not black like you. *Black* black." Apparently, the African American teacher's complexion fell into the acceptable boundary zone.

"You know who you look like?" one of the Mean Girls asked me when I walked into the meeting room that day.

Was she going to pay me a compliment? I hadn't really experienced her hatred directly, but given that everyone had a story about some crazy thing she had said about me, I hardly expected her to say something flattering. A comparison to Beyoncé was out of the question.

"Oh, my God! I can't believe the name isn't coming to me!" She snapped her fingers in hopes of sparking her memory. "It's right on the tip of my tongue!"

I wondered if she was going to compare me to someone in Hollywood, an actress, or maybe a singer? Maybe she was going to say I looked like an ugly actress. But then, who really is ugly in Hollywood? Just then my thoughts were interrupted by her shrieking. She had finally remembered the name on the tip of her tongue.

"Gahhfield!"

———————

"A *cat*? She called you a fucking *cat*?"

My friend Sylvia was beside herself with laughter when I told her. We were no longer teaching together, but she was still my home girl. We talked on the phone at least once a week and traded teacher stories.

"It's not funny," I replied, stifling a giggle. "O.K., it is, but not that damn funny."

Eventually Sylvia stopped, and I could hear her breathing deeply in an effort to compose herself.

"You done?" I snapped.

"Um, not yet. Can you just imitate her one more time?" She burst into laughter again.

To Sylvia it was just a silly remark. But something told me things were only going to get uglier.

By April the heat was stifling. Month by month, the drama from the teachers in the Mean Girls clique escalated with the rising temperature. Divorces, weight gain, menopause, ungrateful children, and anything else that middle-aged women deal with can make a school a hazardous place if their hearts aren't in the right place.

They would stand by the doors of their classrooms, whispering to one another or sometimes playing that childhood staring game, the one where you lock eyes with someone and see how long you can stare at them before they look away. I avoided their eyes as best as I could. Their classroom doorways may as well have been lockers because we were in high school all over again. It was beginning to be clear to me that I would be their next victim.

I began to feel anxious about going to work, my heart palpitating and anxiety sweeping through my body the minute my alarm clock went off. I would stare at my clothes for more than an hour, thinking about what to wear so as not to piss off any of the Mean Girls, something that was extremely difficult when I also had to worry about my wardrobe's setting off my insecurities about my body.

A black woman's body is her power and her shame all at the same time. It was something that was expected to be hidden and something expected to be on display all at once. It was something she owned, and something that others owned. It was something she was told to love, but also to hate. None of us were truly comfortable in it. It was always being watched. It was big, it was full. It was strong, it was intimidating. It was Serena Williams on the tennis court, Tyra Banks on the catwalk, Michelle Obama on the White House lawn; it was something to lust after, laugh at, die for. It was many things, but it was always, always on display. Black women's bodies were always being watched.

As I agonized about what to wear to school every morning, I managed to forget that I had always suffered from anxiety. The Mean Girls and their antics had simply triggered a preexisting condition.

If I had come from a different type of environment, I might have been diagnosed with anxiety as a child. I might have gone to therapy. I might have been taught to understand the origin of my anxiousness: absentee dad and arguing in the home—and not just between my mom and dad prior to their divorce but among family members during our on-again, off-again stays at my grandmother's place, which was always filled to the brim with relatives, love, laughter, and hateful verbal exchanges.

The wicked custody battle between my parents when I was five couldn't have helped. I can still remember the beautiful outfit my mom dressed me in when I had to take the stand in court and testify against my dad: red long sleeves and a cute little plaid skirt, with a front bow. My hair was bound into three long braids, two on either side and one in the back, with barrettes to hold them in place. I don't remember what I said; I must have blocked it out. But as my mother tells the story, I calmly and vividly described the altercation between my mother and father after one of his court-ordered visits, the one that ended with her blackened eye swollen shut and me atop her body on a gurney headed to the emergency room.

I could imagine similar realities with some of my students. They, like me, would never be given a name for their condition, whatever their condition was. They would never learn what caused it. They would only continue to suffer from it with no solution in sight. They would be labeled with words that sought to normalize and uncomplicate a complex, serious condition in need of treatment. They would be considered "high strung," "energetic," "scaredy-cats," "mean," or, my favorite, "one with an attitude," instead of bipolar or suffering from anxiety or post-traumatic stress. People of color, and especially a born-again Christian mother who believed in praying everything away, rarely had much faith in therapy.

Once when a huge bee flew into our apartment, my mother loosed angels to protect her as she grabbed the bee bare-handed and threw it back out the window. Needless to say, she was stung. I believed in healing and I believe in Jesus Christ, but I also believe that Jesus would want us to seek medical help when necessary.

When I was ten and on my way to my first day of middle school, the "morning panic attack" was born. I was deathly afraid of being made fun of, having had my share of pudgy jokes the year before. I didn't get much exercise because playing outside was dangerous, and we consumed lots of chips, candy, and Pepsi. The kids were even bigger and scarier in middle school and so was the building.

As I walked to school I counted my steps, trying to slow my pounding heart. Sometimes after stopping at the light, I would forget and start back up on the wrong foot, causing uneven steps which I would try to ignore until finally I could take no more, hopping twice on the foot that needed catching up. (I know now that I displayed tendencies of obsessive compulsive disorder and that OCD was usually an attempt to gain control of one's life.)

I also began to sweat through the new white button-down shirt that Ma had picked out for me. By the time my mother and I made it to the school—yes, she still walked me to school—my face was puffy and ashen from crying. My eyes had swollen shut as if I were having an allergic reaction to my own tears.

By the time I was sitting in orientation between two girls I knew from the neighborhood, I was having a full-blown attack and could barely breathe. I was heaving so hard that my mother, still watching from the door of the auditorium to make sure I settled in, must have seen my chest pounding. She motioned me to come out, then begged me to pull it together.

"Don't let them see you cry, baby," she whispered. "They will spot weakness and take advantage of it. You gotta calm down. Please, dear Jesus, let her calm down." She knew what I was going through from her own childhood experiences. My worrywart mother was really another sufferer of anxiety.

She said a silent prayer and I felt safe again, but only temporarily. I never stopped longing to be invisible, and I was never really good at not letting them see me cry.

By May, the temperature in the building was about twenty degrees higher than outside, making the air so thick it was nearly impossible to breathe. Sweat trickled down our backs, our armpits, our temples. Students had given up on learning. They fell asleep from the heat, had nosebleeds, sometimes even fainted. Teachers were miserable. Giles would have had to pay thousands of budget dollars to wire the building and install enough air conditioners for the entire school because schools built before a certain time lacked adequate wiring. Considering the fact that property tax determines the budget of a school building, and our school community was listed as one of the poorest in the nation, the funds were just not there. Our kids' comfort while learning, according to law, just wasn't worth it.

Our building was shaped like a capital L with classrooms on both sides of the longer corridor, and only three rooms along the top floor of the short corridor, mine being one of the three. Because heat rises, the hottest floor was the top floor, and for some reason the top floor of the short corridor, where my classroom was, was the hottest of all.

My classroom was a room that usually stayed empty. Because mine was an added position, and all the other classrooms had been filled, this was the only place Giles could put me. The other two rooms on the top floor of the shorter corridor were the library, which had three air conditioners, and the ESL classroom, where Ms. Sales, a Filipino woman who wore sandals and flowery dresses even in winter, taught students whose home language was something other than English, primarily students from Puerto Rico, West Africa, and the Dominican Republic. Although an unlikely pair, Ms. Sales and I were definitely the two hottest teachers in the school. Catching heat from both the Mean Girls and my smoldering classroom meant that I was in Hell.

By now, I had taken the schoolyard jam on the road. The show I'd choreographed and directed at Singletary's school I not only brought to the Old School but perfected, and the students had been invited to other venues to perform. Because I didn't teach just one class, I had the luxury of auditioning students for roles, which made the performances even better. I was able to make the choreography more challenging because I could now pick and choose my dancers.

Leesha, God bless her petite nine-year-old frame, danced better than I did. I tried to picture her all grown up, imagining how talented she would be by the time she was twenty-one if only she could afford real dance classes. Kids like Leesha put some of the talent on television and movies to shame. Unfortunately, most of these children would never get a chance at stardom because their parents didn't know where to look for classes or had no money to pay for them. When I was in school, my music teacher caught me playing his piano by ear without permission, but instead of being annoyed with me, Mr. Graff referred me to a piano teacher in Mount Vernon. Unfortunately, as reasonable as her prices were, my mother couldn't afford more than six months' worth of lessons.

I couldn't get these kids into Juilliard, but I could give them opportunities to share their abilities and to recognize that they had talent. Who knows, maybe one day something would come of it. And if not, at least performing on stage would improve their confidence, have them stand a little taller, speak a little louder, become more visible.

I also had some singers this time around. According to Mrs. Giles,

Kaleef had a real set of pipes. Coming from the 'hood, I had never met a boy who liked to sing because according to most of them singing was feminine. Not Kaleef.

"Hi, I'm Kaleef," he greeted me jauntily when Giles introduced us, sticking out his hand and giving it a vigorous shake. "Nice to meet you."

Kaleef had to be the happiest child I had ever seen. His braids fairly danced on his head. His wide smile revealed deep dimples in the sides of his cheeks. He had enough joy for an entire school full of children.

"Go ahead, Kaleef," Mrs. Giles said. "Show Ms. Lewis how well you can blow."

Kaleef and Giles had a great relationship. Mrs. Giles thought the singing would help with his self-esteem. It most certainly did. His greeting and handshake were like those of a man prepared for a job interview.

Kaleef started snapping his fingers. Giles was now grinning just as widely as the boy, happy to show off yet another gem of her school. She chimed in with the snaps and looked at me as if to say, "Aren't you going to join us?"

I started snapping too, hoping Giles knew a voice when she heard one. I was all about praising children but hated giving them false hopes.

Kaleef pointed a finger at me and began stomping his feet.

I know you wanna leave me, but I *refuuuuse* to let you go!
If I have to beg and plead for your sympathy, I don't *miiiind*, 'cause
   you mean that much to me!
I ain't too proud to beg, sweet darlin', please don't leave me, girl,
   don't you go!

At the word *go*, Kaleef spun around, pointed a finger in the air, and then lowered it until he was pointing at me again. Finally, he bowed a deep Temptations-like bow. I was stunned. I had never met a boy who could sing so well. He had moves and everything. He was definitely a performer and would need a lead in our show. "Bravo! Bravo!" I yelled, clapping wildly.

We performed for state assemblymen and received a grant to help support the school's music program. We performed for a conference of American historians in Manhattan and were interviewed by a reporter from the *New York Times*. Everyone was amazed at the talent of these South Bronx children, and everyone fell in love with Kaleef. Mrs. Giles enlarged a copy of the *Times* article and hung it outside the main office.

As much fun as we were having, there had to be work involved for the production to qualify as legitimate teaching. My students had to write papers about the information I was providing and had to demonstrate that music can tell a story of a community. They were required to include everything I had taught them about the music that had come from the South Bronx, using lyrics, biographical information about the artists, and information about the neighborhood. I bought decorations like jukebox posters and vinyl records to decorate my bulletin board. I made little booklets with musical notes and G clefs on the covers for their essays.

Before I knew it, Giles had unofficially made me the school's musical director. When she had guests, she made sure to stop by my classroom and introduce me as such.

"I'd like you to meet Ms. Lewis. She's our social studies teacher here and she does a lot of Bronx history with the children as well, particularly in the area of music. In fact, because of her, our children have been invited to perform all over the city."

For our holiday show, Kaleef and the entire fourth grade performed as the Temptations. Giles, as my affectionate name for her school suggests, had a deep appreciation for soul and other old-school music, and ever since the schoolyard jam, with the boys wearing those sweater vests and varsity letters, she had been hooked.

"Ms. Lewis," she would say, "you think it would be possible to get a group together to sing some Smokey Robinson?"

When I could find a way to make the old-school theme appropriate, I would use it. If I couldn't, that was fine, too. *A Motown Christmas* was in heavy rotation in my home growing up, and I knew that any holiday song I taught my students would have to have some soul attached. The boys lip-sync'd "Silent Night" wearing red bow ties and shades and performing the signature Temptation steps. "Silent Night" was a Christmas song, of course, but Giles was fine with that. If someone wanted to sing about *dreidels*, she was fine with that too. "Silent Night" was simply a song that our students grew up listening to, just as "Feliz Navidad" was always the final song for every Christmas holiday sing.

One of the huskier male teachers would dress up as Santa Claus, a para or lunch aide would dress up as Mrs. Claus, and the two would greet the children with little gifts of pretty pencils, heart-shaped erasers, and other cute school supplies. We had a large Muslim population that didn't celebrate Christmas, but all the parents loved Mrs. Giles and her ideas. They too were completely fine with Santa, Christmas songs, and Hanukkah songs.

To reinforce the holiday spirit, I made my bulletin board look like a wrapped present, using shiny wrapping paper and silky ribbon to form four quadrants on which I placed student essays written on paper printed with snowflakes.

The theme of the essays was "The Gift of Giving," inspired by an Oprah Winfrey holiday special I'd had my students watch. The special was an account of a visit Ms. Winfrey had made to South Africa, bringing toys, clothes, and school supplies to children who were extremely disadvantaged. The children were so grateful, their reactions were overwhelming to watch. Even some of my most hard-headed kids shed tears. Though my students were poor, they were rich compared with these South African children.

Watching that special helped my students understand that many children around the world couldn't go to school unless they could pay for it. Ms. Winfrey ended the program by saying that she had received the greatest gift of all because the gift of giving was more gratifying than anything she could ever receive. I couldn't have agreed more.

Black History Months were some of the most memorable periods in my teaching career because my children were so thirsty for what we often called "knowledge of self." Black history was not taught year-round, and they knew nothing about their people other than that we were slaves, Martin Luther King Jr gave a speech, Rosa Parks sat on a bus, and cops liked to shoot us.

Through my years of teaching, I discovered again and again just how much our children hated blackness. Sydney was the most heartwrenching example, but the problem showed up repeatedly through the years. And so I taught them about racism and segregation in the Jim Crow era. We looked at court decisions like *Brown v. Board of Education.* I taught about Kenneth Clark's "Doll Test" and "A Class Divided," the latter a documentary about a phenomenal teacher named Jane Elliot who taught her all-white class what it felt like to be discriminated against based on eye color. I taught them about black fraternities and sororities and their mission of education, excellence, and service. I wasn't a soror myself, in part because I attended college on a predominantly white campus and also because I never believed in my ability to handle the pledging process without fighting a big sister, but I still respected the tenets of what they stood for and thought my students should have the opportunity to at least know that they existed.

Of course I taught them about Martin but also about Malcolm and Marcus. They learned the significance of the Pan-African flag and what the colors stood for. I played the racist song "Every Race Has a Flag but the Coon" and explained how the song prompted Marcus Garvey and the Universal Negro Improvement Association to create a flag that united descendants of Africa from across the diaspora. I felt it just as important for my Hispanic students to learn about their African descent. Many Hispanic students were just as brown as if not darker than many of the African American students. Still, I tried to make some lessons culturally specific to them as well. For example, I taught the Dominican students about Rafael Trujillo and his attempt to racially purify the Dominican Republic—this being decided upon after hearing from even the darkest Dominican students that they were "white" or that they were *not* black.

For the bulletin board, I made one enormous Pan-African pride flag by dividing the space into three equal parts and covering them with pieces of red, black, and green paper. Some students wrote essays for the red section of the flag, which symbolized the blood that united all people of African ancestry and the blood shed for our liberation. These students wrote about the fight for freedom for Americans of color. Other students wrote essays for the black section, which symbolized the people, writing about prominent historical figures of African ancestry. The students who wrote essays for the green section of the flag, which symbolized the continent itself, wrote about the landscape of the motherland—her natural resources, the topography, and the abundance of minerals. These boards, no matter how rigorous, differentiated, and creative, would never win our school's "Bulletin Board of the Month" award, not that Mrs. Giles didn't dig it. She just didn't want her white and light-skinned Latina teachers to complain about black pride. Having a black principal, fellow black teachers, and black students was already an uncomfortable situation for some; throwing our pride in their faces would've turned off most. I continued nonetheless. As a public servant, I served my community, not the needs of my colleagues.

Our black history shows, modeled after the ones I had presented at Singletary's school, would always bring down the house. In my first year, Leesha and the rest of her very talented crew of dancers acted out the story of the origins of step, a rhythmically choreographed dance that involved stomping and slapping one's body to make sounds that resembled drumbeats. The skit was performed over songs from *Bring in 'da Noise, Bring in 'da Funk*, the Savion Glover musical that used tap to chronicle the journey of Africans to America and their progress in an oppressive country.

I hired an African drummer to drum some wicked beats while Leesha danced powerfully until being captured. End scene. When the curtains reopened, she sat on the floor rocking softly to the song "Slave Ship," which mimicked the rolling waves of the ocean heard during the Middle Passage. I tried to suggest those waves using two thick strips of blue fabric that kids held at either end. The material flapped as Leesha, dressed in *kente* cloth, performed a beautiful improvisational modern dance. As she danced, her face reflected fear, despair, and frustration.

In the next scene, Tina and Fatou, with the help of our African drummer, ran away from the plantation where they lived, using the cadence of the drum as a signal. Realizing that the drum was being used to plan escapes, Rasheed, portraying a slave owner, performed a monologue (wearing a colonial wig that ran me fifty bucks from the Halloween store) in which he forbade them to ever use the drum again. Once the drum was physically taken away, off-stage the hired drummer started beating softly while the girls stood listening, "remembering" their beloved drum, until finally they copied the sound using two beats, one distinctive beat that Petra made with her body and a complementary one that Gisselle made with hers.

Giles loved it all, and she invited administrators from the school district to observe the amazing talent of her students. I wish I could say the same for the entire school.

Mrs. Pond was also a favorite of the administration. A soft-spoken black woman, she was just a year shy of retirement, but she still managed to do incredible things for the children. She wrote and published children's books and had her students make their own books to be sent out for publication. When she learned American Sign Language, she incorporated it into her teaching. She taught ASL to all of her writing classes and selected the very best students to be a part of a sign language squad. This squad became fluent in ASL and will have that skill with them for the rest of their lives. When Mrs. Giles asked me to plan the ceremony for the fifth-grade graduation, I couldn't think of a better person with whom to collaborate.

Let me explain something about graduation ceremonies in urban settings. Often the song choices are not the traditional "Pomp and Circumstance" but something more soulful and lively. We knew our audience, and our parents wanted to have a good time.

At Singletary's school, the kids walked down the aisle to Tevin Campbell's "Tomorrow," a song that encouraged the children's feet to move with a little more pep without compromising the emotion parents are entitled to feel while watching their children glide down the aisle in their gowns. We also had the kids perform to songs like McFadden and Whitehead's "Ain't No Stoppin' Us Now," a classic that has blasted through the speakers of thousands, maybe millions, of boom boxes in parks and back yards at black family reunions and barbecues. Another popular graduation song in the inner city was Nas's "I Know I Can," in which students rapped and bopped to inspirational lyrics of empowerment.

I knew that Mrs. Pond and I would come up with something amazing. I told Mrs. Giles of my desire to include her, and her eyes lit up. She knew something special was in the works.

Who could do it better than Michael? Michael Jackson was the one artist whose music everyone, regardless of race, gender, or age, recognized immediately after hearing just one soft-spoken word. More important, everyone loved him. I've never met anyone who didn't like at least one Michael Jackson song. His music must have been playing inside the homes of all the kids I taught, because they could all sing the lyrics as if he were some guy who had just hit the charts that year rather than just longtime pop royalty. They did the Moonwalk as if it were the latest dance craze rather than something that had been created in the '80s.

I chose "Will You Be There," the song that became popular from the *Free Willy* soundtrack back in the '90s. Its tempo was just right for an upbeat march down the aisle. The lyrics called for guidance, love, and support, things that both parents and teachers should be offering for the sake of the children they were raising.

The song wasn't preachy; the love and familiarity in Michael's voice was comforting enough for parents to hear his words without taking offense. Still, the song was a reminder that children needed nurturing to grow. As the graduating classes bopped in, Mrs. Pond's ASL squad stood at the front of the auditorium and signed the song in strong, powerful strokes while two little girls dressed in white did a contemporary dance that gracefully interpreted the lyrics. There wasn't a dry eye in the room.

Shortly after the performance, Mrs. Pond informed me of one of the Mean Girls' recent antics.

"Do you know what this woman had the nerve to say to me?" Mrs. Pond was not one for gossip, but she had clearly had enough. She didn't even have to mention a name; I knew exactly who she was talking about.

"That woman came up to me and said, 'Mrs. Pond, you've gotten so fat! What happened to your body? You used to be so much more attractive.'"

This was surprising not only because Mrs. Pond was an older woman but also because she was at least fifty pounds lighter than the woman.

I couldn't believe what I was hearing. Mrs. Pond was like a mother to us all, a veteran teacher who had earned her stripes. She still dedicated hours of her time to her students during her lunchtime and after school, having the same amount of energy as any young, spry new teacher. As a published author of children's books, she was considered the school's writing guru. Messing with her was like breaking the law.

"What did you say to her?"

"I said, 'I guess like you, I've been eating!'" We laughed until tears ran down our cheeks. Unfortunately, my laughter was short-lived.

Seething inside, I recognized the hard, cold fact that an institution of learning, one whose children were even needier than most because they were living in one of the poorest congressional districts in the nation, had a dangerous bunch of bullies on its payroll. I was glad the school year was winding down.

"Lewis, do you know of any teachers looking to transfer?" Giles asked me. "I've got to add some CTT classes, and we don't have enough teachers with special-education licenses."

CTT, or collaborative team teaching, now called ICT for integrated co-teaching, is a level of special education in which two teachers, a general-education teacher and a special-education teacher, teach a full class that is a mix of general- and special-education students.

I actually did have someone in mind. Stella Rabinowitz had worked with me at Singletary's school as a tutor through a program designed to give individual instruction to one student in each class who needed the most help. Because Rebellious Reggie had such trouble working with the group, I chose him to be tutored by her. We had both stayed in touch with Reggie, and earlier that year we had taken him bowling as a treat for his improved behavior and schoolwork.

Stella was awesome. She had just finished her first year as a teacher. The day we took Reggie bowling, she told me she loved teaching but hated her school. I knew Giles would adore her.

"Sure do," I replied to Giles. "When should she stop by?"

"ASAP. We need that spot filled. Tell her it's a fourth-grade class and, if hired, she'd be teaching with Casey."

I called Stella immediately. I knew she would be thrilled, and having Casey Coppola as a team teacher was an added bonus. Though I had never had a long conversation with Casey, he seemed kind and down to Earth. Both were young and full of energy, and both loved our kids as much as I did even if they weren't from their community.

It was the perfect marriage, and Giles must have agreed. As soon as Stella came in with her huge portfolio and dazzled the hiring committee with her responses, she was sold. With Stella on staff, at least we'd have one more white hat, someone on the side of good. Someone on my side.

———————

Summer vacation came right on time. Whoever said teachers had too many breaks needed to first teach a full year before offering such an opinion. Sometimes all it took was just a three-day weekend to give us the little extra sleep and the refreshment necessary to wake up Tuesday morning prepared to take on the world again. By the time holiday, winter, and spring breaks approached, we had almost reached our breaking points. But the big one, of course, was summer vacation.

Summer vacay was the time to do all the things you wanted to do during the school year but couldn't. The myth that teachers stop working at three in the afternoon didn't take into account lesson planning, phone calls, research, and grading papers. Teachers always brought work home because nothing got done during school hours outside of teaching the children, and even if it did, there was never enough time for everything that needed to be done.

Back when I was a student, instead of circulating the room after teaching a lesson, our teachers actually did some of this work at their desks while we worked independently. When people assume that teaching is easy, I think this is the image they have in their minds. But since my becoming a teacher, sitting at one's desk was out of the question. And whatever workload my teachers had in the '80s and '90s was nothing compared with ours, which had probably quadrupled since the school reform movement of the millennium as a result of the No Child Left Behind Act and Common Core State Standards that would follow.

Hours and hours a week were spent collecting and analyzing data, data that was amassed largely for the eyes of administrators. Collecting and analyzing this data sucked hours out of our day because there were so many places from which we had to retrieve it. Some data came from classroom exams, classwork, and homework that was hand-graded. Some data, usually test scores from the countless practice tests students had to take, was available only online.

Because students were always taking exams, this data was spewed out incessantly. It was also extremely specific, and there were several different lenses through which teachers had to read and interpret it. One report showed how much a class as a whole had progressed between exams. Another report showed each student's progress between exams. But the most time-consuming reports to analyze were the so-called item-analysis reports. One of those reports listed the class's average answer for each question. The other broke down each individual question for each individual student, showing the correct response, the child's response, and the skill that the particular question was assessing.

Such a breakdown might seem helpful, but I had two major issues with it. Rather than just providing teachers with the data to inform their instruction, mounds and mounds of paperwork would also be distributed to teachers to *prove* that they had read the data. Instead of simply being able to group the students accordingly, teachers were forced to write up and submit documentation that regurgitated the exact data that was submitted to us. It insulted our intelligence. Did administrators believe that we could not interpret data? What was the point of having a teacher fill out a form that explained who scored the highest, the lowest, whose lexile reading score was high enough to potentially move the student to the next tier? It was already right there in front of us, but the idea seemed to be as if the more paper we used, the more effective a school would be. All the excessive paperwork did, however, was take away from a teacher's actual planning, thus preventing her from preparing the best instruction.

Additionally, the results are hardly the best indicators of student achievement. First of all, these exams sometimes had only one question about a particular skill, not enough to measure whether a child has actually mastered it. Second, as with all multiple-choice questions, a child could have simply guessed, making it seem as if he had mastered a skill that he hadn't. A child might have gotten a wrong answer because he wasn't reading the questions but rushing through the exam because he was tired of being tested or because he was angry about something that happened at home before school even started. A student who was struggling in school might sabotage his own test by bubbling C throughout the entire test rather than actually trying because then it would look as if he'd failed because he didn't care instead of because he struggled in school. There were so many components these exams could not factor in that could be answered merely from teacher observations and classroom assessments. Still, students would continually be formally tested and we would spend a substantial amount of time analyzing this data.

The point of this data breakdown was that some skills were more basic than others, which showed a student's ability to extend her thinking. Being able to infer was supposedly more advanced than being able to recall, and being able to design her own problem was more advanced than both. However, a question that asks a student to infer the season in a reading passage that says a character is wearing a bathing suit is much simpler than my asking Sydney to infer why Kunta was the only slave wearing shackles. With that being said, common sense seemed not to be factored into question complexity, only categories of supposed critical thinking.

_____

The obsession with data only interfered with normal lesson planning. There was never enough time to do what needed to be done. A forty-five-minute prep period might require a teacher to gather books of different reading levels from four different classes because her class set is too difficult for half of her class to read. By the time she has walked up and down stairs trying to persuade teachers to let her borrow their books, her prep period is already over.

A teacher may have every intention of spending most of her prep period writing a daily lesson plan, expecting to need only five of those minutes to call a child's mother. But to make that call the teacher may find herself going through every single number on the child's blue emergency card before she finds one that is still in service, and that number may be the child's best friend's mother's brother, who may give the teacher his sister's number in the hope that the sister may actually have the number of the person with whom the teacher wanted to speak. After a wild-goose chase that has caused the teacher to lose her entire prep period, the number provided may be the same number she had called to begin with, a number that was out of service because the mother hadn't paid her phone bill or had changed her number without informing the school.

A teacher may have anticipated using her prep period to make copies of the following week's assessment only to find a crying child in the hallway who is punching his fist into the wall. Any teacher worth her salt will stop to talk to this child in an effort to calm him down. By the time she has identified the class he was in, figured out who pissed him off, succeeded in making him smile, and returned him to his classroom, her prep time is gone. If this teacher rushes into the copy room to make some copies of her assignment before it's time to pick up her children, she'll likely discover that four teachers are in line ahead of her.

In the end, she has no choice but to go to Kinko's or Staples to make her copies after school with her own money and to do her lesson plans at home along with the list of vocabulary words for each subject she had planned to compile and the class newsletter that she planned to write. Her planned trip to the gym and the healthful meal she had intended to cook, a meal that would have required a stop at the supermarket, would have to be postponed for another night. She would settle for ordering pizza or snacking on leftover pretzels for dinner.

This is why we needed our summer vacation. Summer was a time to take care of our neglected minds, bodies, and spirits by doing such things as traveling, working out, getting medical checkups, taking courses, catching up on reading or, in my case, writing.

―――――――

Since high school, I had wanted to be a writer. Playing with words and ideas and crafting clever ways to deconstruct a traditional literary text in college was more appealing than going to parties or sporting events. The satisfaction I would receive after retrieving the exact word or phrase I was looking for to describe something, or discovering a kick-ass quote to support my thesis, was comparable to things that might seem much more fulfilling, like eating the final bite of an exceptionally delectable meal or finding the pumps I had been eyeing for weeks on sale for 50 percent off.

Teaching was always supposed to be something I did in conjunction with, not instead of, my long-term love affair with writing. However, even weekend writing was out of the question because by the time Saturday rolled around, my mind was devoid of creative juices. And by the time summer vacation arrived, I realized there was something else I wanted to do for a while. Despite the fact that my father was a mostly absent part of my life as a result of his incarceration, for years I had been wanting to visit his family in Georgia, and I thought such a trip would be an excellent summer adventure.

My dad's entire family had moved to Georgia a few years earlier, and they had all begged me to come and visit. I never intended to be distant to them, but growing up it was hard to form any real relationships with them when my father wasn't in my life. They understood but were always ready to welcome me any time I was ready. I couldn't drive, but Georgia wasn't a million miles away. I could just hop a bus and be there in, what, fifteen hours? And it wouldn't cost a fortune. I called to alert my relatives and bought myself a round-trip ticket.

It wasn't long before we had left the city behind. Through the window, I watched the scenery flow by. Sitting there and feeling so relaxed, I ran over in my mind my time at the Old School. While there had definitely been some bumps in the road, overall it had been a good move. I was less jittery. I could enjoy my classes and not worry about whether my students had passed an exam. I was able to explore history and tell the truth doing so. I was less bombarded with all the data nonsense that classroom teachers had to deal with. If it weren't for the Mean Girls, it would have been a perfect gig.

By evening, the landscape had become especially beautiful. The sun was setting, and the orange sky cast a glow on a stunning green backdrop of fields that seemed to go on forever. I pressed the recline button on the seat, closed my eyes, and decided to release my concerns to the wind. I left all fear and doubt behind me, watching it float out of oversized tinted windows.

Because my father's entire family had moved to Georgia, I would be visiting several houses, all within a half-hour of one another. I didn't know any of my relatives well, but the times we had spent together, albeit brief, made me realize that our souls were in sync. It's funny how genetics work.

My aunt Lee Lee was the coolest member of the family and the one who reminded me most of myself. She was a writer like me. We even had the same corkscrew curls. She lived in a condo with no man or children, free as can be. Her sister, Lonnie, was slightly older and more bookish.

She married a brother who was the epitome of a southern gentleman, and they lived in a traditional-looking house with their newborn son.

My granddaddy—and I say *granddaddy* instead of *grandfather* because he was such a cool cat well into his seventies—lived in the type of house I had seen only on *MTV Cribs*, the television show in which celebrities flaunt their multi-million-dollar mansions. Grandpa Jimmy, as his relatives called him, had sold his home on Long Island and was able to use the money to buy a mini-mansion in Georgia because the cost of living there was so much less. He lived there with his third wife, my step-grandmother Candy, whom he had married long before I was born.

Candy was a bona fide New Yorker and, even though legally blind, was the most independent woman I knew. Together they had a child named Kina, who was the center of her daddy's world. Kina was technically my aunt but young enough to be my cousin, being only a few years older than I. She was the firecracker in the family, a mix of her mother's New York grit and her daddy's overabundance of love. The bar for being part of Kina's world was set so high that only the best men, friends, or even acquaintances could be expected to reach it. If you acted in a way that Kina found disrespectful to her or anyone in the Lewis family, she would definitely let you have it. The Lewis women were the embodiment of strength. They were me if I weren't so broken.

Lee Lee was waiting for me at the bus stop.

"Pammy!" she squealed as she wrapped me in a huge bear hug. "My God, girl, you are beautiful!" Lee Lee was always full of compliments.

By the time we pulled up to Grandpa Jimmy's house, I was truly considering moving to one of the most humid places in the country. His house looked more incredible than it did in the pictures Kina had sent me. I'd never seen anything like it. These were upper-middle-class black folk while I was just a kid from the Bronx. Even someone accustomed to a suburban lifestyle would have been impressed.

Grandpa had the biggest master bedroom I had ever laid eyes on. It was the size of my entire apartment, and the attached bathroom was the size of my living room. Each room in the house had its own distinct color scheme of vibrant reds, oranges, and neutrals. Plush, elegantly patterned accent rugs covered brilliantly polished hardwood floors, big lofty sofas sat as proudly as the people they seated, and crystal chandeliers sparkled in the dining room and den.

And the loveliest discovery of all? The works of African and African American art that adorned each room of the house.

A sculpture of a regal Zulu warrior stood in the foyer and could be seen immediately upon entering. Strength and pride radiated from his chiseled bronze frame and his searing, unapologetic gaze. The sculpture seemed to be Grandpa's way of letting everyone who visited know that he loved his people, whether that made them uncomfortable or not.

Nearby hung a trio of African masks, and throughout the house were paintings of African women. Some wore bright flowing dresses. Others wore nothing but billowy wraps on their heads. In the kitchen there hung an image of dignified black women with bowls and buckets atop their heads like crowns. The image of a woman wearing earrings shaped like musical notes and draped in fabric with the pattern of piano keys and melodic brass swirls sat on top of the piano in the den, the same piano I remembered playing as a kid when I used to visit my grandfather's home on Long Island. Upstairs in the bedrooms were images of black lovers making sweet, sensual love, their chocolate bodies melding as one. They called to mind the lyrics of India Arie's "Brown Skin": "I can't tell where yours begins, I can't tell where mine ends."

———————

After all the hugs and kisses, everyone finally sat down to dinner. It was a Sunday, they hadn't seen me in years, and I was in the South, so I don't have to tell you how much food had been prepared. With full bellies, everyone then proceeded to the living room to talk and catch up.

"You know your granddaddy's been going to a senior center and having himself a good ol' time lately, ain't that right, Jimmy?" Candy informed us.

"Really, Grandpa? What do you do there?"

"Daddy does all sorts of things there, right, daddy?" Kina said with a laugh. "He's officially become the senior man on campus."

"Get out!" Lee Lee slapped her knee. "Well, it wouldn't be right any other way, now would it?"

"Sure wouldn't. Daddy, weren't you voted most popular in school or something?" Lonnie stroked her father's hair as she spoke. It was evident that this man was loved.

"Aw, hush up, babies, I'm not *Ebony* Man of the Year or nothing. I am a bit popular, though. It's those Lewis genes, you know? People just gravitate toward us because we're special."

"Here he go." Kina rolled her eyes. "Did you know that this man used to pump that Lewis stuff so hard when I was a kid that I actually thought we were descendants of some royal family? Walking around telling my school friends, 'You can't say that to me. I'm a Lewis.' I used to really think I was some damn princess."

"Used to?" Lonnie shot back.

"She *is* a princess," Grandpa replied. "Daddy's little princess. And, uh, we do descend from royalty." Grandpa looked up at us from above his wire-rimmed glasses.

Everyone stopped laughing to listen to the old wise man speak.

"We *were* royalty in Africa," he said matter-of-factly.

"But how would you know that when we don't even know what country in Africa—"

I couldn't get the words out before he interrupted me.

"Exactly. We don't. So why not believe in the possibility? Whatever we were, though, it damn sure was better than what we became. I'd like to think our stature means something more than an athletic build to work the fields with. Just look at us, Pam. Look at that height. You mean to tell me that strong build doesn't suggest power?"

I had never thought of my body as powerful, more as clumsy. I wished I weren't so tall and that my legs weren't so long, but now that Grandpa mentioned it, I was built. I smiled at the new image of myself that he had given me.

"It all comes down to what you allow yourself to be told," Grandpa continued, taking a long sip of iced tea. "That's why some slaves were always free. They knew their worth. Still got some slaves today, unfortunately. Niggers that don't know their worth. You hear that, grandbaby? Always know your worth. People will lie to you. Try to project their own insecurities on you and tell you you're inferior in hopes that you will believe them. Don't you listen to them, Pam. You come from royalty."

Then Grandpa began telling us about his senior center and the classes he took there. I should have known that he'd be doing something for himself instead of taking care of everyone else at this point in his life. His kids took care of him now, as they should. My mind wandered again to my maternal grandmother, who had taken care of her family until the day she had a nervous breakdown, thanks to the pressure of living in a small apartment with her son, grandson, and granddaughter. Tensions were high living in Edenwald Projects, and often, though we all loved one another, the rage and suffering that we all experienced would erupt, leaving an aftermath of more rage and suffering. The cancer came immediately after, and she died within months. She should have been able to "do her" too, the way my grandfather was doing now, instead of living for everyone else. After years of working and raising children, elders deserved time to enjoy life without worry for a while.

———————

Grandpa did all sorts of things at the center, but his favorite activity was taking African American history courses.

"You take courses at the center?" I couldn't believe it. The idea of people in their seventies choosing to go to school amazed me. What amazed me more was that my Grandpa was one of them.

"Actually, honey, I take two. One pre–civil rights and one post. Here's the syllabus with all the books on our reading list.

"Here's what we're currently reading," he continued. He ran his fingers over the picture of a woman's face on the cover of one volume. On the woman's head was what seemed to be a metal helmet with the lock dangling over one eye. I recognized the drawing immediately. It was a literal interpretation of the idea that this woman's mind was shackled and in need of being unlocked and set free.

"*The Mis-education of the Negro* by Carter G. Woodson," I said. To which my grandfather replied, "We must reprogram our brains, my dear Pamela. Without doing so, we drink the Kool-Aid of whatever society tells us to think of ourselves. Promise me to never buy into their myth."

I promised him by vowing to stop taking sips of the Kool-Aid that I allowed myself occasionally.

———————

Five minutes after I'd crawled into bed, the text alert on my phone went off. It was Stella, who was soon to be hired to work at our school. I had to read it aloud to make sure I had understood the message correctly.

"Hey, so Giles called. Was impressed. Said she's almost positive that she can hire me, but waiting on her budget. Had another interview today. Kinda liked that school too. I don't know girl, it's closer to home and they offered me the job on the spot."

Oh, no! This was not the plan at all!

I texted Giles. She called back, explaining her dilemma with the budget. Poor schools almost always had dilemmas regarding budgets. She couldn't hire Stella. Her projections did not match the money that she would be receiving.

"I guess you'll have to find another teacher now, huh?"

"Yep."

"So, which candidate are you considering?"

"None of them."

"I'm confused." I paused and thought about what she was insinuating.

"So you're going to put a teacher already in the organization down as the special-education teacher in the class?"

"Mmhmm."

I didn't understand how that could be done. She couldn't choose any of the special-ed teachers because they were already assigned. The only solution would be to remove a teacher from a cluster position. But none of them had their special-ed licenses. None of them, that is, except me.

"You and Coppola are cool, right?" Giles asked.

Now I understood everything. She was eliminating the social studies cluster position and putting me in the CTT class. That way she could still create the CTT class without having to hire an additional teacher.

My dream position was gone. The question I was now faced with: Would I be allowed to teach my history, *our* history, with another teacher, a white teacher, in the room?

5
Caught Out There

All summer, I had Kelis's song "Caught Out There" on heavy rotation as I sang along, down even to the scream at the end:

"I hate you so much right now! Ahhhhhh!"

I knew the stress would be coming. Not because I would be responsible for my own set of students, but because of all that came with it: The data monster that had infiltrated all of the schools in the city; the pressure of visitors in and out of my room to check in on me as if I hadn't been teaching for years already; the miracles they would be expecting me to perform that required us to pretend we didn't know that poverty often had a death grip on the achievements of our students. I had to think positive or I would've given myself an ulcer.

I figured I should just come to terms with the fact that I would no longer be teaching history. I decided to think about the pros of collaborative team teaching with Casey.

He was a great teacher, and he genuinely loved our kids.

I would have my own class again and thus have a deeper connection with the students. Even though I had built relationships with many kids as a cluster teacher, it wasn't the same as teaching your own group of children the entire day.

The special-education students in a CTT setting were accustomed to meeting the same expectations as the general-education students they sat next to. They weren't made to feel as though they were different and, as a result, were usually optimistic about their educational experience. This in turn meant they were usually more motivated and tended to be more successful than their special-education peers in self-contained classes—at least, that's what "research" said. It was also true that more money was granted to schools for CTT classes than self-contained classes like the ones I had taught at Singletary's school. With this in mind, it is quite rational to question whether the population of special-education students in CTT classes in any school building is about money or about students.

By now teaching had become a numbers game, although the numbers mattered most in schools in poverty-stricken communities. That was not the case everywhere, as I discovered when chatting with a New York City teacher who had moved to a school in Buffalo. Around the end of the year I inquired about her students' test results.

"Oh, they don't care about that kind of stuff here," she replied.

Here was the operative word. *Here* meant places where children were predominantly white and privileged and therefore not held under a microscope because they were already performing well. They performed well because they were fortunate enough to have been born under different circumstances, circumstances that had everything to do with the color of their skin and the money in their daddies' wallet.

But for children in other places around the country, testing had become increasingly important because the children in these places were failing. The reason for this failure had little to do with teaching and everything to do with broad social and economic problems. Unfortunately, teachers had become the scapegoats for society's ills, and our livelihoods now depended on how well a child performed on a test. As a result, testing was always on our minds.

In fact, testing had become so embedded into the New York City school culture that asking a fellow teacher about her students' test results seemed normal.

Imagine two surgeons having this conversation:

"So, how many died on your table this year?"

"I did better last year. But then, last year was a good year. Not as many knuckleheads coming into the ER, you know? This year, it was damn near impossible to save these people. Lots of successful suicides attempts. Tons of gang-related retaliation shootings. You know I operate in Chicago."

Ouch.

Returning to a classroom teacher position meant that I would again be expected not only to teach but also to do things intended to *prove* that I was teaching. This did not sit well with me at all, as it doesn't with most; however, it was ever the more insulting to me as a teacher of color. I'd done a lot of proving myself already, and I never did well with the idea of shucking and jiving. I didn't work for others' approval, and this new accountability system was even more outrageous than it had been at Singletary's school. At least then, I was still wet behind the ears and eager to learn what I did not know, so having to prove myself was something I was semi-okay with doing. By now, I had already proven I was a good teacher and had impressed not one but two principals with my craft and content knowledge. I wasn't thrilled, to say the least.

I had heard classroom teachers talk about how the educational reform movement of the past decade had kicked into overdrive, but because I didn't have my own classroom, I hadn't felt its effects personally.

I could only imagine what the pressure was like at Singletary's school, where tension had been thick for years. I especially felt for general-education teachers, who would get no pass if their students had failed. Though I had felt pressure to get my special-education students to pass at Singletary's school, teaching a class composed entirely of special-education students meant that it was accepted that some students would score 1, the lowest score, as long as some members of the class had performed on grade level.

Because of students like Jesús, Jennifer, Sydney, Lorenzo, and Reggie, I was always safe. Unfortunately, many general-education students in our communities were performing on the same level as special-education students for reasons beyond a teacher's control. For one thing, testing didn't start until the third grade, and students who fell behind in class year after year were sometimes promoted in the earlier years because their parents refused to let the school hold their children back, or because there were so many young children in the community that those who could benefit from repeating a year were promoted to prevent overcrowding of classrooms. Simply opening another classroom sounds simple, but often schools in poor communities had no money to hire an additional teacher. There was also a space issue. Community schools were not campuses like some of the elementary schools I had seen in other parts of the country. We had an annex that had been built and used for additional pre-kindergarten classrooms, but with the new changes in ed reform, schools were having to share their space with other schools. In our case, the annex was given to a D75 school; however, all across the city whole floors were being taken from schools, sometimes from charter schools that had money. Even though our schools were still poor, a charter school on a different floor could have state-of-the-art technology, renovated classrooms, and brand-new furniture. Luckily, Giles didn't have to go through that, but she still had a space issue and could not open additional classrooms whenever she wanted to.

"Fuck that shit, it's not happening!"

A petite woman wearing pajama pants, sandals, and a head scarf pulled one of the students off the line that Casey and I were standing in front of with the sign that said, "Mr. Coppola and Ms. Lewis. Class 4-402." Casey glanced up at me. Moving from teaching first grade to fourth grade, as he had just done, was already a scary transition for him. Plus he had been traumatized by a horrible experience the previous year involving two parents and a child's coat. Two first-graders had the same NorthFace jacket, and there had been an accidental switch during recess as a result of which the two parents had a fist fight in front of the entire class. This parent appeared to be a problematic one.

"Can I help you with something? What seems to be the problem?"

I had to jog a bit to catch up with the woman before she stomped off.

"It don't *seem* to be a problem," she shot back. "There *is* a fucking problem, and that is that your principal is a fucking retard. I told her stupid ass to not put my son in the same class as Noemi. And lo and fucking behold, I go to drop him off and here go both of these motherfuckers in the same goddamn line. Like, do I have to speak another fucking language or what?"

She was obviously angry. Actually *angry* is an understatement. I tried again.

"Listen, let's see if we can work this out. You're saying you don't want your son in the same class as this girl because they don't get along? Do they have a history of problems?"

I looked over at the little boy she was still gripping by the elbow. He knew not to say a word.

"Don't get along? No, that's not it at all, ma. These two are like Bonnie and motherfuckin' Clyde. They got a history all right. They best friends, and been best friends since they was in the womb because they parents is best friends, *tu sabe?*"

Actually, I didn't know. I was really confused.

"So let me make sure I'm understanding you," I said. "You don't want your son to be in the same class with his best friend? Are you worried that they're going to talk too much?"

"Nah. Buddy works. He needs a little help with his word decoding, but his comprehension is good. And he need that extended time when he takes tests. He's great in math but sometimes reading the word problems fucks with him. But he *works*. He busts his ass. Right, *papi?*"

Papi looked up at his mother and smiled. She pinched his cheek lovingly, then continued.

"So, if they in the same class, it's gonna be a problem. Say Noemi gets into some beef. What the fuck y'all expect Buddy to do? Sit back and watch her get her ass beat? Noemi got beef. Buddy got beef. Buddy got beef, Noemi got beef. You feel me? They go'n be scrappin' every motherfuckin' day. How he expect to learn in that environment? Even his one-to-one ain't gonna be able to help that. Giles didn't think about that shit, did she?"

I had no clue what Giles had been thinking. All I was thinking was that this mother was a mix of sailor and PTA president. She was definitely deeply involved in her son's education. Still, I had to get these kids away from her.

"Casey, take the kids up, I'll meet you in a few. I'm going to go up with Ms.—Ms.—I never got your name."

"Santos."

Ms. Santos agreed to let Buddy walk up the stairs with the class, but she was still cursing by the time we got to Mrs. Giles's door. From the look on her face, I don't think she appreciated our surprise visit.

"Why, hello! What brings you to my office, Ms. Sunshine?"

Ms. Sunshine was laughing by now, but she was still deathly serious. The two of them had an odd relationship. It was obvious that each knew that the other cared, but Giles's sarcasm suggested that her attitude was nothing new. I had a feeling that Ms. Santos was the parent everyone in the school knew not to mess with. I still couldn't figure out if that was a good thing or a bad thing.

"*Ay! Mami*, why must you use such vulgar language in a place of learning?" Mrs. Giles was now mimicking her accent.

She told her, "I had to do it. You know one of the other teachers already had some incidents with your friend Mr. Melendez. I can't put

Noemi in there. Ms. Hemmingway teaches the girls' class and Mr. Diaz teaches the boys, and you know neither of the students can go into the boys' class, *or* the girls' class. They'd fight every day."

Ms. Santos sat on that for a while. "This is true. It'll be drama every day. But I'm telling you, if one fights, they both fight in that room together." She pointed at me.

"Wait, I get why Noemi can't be put in the all-boys' class, and even why Buddy can't be in the all-boys' class, but why can't we put Noemi in the all-girls' class?" I inquired.

Both of them just looked at me. Ms. Santos hissed like a cat.

This was true. I forgot I was experiencing my own bout of cattiness from the Mean Girls. From the sounds of Noemi, she and too many girls didn't mix.

What about that other teacher's class?" I suggested. "You never had a problem with her, right? Noemi's dad doesn't get along with her, not you."

"Ma-ma, Buddy is special ed. He can't go nowhere but your class 'cuz it's CTT. And correction, I *do* got a problem with that bitch. So even if he wasn't special ed, he couldn't go to that fucking bitch. You wasn't listening? My nigga got beef, then I got beef. That's how we roll. Where you think Buddy get it from?"

"Ah."

This was beginning to sound like the Mafia: "La Familia." While I didn't agree with Ms. Santos's methods, I couldn't deny that the bond was one to be envied. I never approved of the violence portrayed in Mafia movies, but there was definitely something to be said about an organization so tight, an organization whose members were so incredibly loyal to one another. I don't use the term *La Familia* to poke fun at Ms. Santos's philosophy but as a form of respect. She and her friends were a family, even if not a biological one.

I imagine that Ms. Santos had grown up as I had, learning to trust only those who had proven themselves to you, who would take a bullet for you, thus limiting her small circle of friends to those she could count on one hand. The school definitely wasn't a place of trust for black and Hispanic single mothers and fathers like her and Noemi's dad. We were just one more institution of authority. Many members of communities like the one in which Ms. Santos lived never believed that the city would ever do a damn thing for them. It was them against the world.

Still, I couldn't believe the level of disrespect spewing from this woman's mouth. And I couldn't believe how patiently Giles responded.

"So you can understand my decision, Ms. Santos. If I had another place, I would, but it's slim pickings. The good thing about the kids' being together with Ms. Lewis here and Mr. Coppola is that there are two teachers in the classroom, two paras, and best of all, the two teachers are both excellent behavior-management specialists."

I was?

"You won't have anything to worry about." Giles had that satisfied look on her face she always had when things went her way.

Ms. Santos clearly wasn't so sure. "Good luck," she said to me with pity in her eyes as she headed out the door.

I had to hurry up and get back to my classroom. It was the first day of school, which meant making introductions and announcing rules and procedures. If I was going to be one of the two teachers in the room, I would need to be there from the beginning.

Teaching collaboratively is not the same as teaching in other settings. A collaborative team-teaching class (the name was later changed to integrated co-teaching, or ICT) was intended to give equal status to both in the classroom. As the latter name suggests, it is truly co-teaching, and neither teacher is above the other.

One is the general-education teacher and the other is the special-education teacher, and the teachers themselves decide how the arrangement will work. Sometimes the special-ed teacher works only with students assigned to her. More often the teachers take turns teaching different subjects. Casey and I decided that together we would conduct the reading workshop, which consisted of different reading groups organized according to students' abilities. Casey would be the lead teacher for science and math, and I would be the lead teacher for writing and social studies. When I was up at bat, he would work with our lowest group, and vice versa.

To work properly, team teaching has to involve a perfect marriage. If the two teachers mesh well, if they communicate well and complement each other, it's a match made in education heaven. But if they don't like or respect each other or if one of them is controlling, expect tension, bickering, and an eventual breakup.

Having two teachers in the classroom made sense in many respects. Two teachers meant better behavior management, more time devoted to planning instruction, even much-needed breaks from talking to students all day. But because co-teaching had become a mandated and more popular program of special education, there were ever more CTT classes per grade level, which meant more marriages and a smaller pool of teachers from which to choose. Expecting that any two teachers chosen at random could be thrown together and be more effective as a unit than individually was as insane as believing that any man and woman in the world could get married and offer a better home life for their children than either could do alone.

Even at the age of five, I knew better. My parents, who were then separated and in the process of getting a divorce, were prepared to give their marriage one more try for the sake of their only child. Their thinking was that whatever their differences, having both parents in the home would be best for me. Thankfully, they made the wise decision to ask me my opinion, and fortunately, I responded logically rather than emotionally, despite my age: "Thanks, but no thanks."

So far, Casey and I were off to a good start. Ms. Santos clearly was someone I should have handled. I had realized that more often than not I would get a free pass with some of the parents of minority students, one that Coppola, with his blue eyes and blond hair, would often be denied. Though, as with the case of peoples who are oppressed, sometimes being white and male worked in his favor. Many of our students admired his hair and his eyes similarly to the way they focused on my lighter skin and hair. This adoration for him, however, changed immediately when they became upset with him; immediately, he would become the oppressor, and all of a sudden, his straight hair and light eyes no longer mattered. Some of our parents of children of color felt uncomfortable with white teachers, and with those parents I took the lead. And even though we had more Hispanic students than black students, these parents usually accepted me because I was a person of color, because I came from the bottom, and often because they thought I was Dominican.

In any case, it was now introduction time. I had left Casey to perform the ritualistic dance of dominance alone. I hadn't wanted that to happen, but as it would turn out, I didn't have a choice.

"Ms. Lewis, slow down! Can I borrow you for just one minute?" A charter member of the Mean Girls posse was yelling to me from her classroom.

What now?

I poked my head through the door. Shocked that she was speaking to me because she often ignored me when I said hello, I walked into the room to see what she wanted.

"In a bit of a rush," I said cheerfully, "but what's up?"

"Well, I'll be brief. But you are the perfect example of what I was just trying to illustrate to Grace over here."

She pointed to a little girl at a desk playing with her hair.

"I asked the class what they wanted to be when they grew up," she continued, "because I wanted to give them information on the steps they'd need to take to get there, like you know, Ms. Lewis, if, say, you wanted to be a teacher, you'd need to get your teacher certification and—"

"Uh-huh, I get it."

"So anyway, Grace says she's going to get married so that a man can take care of her. Can you believe that? We're in a new millennium, and this child just looked me in the eye and said it with such matter-of-factness! I had to check for fever!" With each sentence, her voice seemed to grow louder.

"So, I say to her, I say, now listen here, Grace. We women are supposed to be independent. You can't have a man taking care of you. See, that's where you came up."

Where I came up? How on Earth did this woman manage to get me into this conversation?

"So I say to her, I say, 'Now, just because you're pretty and a man will probably do whatever you ask him to, it doesn't mean that you should let him. Ms. Lewis is pretty.'

"And then I said, 'Now, kids, if Ms. Lewis wanted to have a man take care of her, she could, but she didn't.' You have your master's degree, right? Tell them you have your master's."

Reluctantly, "I have a master's."

"And you are an independent woman because although you're pretty enough to have a man take care of you, beauty fades. You see, class," she added, turning to her students, "what you have in front of you is an attractive woman. But she won't be beautiful forever. If she had a man taking care of her, she'd run the risk of his leaving her after her beauty was gone for a younger, more attractive woman. And then where would she be? And who knows? Ms. Lewis could even get into an accident one day, and something could happen to that pretty face of hers. Then what?

"But," she added, tapping her temple with her index finger, "luckily, Ms. Lewis was no dummy. She made sure she got her master's."

Was that a threat?

I managed a smile and walked out hastily. Turning the corner, I saw someone walking toward me and realized it was another woman from the crew.

Great.

She was sure to have something evil to say to mess up my first day even more. But whatever she had to say, I wasn't going to let her know that she was getting to me. I smiled with my eyes, hoping I would be met with the same reaction. Instead, she looked me straight in the eyes and walked right past me.

So now she's not speaking to me at all?

Over the next few weeks, I had my answer. She and the rest of her older cronies were giving me the silent treatment. I was officially in high school again.

Casey proved to be quite the cool dude. He genuinely loved our kids. We were a dynamic pair, both viewed by others as intelligent but rough around the edges, though we came from entirely different worlds. In fact, we did so well together our first year that Mrs. Giles suggested that we loop with our class to the fifth grade—that is, move with our students up to the next grade.

We thought it was a splendid idea because we complemented each other extremely well. We were close in age, and though different culturally, we hadn't grown up too far from each other. Casey was one of those white boys who could fit into a group of brothers and hold their own. Because of this we even hung out together during our off hours. He knew about my love life and I about his. Because this was his first time teaching an upper grade, he was totally fine with receiving help. Still, he was a great teacher. It really was like a model marriage.

I could see, though, how he might feel that Giles didn't respect the marriage. Given the growing emphasis on accountability that had swept our school and the rest of the city, teachers were required to be involved in more decision-making activities than ever before. Having teacher input was a good idea, but this involvement also meant more work and thus more energy being stripped from one's classroom.

It made sense for Giles to include as many co-teachers as possible on the committees that did this extra work because there'd always be another teacher in the room to manage classroom responsibilities. And because I was being given so many out-of-classroom responsibilities, Casey was often left to do most of the classroom prep on his own. I was on the hiring committee, the RTI (Response to Intervention) team, the Inquiry team (an investigative team that targeted select students who were academically at risk), and the curriculum mapping team. You name it, and my signature was on the attendance sheet. I was also always sent out to attend workshops and often to turnkey the information during our school's professional development.

I felt guilty for leaving Casey to handle our classroom alone so often. Many times, while I was off attending a workshop, a substitute teacher was put in the room with him to provide support. Much of my prep time went to committee work and meetings. One day a student named Gabby asked me if I was an administrator because I was always doing something that in her nine-year-old mind looked "administrative."

I enjoyed learning about such issues as school budgeting, and I took seriously any work that helped advance our school's standing, such as developing an instructional focus for the year, drawing up comprehensive education plans, and writing grant applications.

In addition, having fancy titles and positions and being able to add certifications, training, and committee membership to one's résumé offered many benefits. It sounds more professional to say that someone is a "consultant" or a "leadership coach" or a "coordinator" than "teacher." It looks good to be able to say that you have had training in this or that, that you have piloted a new program or provided professional development to an entire faculty. All of these things represent great leadership opportunities, and administrators and superintendents value such titles.

At the same time, resentment builds toward those who are not on the front lines, toward those who don't do the dirty work full time. They lose their street cred, the same way a police officer who sits at a desk all day gets less respect from those who battle crime in the streets. My co-teacher relationship was bound to deteriorate.

Prepared to take my dramatic turn, I faced the board, holding an eraser in my hand like a microphone, ready for the beat to drop for the instrumental to Beyoncé's "Ego." My version was called "Intro," and it was intended to help students understand how to write a strong introduction using a thesis statement.

Once I heard the cue, I was on. I turned around sharply and began in a low voice:

> Don't let your readers get lost, you need a strong intro, call in the
> big boss,
> For real, I wanna tell you how I feel, I consider my thoughts and
> ideas a big deal,
> Why? Well, my thesis begins from the start, but I'm not gonna
> prove it,
> I'd rather prove it in the body, and show you something, I believe
> inside,
> No need for me to lie.
> It's *solid*! *Organized*! It's so *strong*! Perfect *fit*!
> Not too *much*, just the right *touch*,
> I gotta thesis and I can back it up!
> I gotta strong intro! *Such* a strong intro! It has *just* the right info!
> Not too much, I gotta thesis and I can back it up. I can back it up,
> I can back it up, I write like this 'cause I can back it *uuuup*!

I froze, still with the eraser serving as my microphone. The kids clapped and hooted and hollered. Casey gave me a standing ovation. The kids took off to review the introductions they had written the previous day. Using the song as a guide, they expanded, edited, or enhanced their introductions, ensuring that they were strong and clear and included a thesis statement of an idea they felt strongly about and one they could prove eventually but not in the introduction. Casey and I circulated around the room, looking over their shoulders to see if they knew what they were doing. The approach seemed to be working.

Then Casey sent a signal to me.

"Ahem, Ms. Lewis, you've *got* to see what Summer wrote. She really did an excellent job."

Casey's bulging eyes told me that he wasn't as impressed with Summer's work as he seemed but wanted me to look at something else. I walked over to them and followed his eyes to Summer's neck, where I saw a big purple hickey. I wasn't surprised. Summer was older than the other girls in our class and was the first one to deal with raging hormones. Her behavior had been completely out of hand lately, and most days Casey just couldn't take it. But Summer adored me, so she bit her tongue when speaking to me.

"You could be my momma," she'd always say. We did resemble each other.

I had an idea. Giles had asked me to practice with the group of three girls I had selected for the school's forthcoming holiday performance. It was nearly 11:30, the time set aside for the practice, so I led Summer and the other girls away, planning to talk to her alone after the practice session.

The three girls—Summer, Jordan, and Gabby—had practiced their steps for two weeks. Their routine was nearly perfect, and they were thrilled that all their hard work had finally paid off.

Summer and the rest of the girls had been carefully chosen for this particular presentation. Schools often made every student in the class participate in a song or a dance for the purpose of inclusion, but I didn't operate that way. I believed that everyone deserved the opportunity but that only those who made sense to be chosen for something should be selected. I didn't believe in entitlement; that's not the world we live in, and it kept our students complacent with mediocrity. For that reason, I found strengths in my students and always gave opportunities as they arose based on those strengths.

When it came to performing, I understood that not every child was musically inclined or a talented dancer, and even those who were had different strengths. Some children were graceful and could do a contemporary dance number that would bring anyone to tears. I wasn't that child, and frankly, I had to hire a Fordham intern to teach those types of dances to those children. Some had an amazing ability to interpret any drum beat thrown their way. To those kids I taught African dance, step dancing, hip-hop, reggae, and Latin dance. Some had Caribbean rhythm but couldn't do the running man, a classic hip-hop move, to save their lives.

Some kids had two left feet but could sing like nobody's business. Some weren't into performing at all, and I had to respect that and find something else they could contribute to a school assembly, assigning them roles like stagehand. When Frankie and Curtis refused to perform for the "History of Step" show that depicted the Middle Passage journey from Africa to the Americas, they were the ones who stood at either side of the stage and used a strip of bright blue fabric to suggest waves.

Summer, Jordan, and Gabby could dance to anything. They were my top performers and would invariably be the stars of any school production. During this practice session, they begged every teacher who walked past the door to stop and watch them perform. After each performance, the teacher applauded, first because they really *were* great and, second, what kind of teacher would not want to make three little girls feel special?

Marriott Hotel to perform our "Story of Our Community Through Music" show for the Organization of American Historians, they danced their little behinds off. Their performance had been the subject of an article in the *New York Times*, too, so Giles was thrilled. Along with bragging rights, Giles sought publicity because publicity nearly always brought money that was essential for a school located in one of the nation's poorest congressional districts. These activities also meant that the kids were truly enjoying themselves, and happy children meant learning children.

I enjoyed what I was doing, and I did my best to make sure that the kids enjoyed themselves too. One would think that motivating children to learn was something teachers could appreciate. None of that mattered. I was rocking the boat of seniority.

After the students finished practicing, I told the other two girls to go back to class and took Summer with me to the teachers' lounge so we could talk. I was glad I did. She opened up to me about everything she was feeling, feelings that, now exposed, led to tears. Summer wasn't one for crying, so her tears represented how emotional she was at that time. Growing pains, we had all been there, and I let her know she wasn't alone. Our talk did her some good.

Just as we were wrapping things up, two older teachers, a man and a woman, with whom I hadn't had much communication up until then walked in and sat down at the other side of the table. They looked at Summer and saw that her face was red and ashen from crying. Unconcerned, the woman began:

"You know, I thought this was a teachers' lounge," she snorted to her male colleague.

"I thought so too," he said back, almost as if he believed that he had been wrong to assume as such.

"I don't know what kind of teacher would think it's O.K. to bring a student into a teachers' lounge meant for teachers to take a break from children for forty-five minutes."

"I don't know either. Can't say I'd do something like that. Wouldn't want to keep teachers from enjoying their lunch."

Summer communicated, "Is this bitch serious?" to me with her eyes.

"Apparently so," my eyes told hers back. "But it's O.K., I got something for her. Watch this."

I could feel my crazy creeping up. My hands were trembling, and a typhoon of tears rose to my eyes. As much as I wanted to play it cool and act like I could take such hatred in stride, it hurt to be mistreated for no

Apparently, there was one such teacher.

An older black woman from the South, one particular teache the most ornery woman I ever met. She was the original Mean Gir with no crew. She never particularly liked me, and she made sure I l it by the look on her face whenever I said hello. As she walked pas rehearsal room, Summer called out to her to come in. After rolling eyes, she entered, clearly unenthusiastic about the idea.

The girls didn't notice. They were too excited about the chan show off.

As soon as I pressed the play button for the music and the girls gan to move, she began to read the sheet of paper she was holding in hand. After a few seconds, the girls took notice and looked at me for port. I waved at them to continue.

"*I'm* watching, girls," I called out cheerfully. "Keep going."

The three continued their performance, but it had become slig lackluster now that their feelings had been hurt. The teacher contin to read, not looking up once.

When the girls ended the number with a dramatic pose and the mu stopped, she finally raised her eyes.

"Y'all finished yet?" she demanded.

"Yep, done," I replied on the girls' behalf.

"Good," she snapped, storming out of the room in her usual surly v

When the door slammed, my girls stood there in shock. Their e darted from the door to me and then to one another, confused as to wl they had done wrong.

"It's not you, girls, it's me," I told them consolingly. "You danc beautifully. She didn't want to watch you because I choreographed Don't take it personally. It's guilt by association."

But how could they not? These were children.

The whole incident forced me to realize something. What I was doir was frowned upon. I knew that Giles had hired me not only to teac but also to be fun and artistic, the same way she'd observed when she a tended my schoolyard jam at Singletary's school. Giles believed in rigor ous instruction and all the new initiatives that had come down the pik meant to close the achievement gap, but she never sacrificed the chil dren's happiness. If I ever become an administrator, I will always remem ber that valuable lesson: Work hard, but play hard too, or, better yet, lear to disguise work as play.

As a teacher, that was what I strived for on most days. My kids learnec while simultaneously having fun. When my students were invited to the reason. It hurt even more to know that there were adults in teacher positions who didn't love children.

"What kind of teacher?" I demanded of the pair. "I'll tell you. The kind of teacher who brings a child who is extremely emotional and in need of some personal attention into a teachers' lounge, which happens to be the only empty place in the entire school that she could find. Me! *I* did that! *Me*! You know why? Because my brain is programmed to think of my children before I think about some teacher's lunch break."

They both looked at me indifferently. Summer watched in astonishment and—I hope—with pride, pride in her teacher's decision to choose students over contractual bureaucratic bullshit. The two despicable teachers were right—we teachers were obligated to have a space to ourselves. I just didn't think that right superseded a child's well-being. I got up and stormed past them with Summer at my heels. It was going to be a long year.

"Mr Coppola, it doesn't hurt, it's just oil!"

I walked back into my classroom to the sound of Casey yelling while Jordan chased him around the room with a tiny bottle in her hand.

"Get that hocus pocus away from me!" Casey yelled. "Don't you touch me with that, Jordan!" He slowly backed away, moving behind his teacher desk, which served as a barrier between him and the oil in Jordan's hand.

"Mr. Coppola, I just want to anoint you with the blood of Jesus!" Jordan replied. "It's not really blood, it's just some corn oil from my kitchen, but I blessed it so it's holy. It's not going to hurt you. It's going to help you!"

It was clear that I needed to intervene quickly. Casey had clearly confused this born-again Christian child with a voodoo practitioner. I chuckled at the thought of what he would do if he knew that some of our students did actually practice Santería, a religion rooted in African Yoruba practices. Many Hispanics practiced this religion, often in secret, a tradition that began in Caribbean slavery, because all things African were banned. Santeras prayed to hundreds of *orishas*, spirits that represented several manifestations of God, and performed rituals as all religions did, but they were often more traditional than most, thus something of which many close-minded people would be afraid. If Casey was bugging out over some corn oil, he'd quit his job if he knew that any of our children were participating in Santería rituals. Luckily for him, the children who did learned early to keep it a secret.

"Jordan, leave the poor man alone and sit back down," I said firmly.

The whole scene struck me as comical, but from the looks of Casey, a person might have thought that Jordan was aiming a gun at his head.

If Casey had been a member of the community, he would know a thing or two about anointing with oil. Many of our black students were Baptists or Pentecostals, and metaphors like the blood of Jesus and lively rebukes by Satan were a standard part of their religious upbringing. Coppola had grown up Catholic but didn't go to church as an adult. And even if he had, the only handlers of oils and holy water he would have been accustomed to were priests.

Our students had grown to love Casey enough to forget the differences between them. Incidents like this one served as reminders of those differences. Luckily, with Casey, these differences in beliefs and customs, like his intolerance of fifth-graders' wearing clear lip gloss or earrings other than studs, were trivial. But there were other teachers whose cultural differences clashed greatly with those of the students they were teaching. The children, offended by these differences, would often jump to conclusions and label these teachers racist. Sometimes the label was accurate.

Jordan finally stepped back.

"O.K., well, will *you* let me anoint you then?" She gave me a look that let me know she was aware of our kindred holy spirits. "But first you must read this prayer."

Basically, it was a protection prayer rebuking Satan and his demons from entering and disturbing one's life. Apparently, she had anointed half the girls in her class by dipping her finger in the bottle and putting the sign of the Father, Son, and Holy Ghost on their foreheads. While it was tempting to allow Jordan to anoint everyone in the class in order to keep any demon spirits from interfering with our instruction, I explained to her that we were legally required to separate church and state in school.

Feeling the way a pastor must feel when no one answers his call to walk to the pulpit and join the church, Jordan sat back down, looking defeated. She folded her prayer into a little rectangle, took out the tiny green pocket Bible that she carried to school every day, and slid the paper between the gilt-edged pages.

"Well," she said with a sigh, "I guess the devil won *that* fight."

Spring break was finally here and as usual arrived in the nick of time. It had been a trying few months, and I just hoped the second half of the year would be better.

Buddy and Noemi were a handful by themselves. Ms. Santos was right about Buddy. He worked. He was the hardest worker of all the boys. He struggled in reading, but he had a tremendous work ethic. The problem was that when he got frustrated, he would lose it, balling his fists and slamming them into his head, using profanity and throwing tantrums. He also would fight at the drop of a dime. Once he became so upset with two of the members of the Mean Girls for telling him to be quiet in the hall that he threatened their lives.

Clearly, Buddy was used to adults' handling him with care, aware that he suffered from emotional issues. But after this incident, despite the fact that Buddy was so small that he could pass for a second-grader, the two threatened to call the police if Giles did not take action. Buddy would have to be suspended.

Predictably, Ms. Santos had a fit when she learned what was going on. She came into Giles's office, guns blazing, ready to attack whoever had made the call to suspend her son. In an attempt to appease both her and the two teachers, Giles came up with a Plan B. Buddy would attend another school for a week, a school down the block with which Giles had an exchange arrangement. Even this was an extreme measure for Giles, who was often criticized by staff members who wanted students to face tougher consequences. When a student with behavioral issues was sent out of the room to the principal's office, he could easily be found lounging in her office with a candy bar or some tasty snack she had bought for him. There, she would bond with the student, and talk to him rather than punish him This was what Buddy was used to, and the idea of real punishment was something that neither he nor his mother could accept. But Giles had no choice. The Mean Girls had forced her hand. If she didn't do anything, Buddy would be facing a police charge, which was definitely worse.

For children, being in a different school was often frightening because they were out of their comfort zone. Predictably, Buddy was terrified. He pleaded with Mrs. Giles not to move him, but it was no use. He would be attending the other school the next day.

That night, right before I went to bed, I got a call from Ms. Santos. She wasn't her usual aggressive self. Instead, she was in panic mode. Buddy had gone off the deep end, and even she couldn't rescue him. His one-to-one para, Ms. Delgado, would be accompanying him to the new school, but that didn't ease his mind. I could hear him screaming in the background as if someone were trying to kill him.

"He won't stop! He won't stop!" Ms. Santos was yelling almost as loudly as her son.

"What happened?"

"You *know* what happened! Look what y'all did!" She began sobbing.

I tried to calm her down by telling her it hadn't been my decision. But it didn't matter what I said. In her eyes, I was the enemy.

"You were in on it! You was even in the principal's swivelly chair!" It was true. When she arrived in Giles's office, I had been sitting in her chair because I was working on her computer.

"Ms. Santos, I was completing something that was only accessible through Giles's computer," I replied. "I am not an administrator. I am your son's teacher. I am not against you. I am with you. So is she. Now, how can I help him right now?"

"I don't know," she sniffled. "Maybe you can talk to him?"

At that moment, I sympathized with her. She was trying as best as she could, and doing a pretty good job despite her occasional emotional outbursts. It was hard to raise any child alone, especially when you feel as though the world is against you. Santos had a deep resentment toward the school system as a result of her experiences. I never asked how deep these experiences ran, if they were only since Buddy's schooling or her own as well. Either way, she was used to fighting for their rights, and she was the best damn advocate for a child that I have ever known.

"Sure. I don't know if it'll work, but I'll try. Put him on."

"*Papi!*" she yelled to him. "Your teacher is on the phone."

I could hear her pleading softly with him before he finally let her put the phone to his ear. It got quiet, so I figured he was there.

"Buddy? It's Ms. Lewis, honey. Baby, don't cry. You're going to make me cry. You don't want that, do you? Look how upset you've got mommy. You gotta be strong so she can be O.K. She needs you to try, sugar. Just calm down for me, please."

It was true. Buddy came by his emotions honestly. His mother was just as emotionally driven as he was, and the sight of her child having a crisis would send her into a heightened state of her own. I knew all moms loved their children, but Ms. Santos loved harder than any mom I had ever seen. Because Buddy dealt with a lot of issues at school, that meant she often expressed her love through being defensive and ready to kill for her son. Ms. Santos would literally kill a man over her son if she had to. And he was the same for her. I figured the only way to calm him down was by making him realize that his own behavior was detrimental to his mother's well-being. It was the same strategy I used on her. They would do anything for each other. They'd die for each other, but they'd also live.

Buddy stopped sobbing but was still gasping for air. We did breathing exercises until he was calm. His mother rocked him while I spoke to him softly. Before I knew it, he was asleep.

Calmer herself now because Buddy had finally stopped screaming after three hours, Ms. Santos redirected her anger at the right person.

"I fucking hate those fucking *putas.*"

"I know, Mommy. I know. Me too."

Noemi's father, Mr. Melendez, had been suspicious of Casey from the beginning. Casey and I never discussed the subject, but we both knew it was because he was white. Whatever experiences he had had in his own school career or Noemi's early childhood education had made him distrust the entire profession as well. In his mind, educators were definitely not on the same side as parents. We were the enemy. The only reason he was cordial to me was that I would code-switch when speaking to him. Instead of saying, "Good morning, Mr. Melendez," I'd say something like, "What's good, pa?" Casey was one tough little white boy, but to parents like Noemi's dad, that didn't matter. He wasn't from the Bronx and he was white. Even worse, when he dressed down on Fridays, wearing a hoodie or jersey, he looked like an undercover detective.

Sometimes, my code-switching made Mr. Melendez a little too comfortable, as was evident by a letter he wrote us about this time.

"What's good?" it began. "I was just writing ya'll to let ya'll know that I want that nurse to make sure she gives Noemi her asthma medicine every day before gym class 'cause if she don't I'm gonna sue her ass. Word to everything I love. Cuz she got the asthma real bad. Ight? Peace, Mr. Melendez."

Casey laughed after he read it. So did I. As teachers, we connected on the absurdity of such an informal letter. But deep down I was kind of tickled. The letter made me realize how torn I was in situations like this one. On the one hand, I was a teacher, and I was sick of the abuse we experienced from parents, administrators, and everyone else. On the other, I felt like I just wanted to pull Mr. Melendez aside, show him the correct way to write a letter, and make a joke out of his original, tell him, "*Papi,* you *know* that letter was a hot mess, right?" He would have probably laughed, and then we would have worked on his getting it right. Being in a co-teacher position, particularly with a white man, I was losing a bit of myself. Some would argue that that was a good thing. Talking with a *blackcent* was *ghetto,* right? At least, that's what I've been told.

———

Noemi was incredibly bright. Not only could she pass an exam and get a 4 with her eyes closed, she was charismatic and a natural leader. She reminded me of Lorenzo, my favorite student from Singletary's school.

One of Noemi's problems was that she was an attention vampire, demanding all of me at all times. Her desk was parked right next to mine, and I let her stay with me during all of my prep periods. She would be the sweetest kid ever as long as I was making her feel like the only person in the room. But the minute my attention went to someone else she would turn on me. One minute I was the best teacher she ever had, with a bracelet that said so, a gift she gave me one day as a thank you present. The next I was the worst teacher on Earth, all because I picked someone other than her to answer a question.

In these moments, Noemi would pace around the classroom and refuse to sit down. A few times, when Casey was there alone, she even ran out of the room. She never left the building, but she wanted someone to chase after her. Until one day she changed the rules of her game without telling anyone.

I was in my classroom eating lunch when I got a frantic call from Ms. Delgado.

"Noemi is gone!"

"What? You mean she's walking the halls again?"

"No, I mean, she's gone. Like out-of-the-building gone. They interrupted my lunch to tell me! I'm on my way out the door!"

Ms. Delgado was panting. I could hear the sound of traffic in the background. Our school was on the corner of a busy thoroughfare filled with honking cars that sped around corners well over the speed limit. On more than one occasion a child had been hit crossing the street. Ms. Delgado was rightfully concerned.

"I'll call you back! Bye!"

This had all started because during recess Noemi used to run away from the fifth-grade area into the lower yard, expecting Ms. Yari to chase her. She and Ms. Yari, who handled disciplinary issues, had developed a close relationship because she had been sentenced to so many in-house suspensions in the S.A.V.E. room, where students went for a few days when the teacher needed a serious break from their behavior. Out-of-school suspensions were hard to come by and were decided upon only for very serious altercations, such as death threats, as Buddy had learned.

Tired of this game, Ms. Yari had called out, "Noemi, you're getting too old for this. I'm not chasing you!"

Noemi went ballistic.

"You not chasing me, Ms. Yari? I'm nobody, right? Let's see if you chase me now!"

She was caught right in front of the school. By the time they placed her inside an empty classroom, she was being so unruly that the security guard had to be called, and even she could not get her to calm down. Ms. Yari called my classroom phone and asked me to come down. The three of us sat there with Noemi, trying to calm her. For more than an hour, she continued to scream that Ms. Yari didn't love her, that she wouldn't chase her, that she was nothing to anyone. Only when she saw both of us crying was she placated. She grabbed our hands and stroked them affectionately, as if to say she was sorry.

As far as Giles was concerned, this episode was the last straw. All year she had been threatening to change Noemi's class and assign her to a teacher who would not stand for this behavior. You guessed it. One of the members of the Mean Girls was set to take her in, the same one who already had beef with Noemi's dad, Mr. Melendez. Giles argued that Noemi would grow restless with the attention-seeking stunts in her class because this teacher, being the Mean Girl that she was, wouldn't care enough about Noemi's feelings. Giles thought we were coddling Noemi too much and played along with her hijinks. At least that's what she told us. I couldn't understand how she could say that we weren't strict enough when she didn't believe in punishment but love herself. Now that I think of it, I am sure it was a scare tactic.

"So, that's it?" Noemi cried to me. "I'll be moved and that's the final word? Is there anything I could do to change her mind?"

"I don't know, Noemi," I said. "You heard her." It was sad. *I* was sad. I loved Noemi even though she drove me batty. I worried about how she would fare in a Mean Girl's care. But there was nothing I could do.

"What if I wrote Mrs. Giles a letter to persuade her?" she suggested. She was so smart.

"It won't hurt to try." I still carry the letter in my wallet today.

Dear Mrs. Giles,

Mrs. Giles, please don't change me. I really, really, want to stay in Mr. Coppola's and Ms. Lewis' class. Please give me one more chance. And I don't really think this other class is the best class for

me. [The teacher] has problems with my dad and my dad has problems with her, and I don't want to get in the middle of that. And
also there's a lot of kids from my third grade class, and I don't like
the kids from my third grade class because they are all mean to me.

I will do a lot better if you give me one more chance. And also, if
you give me one more chance, the only things you would hear from
the teachers would be good things, I promise you. The teachers are
nice to me because whenever I'm angry, they listen to me, and they
care for me. For example, Ms. Yari, Ms. Lewis, Mr. Coppola, and
Ms. Delgado all listen to me and come running whenever there is
a situation.

That nasty teacher would just let me stay running around. Ms.
Lewis and Ms. Yari were crying. And if you change my class, I
can't show them that I can change. Remember, Ms. Lewis and Mr.
Coppola won't let me run out of the class like that other one.

Circle yes or no to changing my class.

Yes or No

From,
Noemi Melendez

––––––––––

In the end, Noemi remained in our class. Things seemed to be getting
better with her and Buddy's mom because the same oath that guaranteed
beef with all of them if one person had a problem applied in good times
as well. If one of them was "feeling us," the rest were approving of us
too. Noemi was definitely "feeling" me and Coppola, therefore so was
her dad, which meant that Buddy and Ms. Santos were too. Santos had
already begun to come around after I helped her calm Buddy over the
phone. It was the era of good feelings.

Until Casey screwed it all up.

We were all set to have our Easter/spring break party. Cupcakes, candy,
and chips had been bought. Pizza was on the way. We had warned the
children ahead of time that they had to be on their best behavior up until
the party or it would be canceled. If only a few children misbehaved, they
would not be allowed to attend.

Unfortunately for Buddy and Noemi, they got into a fight with some
children from another class during recess the day before the party. No-

emi, as usual, was the mastermind behind the entire thing. She had issues with another boy and knew that hot-headed Buddy would be ready and willing to fight any opponent. All Noemi had to do was point Buddy in the direction she wanted him to go, wind him up, and then let him loose. Once the fight was on, Noemi egged Buddy on to make him fight harder.

"You gonna let him do you like that, Buddy? Oooh, he punched you real hard! What you gonna do about it, huh? That's all you got?"

In response, Casey and I told the two of them that they wouldn't be allowed to attend the party and would have to stay in the S.A.V.E. room with Ms. Yari. Of course Noemi had a plan. In an attempt to crash the party, she told Ms. Yari that she needed one of her books from her classroom. We were only a few doors down, so Ms. Yari agreed to let her go.

When she got there, she saw the joy on everyone's faces and immediately melted. The tears were about to flow when she looked in my direction, waiting for me to stop her from leaving. I gave her an "I'm sorry" face, which pretty much said, "I still love you, but you don't deserve this right now."

She then turned to Casey, hoping that he might have a change of heart. But when he saw her sad face, instead of feeling sympathy for her he felt a grim satisfaction.

Noemi and Buddy were the golden kids of the class because everyone walked on eggshells around their parents. They got away with so much more than the other children, and this recent fight was only one of several things they would have gotten away with in the past month.

Casey didn't feel sorry for Noemi in the least. He looked her straight in the eye and smirked ever so slightly.

In an instant, Noemi's expression changed from heartbroken to vengeful. If I'd been able to read her mind, she was probably thinking, "You stupid, stupid white motherfucker. You done fucked up now."

It was already evident that Noemi pulled the strings. She was already going over her meeting agenda in her mind. Buddy would nod in agreement as she met with the two parents to discuss next steps on what should be done. It was officially on.

By the time I got home, I had ten missed calls between Ms. Santos and Mr. Melendez. I dreaded calling them back, but I knew I would seem to be avoiding them if I didn't. I decided to call Ms. Santos, because she was probably the more irate, even though Noemi wasn't her child. She could relay the message to Noemi's dad.

"Why'd you let that white piece of shit taunt Noemi like that?" she demanded.

"Um, Ms. Santos, I didn't let him do anything."

"But you were in the room, right?"

"Yeah, I was there."

"So you're saying that didn't happen?"

"I didn't see anything."

"That fucking white cocksucker was laughing at her, rubbing it in her face!"

I didn't know what would happen if I told on Casey. Santos might have tried to do something crazy like accuse him of child abuse, and the way the system was these days, she might have had a case. Even worse, the parents might have waited for him after school, and something told me that these two jumped adversaries rather than fight one-on-one. Even if Santos flew solo, she would still kick Casey's ass. I was sure of it.

Although I thought Casey had been wrong to smile, it was, after all, just a smile. Could a teacher go to the rubber room for a *smile*?

"I didn't see all that, Ms. Santos. Like I said."

"So you're saying the kids are lying?"

"I'm not saying anything at all. I'm saying I didn't see that. I was reading papers and I wasn't really paying attention."

"Yeah, *i-ight*."

She knew I was lying, but she also knew she wasn't going to get me to agree to anything that would get Casey in trouble. Loyalty wasn't just something that had been instilled in women like Santos. The 'hood had taught *me* some things too. Casey was my co-teacher, and I was going to have his back. When it came to loyalty, Santos knew that I abided by the same rules of the streets, and Rule Number 1 was "snitches get stitches." Not that I really worried that Casey would inflict pain upon me if I ratted him out, but the rule applied nonetheless.

The downside to loyalty is that you suffer the consequences of another's actions. Remaining loyal to my co-teacher was the equivalent of repping a gang, or claiming a set—making clear where your loyalty lay. And as with any gang war, once you were part of that gang, you inherited their beef. If Casey was the enemy, I was automatically guilty by association the minute I pledged my loyalty to him.

In the wake of that smile, the kids and their parents made a pact with one another to never say more than three words to either of us again unless it was absolutely necessary. Parent–Teacher Night was an exception. Unlike many parents, Ms. Santos and Mr. Melendez never missed a single conference. But even during the parent–teacher meeting, the two directed their questions to me and ignored the "fucking white cocksucker" next to me; apparently Casey had lost his right to a surname.

Noemi, for her part, gave up on school, which didn't matter when exam time came; she still got one of the highest scores in the entire grade. In class, however, she put her head down, having lost interest in anything either of us had to say. Noemi had such potential to be a leader, but instead of helping others to understand lessons the way she used to—Noemi was so intelligent and charismatic that she could almost take over a lesson in math, her strongest subject—she became invisible.

In addition to her lethargy, everything that came out of her mouth was condescending, mean, or disrespectful. She questioned our teaching and blamed us when she couldn't understand something. Because she was so intelligent, she was able to make the most innocent comment sound abusive, threatening, or inappropriate. We learned to watch everything we said around her because it would get back to "the family." Coppola refused to even talk to her for fear that anything he said might be held against him in their court of law.

———

The children were angry at us. But if it hadn't been for their parents' telling them not to speak to us, they would have gotten over it, as children do. They would answer us if we asked a question, but that was all we got out of them for the rest of the year.

It didn't matter that Ms. Santos had hugged us both and cried earlier that year when she saw how much Buddy had improved in reading since being in our class. It didn't matter that Noemi got more attention than everyone else in the class combined, or that she had fought hard to stay with us because she knew she was loved. It didn't matter that I had stayed up late at night to calm down Buddy and his mother.

Who could have known that a smirk could destroy all our efforts to prove to these parents that we were on their side? For them to go to such lengths to dissociate from us illustrated only how unbelievably important allegiance was to them. There weren't many people in this world whom they felt they could trust. That they had even contemplated making us honorary members of their makeshift family, that they had dared to believe that we loved their kids like our own, made the smirk as painful as a stab.

In their eyes, Casey had abandoned them. And by siding with him I had betrayed them too. Even after all the hugs, the tears, the heart-to-heart talks, the praise, the laughs, when Noemi and Buddy graduated and went on to junior high, their vow of silence remained. If Casey or I saw either of them on the block, they wouldn't stop, say hello, or even smile in our direction. I couldn't help but mentally play Isaac Hayes's "Walk on By" as the soundtrack to our relationship's tragic end whenever I spotted one of them on the street: "If you see me walking down the street, and I start to cry, walk on by."

It was as though we all were moving in slow motion, each step echoing the melancholy bass melody as we walked in opposite directions, eyes catching and then falling away. Noemi and Buddy were the kind of kids I would have remained in touch with forever if it had not been for that smirk. I love them still.

As the days and months passed, I began to wonder if I had sided with the wrong faction. Parents like Ms. Santos and Mr. Melendez were very difficult to form relationships with, and it was easy to write them off as unfit or bad. I cringed when they cursed in front of their kids and wanted to scream at them to stop. But when I sat down and reflected, I realized how much I could still understand them, and I found myself empathizing with them more quickly than teachers who were not of color or from their neighborhoods would have. When I stripped away the language, the attitude, the vindictiveness, what was left in their place were *good* parents, parents who were extremely active in their children's education, parents who *loved* their babies and would walk through Hell for them if they needed to. Their passion sometimes got the best of them, but I was no stranger to that myself. Passion is part of the struggle, and the way we survive.

Ms. Santos and Mr. Melendez were my *melanated* people. I didn't have to speak Spanish. I viewed them, like most Hispanic people I knew, as Africans just the same, just dropped elsewhere in the diaspora. They were from the 'hood. I didn't have to be from their 'hood. Hood is hood, and therefore Edenwald's was just the same as theirs. If I wouldn't stick up for them, who would?

————————

"Hey, girl, so listen," Ms. Williams, the speech therapist, called to me one day. "Coppola called to ask me to help him write a song for a lesson. You guys O.K.?"

The fact that Casey had asked Ms. Williams for help with a song reveals how ridiculous he was being these days. Ms. Williams sang in her church choir, but there had never been any mention of her having any songwriting ability. I, on the other hand, wrote songs all the time for educational purposes and was called on to help for all the school's musical performances. I was also his co-teacher, someone who taught the same students he did and therefore knew what instruction they needed, unlike Ms. Williams, who had no idea what was in the fifth-grade curriculum. It was clear that Casey didn't want to ask me for help even if I was the best person to ask.

"Yeah, I mean, I thought we were cool," I replied. "That's strange."

"Exactly. Shouldn't you be the first person to ask?"

"That would make sense. So what was it for?"

"A math lesson. He wanted to change a rap song to teach division."

"Cool. I could've helped him with that." I truly could've. I had "bars," or clever rap lyrics. "I guess he didn't want my help. So what did you come up with?"

"That's the thing. I don't write songs. I got a few lines, but nothing really. Can you help me?"

Despite Casey's decision to not request my help, I ended up helping anyway. And it didn't stop there.

He had the bright idea that he alone would make a test-prep Power-Point presentation for the forthcoming social studies exam. That might have been because he had been deeply involved in our test-prep work the previous year, when the test was on science, the subject he taught in our class. But because I was the one who taught the class social studies, was familiar with the fifth-grade social studies exam as a result of having taught fifth grade for three years at my previous school, and had been the only social studies cluster teacher in Old School history, it seemed only logical that I would spearhead the fifth-grade social studies exam prep, right?

There was no way Casey could have thought that he would do a better job than I. He was the first to admit that he didn't know history, wasn't interested in history, and never paid attention to history when he was a student. He couldn't possibly have thought that he could teach a subject he had never taught better than I could. Or had he?

This seems like pettiness, I'll admit. But even the most unintentional slight could look suspicious to minorities who are so accustomed to racist beliefs against them. It was that double-consciousness kicking in again, that need to try to think like the oppressor, to get into their heads, to figure out what each word really meant, what each action really signified. It follows you in every aspect of your life, and so it lived in my teacher world as well. Racism was never overt in these days, and neither was sexism. When a woman was not offered a position at work or was making less than her male counterparts, no one would ever say it was because of what was between her legs. It made humanity sound primitive, a truth that was thick and bitter, like Mylanta. A friend of mine just recently got into a Facebook battle with a white woman who was disgusted that an underwear company would be expanding the color nude to include different shades of beiges and browns, because nude as we know it would not give someone with mahogany skin the appearance of being naked. This white woman actually waged a Facebook war in defense of keeping the color nude exclusive to one color, one color that benefited only one skin tone. She would never claim racism. Racist bullshit happens over seemingly trivial details too. It creeps into places one would least expect, seemingly impenetrable places like pebbles in tightly laced sneakers.

As a person of color, I was always on the lookout. Not asking your co-teacher who was extremely musically inclined to help with a song, or to take the lead in a subject that she knew better than you, offered many possible scenarios. But all the scenarios led back to the same question: Why did he feel entitled? Maybe he thought he could teach it better? But what about him would make him think he could teach it better if I knew the subject better and had been teaching longer? Maybe the way I taught history was not appropriate in his eyes. I taught history through a lens that was brutally truthful, and I did not hesitate to tell my students how ugly history could be. All the facts they needed to know would be included, but if there was a perspective that had been ignored, I would spotlight it. Maybe he didn't like my perspective. But if so, what was wrong with it?

He could have probably done without my added two cents about Malcolm X when he was teaching variables in math, and the time I gave the students the speech by the Wampanoag leader Frank James about the

Native American National Day of Mourning to read over Thanksgiving break.

Maybe it had nothing to do with the way I taught history. Maybe it was about control. Maybe these decisions were his way of marking his territory, sticking a flag in the hard linoleum and claiming, "This is *my* classroom!"

Whatever his reasons, Casey decided to make this PowerPoint presentation himself. Because he didn't know a lick of history, not even simple fifth-grade history, he took home a textbook and gave himself homework. Because this crash course in history took several weeks, the presentation wasn't finished until just two weeks before the exam.

After he was done, he asked me to look over the presentation. I guess he figured that wouldn't give me enough time to take ownership of or ethnify it. I looked over what he had done, only to discover that he had spent hours adding information that wouldn't be on the test. Hell, much of the material he included wasn't even in the curriculum. I asked him what book he had used and he pulled out an antiquated thing that had been written in like 1972.

"Where are the Iroquois?" I asked. "You didn't even put in the Iroquois. The test always has questions on them."

"They do?"

"Yes, and the Erie Canal, I don't see that either."

"I didn't put it in."

"Well, there's always a graph or even an essay question about the Erie Canal."

"Shit. O.K. What else?"

I began flagging slide after slide. In the end, I had to help him redo the entire presentation, and it was finished so late that the kids were able to use it for only a week.

———

I couldn't help but think of history and all the moments in which my ancestors were invisible because white people felt they owned the world and everything in it. I couldn't help but think of how the Native Americans were so easily fooled into giving up their land because the European way was something they could not conceive of, being a people who did not believe in ownership in the same way, especially in terms of land, which was something that should be shared. I thought about the arrogance it requires to stick a flag in some dirt and claim the land as one's own.

Memories flooded my mind as if I were actually there. I was the native whose hair was cut and clothes were stripped from his body, sent to a school to learn the Western way in a collared shirt and slacks. I was the little slave girl who was given *permission* from her master to learn how to read. A righteous anger flooded my whole being and made me realize just how much healing was still needed for our people, me included. At that moment, Casey was no better than a slavemaster calling shots.

At the same time, I couldn't help but wonder if this was all in my head. Did race have anything to do with his need to control our classroom? As my relationship with my co-teacher crumbled, I asked myself the most disturbing question of all: Would I be doomed to always worry about the intentions of every white person I ever knew?

The question reminded me of the way so many of the parents viewed Casey and other white teachers, and sometimes me. When I taught my own class at Singletary's school, I didn't have beef with the parents of any of my students. Only when I put myself on the side of teachers and had to teach side by side with another individual did I become one of them.

There was another issue. Even some students who had originally loved Casey were learning to hate him because they didn't like it when he disciplined them. I could discipline them all day and it wouldn't matter.

"But he's so mean!" my students would say when he was stern.

"I could be mean too," I'd say in his defense. In fact, I could be way meaner and more intimidating if I had to be.

"I don't know, it's just different."

"What makes it different?"

"I don't know, it just *is*!"

Race mattered, but no one wanted to admit to it.

———————

The next troubling event occurred a few days later. Around noon, a boy came in with a stack of copies and asked for Casey.

"He stepped out for a minute," I replied. "What did you need?"

"It's O.K.," he said, turning to walk out of the room. "I'll just come back."

"Wait, are those the copies of the fifth-grade homework for the week?" I asked. "You can set them down on that table by the door."

"I'll just wait until he comes back," he said with a bit of a tone.

My paras looked up and we glanced at one another, shocked by the nerve of this ten-year-old.

"You don't need him to come back to give us *our* homework packets," I said. "I'm the other teacher in this room, and these are the other para-professionals in the room. That counts four adults in this room that you can always leave copies with. I'm not asking you, I'm telling you to put the homework copies on the table."

"I was told not to give anything to anyone but Mr. Coppola," the boy replied curtly.

"By *whom?*"

Changing my mind about waiting for an answer, I pulled the hall pass from under his arm. I should have known—it was signed by one of the Mean Girls.

I snatched the copies out of his hand and counted out the number needed for our class. Then I shoved the remaining papers into his hands and told him to hurry back to his teacher.

I couldn't wait to tell Casey what had happened. He would understand my frustration. This was an all-time low, even for a Mean Girl. She had stooped to allowing children to disrespect me, something teachers simply didn't do. It's against our code of ethics, like a doctor giving a patient a prescription pad and a pen.

Casey and I decided to eat lunch at the diner down the block. It had been a while since we had eaten lunch together, and I thought this would be a great way to ease some of the tension that had been building up between us. Soon we were laughing and giggling like old times. I almost forgot what I'd wanted to talk to him about . . . or that I'd had a mental image of a whip in his hand just the previous week.

"I just remembered! Guess what happened when you left the room earlier? A kid came to the room to give you the homework copies and wouldn't leave them with me. He said his teacher told him not to hand anything to me. Can you believe that?"

Casey's expression suddenly turned awkward. This wasn't news to him.

"No, see what happened was we were having an impromptu grade meeting," he began.

"Without me? Why wasn't I notified?"

Casey just bowed his head.

Whop-eesh! The image of him cracking a whip was back and in full effect.

"And I was telling them how things are forever getting lost in the classroom because there are so many adults in here. And so we came up with an idea so that nothing gets misplaced anymore. We decided that they were just going to send things to me from now on."

We decided? I could have punched him. Instead I just smiled and acted as though it were a marvelous plan. Just marvelous that he decided to have a meeting with two teachers—white-skinned Latinas—who didn't even share a classroom with him and make decisions as to how the classroom would be run without involving the teacher and paraprofessionals who actually worked in that room, all women of color.

It would have been simple to just have a classroom meeting to establish where certain things would go, although we already had a plan in place. Homework sheets were kept by the front of the board near the door. It was Casey who was so absent-minded that after he picked something up he would put it down and forget where he left it. Even if he wasn't being racist, I was angry that he did not at least realize how his actions appeared. We weren't his wenches; we were educators who shared equal responsibility in the room.

I wanted to scream at him, "If you haven't noticed, you're a white man! That means you can't make decisions without including the three black women in the room because it makes you look racist and sexist. Especially one who has *more* seniority than you! Can't you see how oppressive that is?"

Casey's inability to see the larger picture ruined what could have been a healthy co-teacher relationship. My inability to keep it real with him either prevented things from getting uglier or foiled all chances of growth. I always thought he was the coolest white guy I had ever met; maybe I underestimated his ability to grow. Maybe if I told him how his actions were making me feel, he would be understanding and even apologetic. It was too risky to take a chance. If he didn't appreciate my truth, instead of just being annoyed with his actions from time to time I would be no longer on speaking terms with him. I picked my battles, and once again, I lost my voice.

Casey was supposed to be my backup, my ace, the way I had been for him. I had already sacrificed my reputation with Noemi's and Buddy's parents for him. I had been his "ride or die." But he clearly wouldn't be the same for me. He had committed an even worse sin. He was schmoozing with the enemy, and I had no doubt that the fires of his innate sense of superiority to me, whether based on his color or not, had been fueled by the Mean Girls.

It turned out that Casey wasn't the only teacher the Mean Girls had tried to turn against me.

Ms. Gutierrez, another upper-grade teacher I had made friends with, informed me that when she first came to the school, they told her to watch out for me and not to speak to me because I was a good-for-nothing who didn't do any work. My being black made the accusation stick. Of *course* I was lazy!

Gutierrez stayed away for a while and then started to hear my name on the loudspeaker, being asked to attend meeting after meeting. She saw that I was asked to take the lead in planning all school performances and graduations, choosing and teaching songs, creating choreography, selecting themes. She attended all the professional development workshops for which I created PowerPoint presentations. Despite attempts by the Mean Girls to keep me isolated and miserable, Gutierrez and I became friends. By the time we had begun to hang out after work, she finally confessed to me, "You know, I was leery of you when I first met you because that crew told me you were lazy and Giles was paying you to do nothing. They couldn't have told a bigger lie. You do everything around here."

By now, I, along with the other so-called favorites, was being firmly ignored by the crew. We were called "favorites" because we stayed after hours and came in on Saturdays to complete required paperwork. We helped Giles with anything she asked because we wanted to improve the school, which in turn would improve the lives of the children we served.

––––––

Mr. Spencer wanted to meet with me. He was one of the assistant principals, and everyone loved him, even the Mean Girls. Mr. Spencer was one of Queensbridge Houses' finest, along with the rappers Nas and Marley Marl. Queensbridge was the largest housing project in the United States, and *rough* wasn't the word for it. Mr. Spencer was Costa Rican, but he looked and sounded like a black man who came from mean streets, even when he fluently translated the Spanish of many of our immigrant parents. He had that grit that we all had, but unlike some who allowed it to be their demise, Spencer used it as proper fuel to propel him further down the road to success. He had what the kids called swag. To all the female teachers he was "Suave Spencer" behind closed classroom doors.

The school's previous administration hadn't valued him, not realizing how significant it was that a black man from one of the wickedest projects in New York City had become a school leader. But when Giles took over as principal, she quickly formed a rapport with Spencer. She realized how much value he had to the school organization and gave him the kinds of leadership opportunities he deserved. He had great relationships with everyone, especially the students and the parents.

While Ms. Ferguson, our other assistant principal, was well versed in different teaching methodologies and curricula, Mr. Spencer was hands-on, ensuring that everything in the building ran like a well-oiled machine. He drew up all of the prep schedules and never missed a beat. If a teacher had to lose her prep time, he made sure to give her an additional prep period the following day. Spencer was the first one in the building in the morning and the last one to leave at night. Even people who had problems with black leadership seemed to love Mr. Spencer because of his humble spirit. Everyone loved him. And although he was no longer in the classroom, he sincerely loved the kids.

"Ms. Lewis, can I talk to you a minute?"

Spencer had been in the classroom for all of two seconds before Buddy ran into his arms. Most of the time Buddy hated the world, but he adored Spence.

It was the first week of school after spring break, and the students had only a week to review before the state exams. Buddy especially was feeling the pressure, knowing that he had reading difficulties. He still had his mother to deal with when he got home, and Ms. Santos was a deeply involved parent with extremely high expectations. Seeing the anxiety on his and the other children's faces, Mr. Spencer sat down and started talking.

"You guys ready for the test?" he asked cheerfully. A nod here and there. Buddy bit his nails.

Spencer hunched over and clasped his hands, prepared to say something that departed from his usual breeziness.

"I just wanted to say something to you kids," he began. "I know you're scared. I know you feel like everyone expects you to fail because you have a reading problem or you get distracted.

"Listen. I was you. School didn't come easy to me either. And I had the odds against me. I couldn't speak English well, and they made fun of my accent. And, I stuttered. I still stutter sometimes. Plus my brain wouldn't always remember everything. I would forget what I learned really quick, you know? I was in the class where they put the kids that needed the most help."

Spencer dabbed at his eyes as he continued.

"I wasn't supposed to be anybody. They told me that. I wasn't supposed to be anyone. So I studied anywhere I went. I kept flash cards in my pocket and would read them everywhere I went, even while taking the train to a party. Any time I could study, I did. I worked harder than anyone I knew because I had to. It paid off in the end, and I had the highest GPA in my undergraduate class."

All the kids got up and started clapping. This was Spencer in rare form. Before he left, he had one last thing to say.

"Kids, don't let anyone tell you who you are, not even yourself. Never doubt yourself. But you gotta try hard. Harder than you've ever tried. When you get frustrated, don't give up, just try even harder until you get it because you will. You have my word. Now give me your word that you will never, ever give up."

The entire class pledged. Buddy stopped biting his nails long enough to raise his right hand and solemnly swear to give his best, his whole best, and nothing but his best. Grit wasn't the only thing Spencer and I had in common. He empathized with our kids and saw himself in them, as I had seen myself in them. We were all from the bottom, and he wanted them to make it just as badly as I did. Education was our profession, but our students' success was quite personal.

"Oh, I almost forgot. Ms. Lewis?" He motioned me outside.

If I had known that his plan had anything to do with making nice with any teacher who didn't deserve it, I would've vehemently declined to participate. But before I knew it, I was sitting in Spencer's office in an effort to resolve what he described as a "conflict" between me and a fellow teacher with whom he happened to be good friends. Remember Finch, the surly old woman who wouldn't even applaud my students' performance? Neither of us had anything to say to each other. Spencer just sat there staring at the both of us, waiting for one of us to begin. Finally, I spoke up.

"It's really nothing, Mr. Spencer," I pleaded. "We don't have to do this. I appreciate what you're trying to do here, but I don't need friends, and I am totally O.K. if she doesn't like me. We're professionals. We don't need to be BFFs. Now if you don't mind—"

I tried to get up, but Spencer held my hand. "Wait, there has to be a reason, a misunderstanding. Both of you are wonderful people."

Apparently he didn't realize that women would react differently to him than to one another. Nor did he consider how much envy could spiral out of control once you added race and color to the story. Finch was an old woman from the South, and this was the first time I ever had to wonder whether a black woman might have hated me because of my appearance, specifically my skin color and hair. My mother had warned me my entire life that something like this could happen, having experienced her share of this sort of hatred along with her siblings. The problem went as far back as my grandmother, who never identified with any particular race but was clearly a mixture of something.

As the story goes, my grandmother was identified as white on her birth certificate. But when the county clerk took one look at my grandfather on their wedding day he crossed off the word *white* on my grandmother's birth certificate and wrote the word *colored*, saying, "You wanna marry a nigger, then you be a nigger too." I had to see her birth certificate with my own eyes before I believed this story, thinking at first it was my family's attempt to claim "whiteness," as some black folk tend to do.

Nana may have been white on paper, but she lived in the mountains of Virginia among poor black folk who probably understood her to be colored too. Despite a photograph of my grandmother and her best friend, Hesseltine, hand in hand, the two of them looking like an illustration of the Paul McCartney and Stevie Wonder song "Ebony and Ivory," Nana told stories for days of her fights with the "black girls" over her hair, one story involving her long auburn braids' being dipped into the ink jar students used when they were writing in school.

A generation later in New York, her daughters suffered tremendously. They were jumped repeatedly after school because other girls were angry that the boys preferred their lighter skin and longer hair. I never had a fellow sister hate me, so I couldn't relate to my mother and grandmother.

As my mother and grandmother talked about these envious women with contempt, I couldn't understand how the women in my family could feel like victims. Sometimes their hateful words embarrassed me, making me think that they may have deserved everything they received, every hair tug, every scratched face, every bloody nose, every blackened eye. How could they not understand why some darker women hated them? In the world of blackness, they were the privileged ones. They should understand the resentment just as whites should understand ours.

After feeling that I might be getting a taste of the same thing for the first time, I could finally relate to how angry the women of my family had been. I used to assume that my mom and her siblings had done something to deserve the treatment they received. Now I knew they had done nothing wrong because I had done nothing wrong.

As I sat there looking at this woman's face, a face that was looking back at me with such contempt as if I had actually done something to deserve it, my blood boiled. Maybe it wasn't my hair or complexion, but she hated me for something. Maybe it was because I was from the 'hood and too "ghetto" for her liking. Maybe it was because I was young, or because she thought I was cute. Maybe I carried myself with too much confidence. Who knew? Something about me, though, enraged her in ways that defied logic.

And so I said to Spencer: "You really want to know what the problem is?" Turning toward her, I continued, "I am young and vibrant while you are old. I am intelligent and well educated while you are ignorant. And worst of all, I am attractive. I am all things you are not. If I were you, I wouldn't like me either."

With that, I got up and sashayed out of Spencer's office, mimicking my mother's famed switch the entire way.

Admitting to my attractiveness had nothing to do with my skin color. But if this woman in fact *did* hate me because of my skin color, she would assume that I believed myself to be attractive because of it. A light-skinned black girl could no more admit to being attractive without everyone's assuming she believed that her complexion had something to do with her attractiveness any more than a dark-skinned black girl could admit to not liking a light-skinned black girl, a Hispanic girl, or a white girl without everyone's assuming she was jealous.

We were all trapped in a perpetual state of vicious colorism that would never be cured until we began to be honest about its existence. In retrospect, I wish I could have handled her mistreatment differently; my actions probably set light-skinned girls back a hundred years.

Spring break had come and gone and school was back in session, which meant test prep and more test prep. There had been so much test prep for the past few weeks that the kids needed a break. At this point, they either knew the material or they didn't. We decided to stop stressing everyone out, even though the English exam was the next day.

One of the big events on the horizon was the school's pep rally. But this wasn't a typical pep rally. It was a test pep rally.

First the kids made beautifully colored signs with slogans like "What are we waiting for? For four to be our score!" Other catchy slogans: "Eagles soar high, not low. So ones and twos know where to go!" and "One, two, we're not looking for you, three, four, we're busting through your door!" The day before each exam, the children marched around the school with their signs, chanting and hollering and having a good time.

Then they filed into the auditorium, where the school's cheerleaders, wearing their pretty skirts and pom-poms, revved up the crowd. I loved the test pep rallies. I just wish they had been for actual games.

The day my students finished making their signs, we still had a half-hour to practice our skit and dance for the Leap Leadership assembly. Leap Leadership is an organization designed to help young people develop the skills they need for success in life. Every Wednesday, a Leap Leadership consultant came to our classrooms to discuss what it meant to be a leader and played games with the students that involved teamwork and conflict resolution. When it was time to create a skit for the Leap Leadership assembly, I knew exactly what I wanted to do.

———————

Over the past few months, Gabby hadn't been her usual self. Normally she dazzled, she wowed, she glowed. But recently she had stopped participating in activities, which made me wonder if she was having problems at home. But that seemed unlikely. Her mom deserved a parent-of-the-year award, she was that amazing. All three of her children were straight-A students, and she didn't even speak English. She couldn't help them with their homework, but she instilled in them a belief in the value of hard work. Gabby was the last student I would have expected to have problems at home. Something else was wrong.

Who would have known that there was a little crew of evil girls right under our noses, and that they were picking on Gabby? She wasn't the typical target of bullying; in fact, she was Miss Popularity. She was gorgeous, kind-hearted, and smart. Everyone wanted to be her friend, and she in turn was friends with everyone. Except for them.

Gabby figured that if she removed herself from the spotlight, they would go back to being her friends. She didn't want to be praised for her high scores on her exams and she began claiming she didn't know the answer when called on. The problem was brought up during a Leap Leadership session, and together as a class we decided that this would be the subject of the skit the class would perform. All the students would play themselves except for Mila, who jumped at the chance to play teacher.

———————

When the tests were finally over, we finally had a chance to focus on the show. Our students were elated. The school year wasn't over officially, but the exams were. And the performance was going to be incredible.

As each group went up on stage, my kids became more and more excited. We were supposed to go last, right after one of the members of a Mean Girl's class.

I sometimes wanted to stop doing everything so "big" because I figured if I weren't in the spotlight, no one would talk about me. Giles must have been thinking the same thing because she stopped publicly congratulating me for things. During one performance I coordinated that made the local news, she got up on the stage and thanked everyone but me, even the members of the audience. At first I thought it was unintentional, but after a while, I realized what she was doing. Whenever I did something praiseworthy I would receive a private thank-you note from her in my mailbox while others got public shout-outs in our weekly newsletter.

When it was our turn to go on, my students found their marks on the stage, and I took the microphone, prepared to introduce them and the theme of their skit. I popped in the CD to which Gabby and Jordan had added their voices.

The song was called "Took the Night" by an artist named Chelley. It was a song fit for a diva, with hard-hitting bass and repetitive loops typical of House music. Some of the words had been changed to make the lyrics more appropriate for a class of ten-year-olds. While Chelley sang, "Every time I step into the club," our version included the word *class*. *Bitches* became *people*, and instead of hair that looked just right or dresses that fit tight, Gabby and Jordan sang about their answers' always being right and grades that were tight, which meant good. They didn't "take the night," they were "out of sight."

As I got ready to speak, the fifth-grade teacher Mean Girl representative decided to hit below the belt again.

"Come on, class. Let's go!" I wasn't surprised that she was walking out on my students' performance. I *was* surprised by my reaction, however, and so was she.

"Excuse me," I said evenly.

She whipped around her head and glared at me. Her students, standing in front of their chairs, froze.

"I said let's go!" she ordered her students once more. They looked at her and then back at me, torn between obeying their teacher and their own desire to watch the rest of the assembly.

"The kids will only be up on stage for five minutes and seventeen seconds," I said to her. "I see you have things to do, but do you think it could wait just five more minutes? I don't want your class to miss the show. It has a really important theme."

Her students looked at her, then at me, then back at her, and finally made their decision. They sat down. She stormed out of the auditorium. It was a small victory but one point for the underdog. One of the students' parents even complained to the administration about her behavior. She couldn't believe how petty a fellow teacher could be to a colleague. More pebbles in seemingly tightly laced sneakers.

———————

For the most part, my students acted out exactly what had been happening in class, adding a little bit more to the story to get the point across. Mila, playing the teacher, announced to the class that Gabby had achieved the highest score on the last math exam, urging everyone to give her a round of applause. Instead, Diamond and her crew gave just a clap or two and a look of disgust. When "class" came back into session, and "Ms. Mila" asked questions, Gabby pretended not to know the answers while Diamond stared at her intimidatingly.

Ms. Mila, being an observant teacher, recognized that Gabby was behaving oddly and began to figure out what the problem was. She discovered that Gabby was feeling pressure to dim her light. Ms. Mila told Gabby that she was a star and should shine, despite how others might respond. The message was to never give less of yourself to appease others, and to expect envy but to take it in stride. This may be something that some people could do naturally, especially those who'd grown up with confidence, those whose world told them every day that they were awesome. But if you're a kid who comes from the bottom, when someone tries to stomp out what little bit of confidence you may have gained, the damage could be irreversible.

After the skit, Gabby and Jordan began the song:

Hate, hate . . . hate, hate, hate, I don't care what people say,
I don't even look their way, look their way, look their way,
Every time I walk in the class, they're hating on me, they're hating
    on me.
All my answers, right and my grades, tight, all eyes on me, I'm out
    of sight! Out of sight! Out of sight. All eyes on me, I'm out of
    sight!

As Gabby, Jordan, and Summer burst into a complicated step during the fist-thumping, heavy bass dance break, the rest of the kids in the class came out from behind the curtains in two lines, confident, happy, and completely sure of themselves. Although they were pretending to be runway models, they weren't showing off trendy clothes or physical beauty. Instead, as each of my students had five seconds of fame on the catwalk, I announced some fantastic fact about them. As Marie sashayed down the stage, I announced that her grades had improved ten points since the last marking period. When Idris walked down, I announced that he answered the winning question in the math bowl that our class won. The "haters" who sat at their desks with attitudes were pulled out of their chairs by other students in the class, echoing the phrase I grew up hearing, "Don't hate, participate."

When the performance was over, our school's head Mean Girl teacher strolled back in to retrieve her class. Summer just looked at me. "Hate, hate . . . hate, hate, hate, Ms. Lewis," she said with a shrug. Together, we headed out of the auditorium, arms locked in solidarity, with a fierce stride that would have made Naomi Campbell and Tyra Banks proud. Could I have used a dose of humility? Of course. But I had been backed into a wall. I was still young and dumb, and I had yet to develop the maturity to handle a bully.

Graduation was the most wonderful time of the year. It could be argued that teachers of graduating classes should be paid less than other teachers because the image of their students walking down the aisle was compensation enough. Even if you taught in a school with no air conditioning, the day was always a joyous occasion. At an Old School graduation, we brought extra Kleenex to mop up the combination of tears and sweat from our faces amid the flashing of cameras that were sure to catch us melting.

The singing usually brought everyone to their knees. In fact, the songs were selected specifically for the purpose of making parents cry. At the Old School, we usually performed two songs, one that was cute and appealed to the kids and another that did the job if the first one was too cool to induce waterworks. As usual, Giles asked me to take charge of the music.

The Mean Girls who taught fifth grade with me had made an issue out of every song I had chosen for the graduation ceremonies since I began working at the school. Usually their objection was that the song was too "ghetto." The previous year, my picks had included Marvin Sap's "Never Would Have Made It," a gospel song that praises God. As Marvin sang, "Never would have made it without you" to his Lord and Savior, my students sang along and pointed to their parents, who faced them in the audience.

For the recession march, the graduates had stood by their seats, waving farewell to their beloved school community and singing along as Jay Z crooned his sampled line in "Death of the Autotune": "Lada da da, lada da da, hey hey hey, goodbye." "Death of the Autotune" had a sophistication seen in much of Jay Z's recent music, a sophistication that symbolized his evolution from young street hustler rapper to three-piece-suit-wearing business tycoon. Our students weren't babies anymore but pre-teens maturing into young men and women. When the crooning ended and the beat dropped, the fifth-graders were to stop waving goodbye and bop up the aisle in sync and with the sophisticated swagger of the middle school students they would become in September.

This was their exit song, their caterpillar-that-had-turned-into-a-butterfly song. The parents got it. The Mean Girls didn't. In their disapproving eyes, my nod to Jay was "'hood."

This time around, I decided to play it safe and choose a nice ballad. It was the year Whitney Houston died. Being a Newark girl at heart, Whitney resonated with people in similar communities all over America, and we mourned the loss of our talented, tormented sister.

We had forgiven her the demons she had battled for her entire career, and we played her greatest hits in our living rooms, crying for weeks after the news broke. Black churches prayed for her mother, Cissy, and her child, Bobbi Kristina, who would herself die some years later in an assumed suicide, as if they were members of their own congregation, which they were in spirit.

When I was five, I sang "The Greatest Love of All" for my school's graduation, and for years to come that song would go down as one of the top five graduation songs for communities such as ours. I felt it was time to resurrect the song, not only because of the appropriateness of its lyrics but also as a tribute to our fallen angel. There was no way anyone could call this another one of my 'hood creations. Whitney's voice was so clean that she had often been labeled a sell-out and criticized for not sounding "black." Her voice transcended race.

In previous years I had won the battle of the graduation song. But this year the Mean Girls refused to let up. They discussed the issue with anyone who would listen. I would see them slithering from classroom to classroom, whispering with their fellow teachers. They brought up the subject yet again in the meeting of fifth-grade teachers, where the few other teachers who happened to be in the room overheard their rant about the need to pick another song.

Two of the teachers, Ms. Tibbetts and Ms. Evelyn, were born-again Christians and West Indian, which meant they usually chose to turn the other cheek when it came to disagreements but had the heat of a Scotch bonnet under their tongues simmering for special occasions. They listened, intrigued, as the Mean Girls spewed their hatred about a song that promoted self-worth and love.

Tibbetts was new to the school and knew nothing about the bullying that went on there. And so when the Mean Girls began to complain about the song, she responded, "What's so bad about the song? They sang it at my former school's graduation and the parents loved it. It's a beautiful song."

"I personally love the song too," one of them simpered. "But unfortunately, as teachers, it's not really about what we want, it's about putting children first."

Tibbetts saw their behavior as catty nonsense, so she continued.

"You guys don't strike me as teachers who give in to children's wants," Tibbetts replied.

Each of them froze. No one had expected Tibbetts to question them. No one ever questioned the bullies.

Pissed, they stormed out and headed straight to Mrs. Giles's office. It wasn't long before I was called in to the principal's office like I was a misbehaved child. I, of course, was held responsible for the incident, not that it could be called an incident.

After discussing it with Giles, I had a solution. Maybe if I spoke to them, I could explain to them that I had nothing to do with what Tibbetts had said. I was tired of being unable to be real about a very obvious reality. There would be no more ignoring the elephant in the room. These women were out to get me, and I wanted to know why. Maybe confronting the problem could end their issues with me, as long as I confronted them respectfully.

When I saw one of them in the lobby, I made my move. "Hey, can we talk for a sec?"

"About what?" she snapped.

"Just stuff. Don't want to get into it in front of all these people." Parents, students, teachers, and security guards were milling around.

"You'll have to tell me what it's about," she insisted.

"O.K., well, I want to clear up some things that I think you think I took a part in which I didn't."

Her expression seemed to change for the better.

"O.K."

"O.K.?"

"O.K.!" She was getting annoyed. I thought I had better thank her and keep it moving before she changed her mind.

"Great. Well, when you're on prep today, just stop by."

"O.K."

This apparent truce was short-lived. As I was heading up to my classroom, Ms. Ferguson, the assistant principal, stopped me in my tracks.

"Did you just threaten a teacher? I was just told that you threatened someone."

The accusation hurt me to my core, considering that I had done such an excellent job of containing my anger. It was against my nature to look away if someone stared me down. But when I became an adult, I understood the consequences of fighting physically or verbally and did my best to ignore being disrespected. The Mean Girls, however, took advantage of the fact that I never retaliated.

There had been nothing in my demeanor that they could have interpreted as a threat. They were the ones who were intimidating. They were the bullies. How typical to make the black girl the aggressor. And how easy would it be for someone to believe it.

We were stereotyped as angry and confrontational, and in communities like the one I came from, we often had reason to be. It was as if these white and white-skinned Latinas knew what was brewing inside me and all their actions were attempts to make me erupt and to leave me with no one but myself to blame if something happened to me. Another teacher had already left the school in part because of them. She hadn't been afraid of them; she'd been afraid of what she would do to them if she stayed.

"Those women are going to make me lose my job," she'd worry. I think that was part of the Mean Girls' plan. She eventually got out and moved to teach at another school before her anger could get the best of her. Meanwhile, I tried to not let it get the best of me.

Luckily Giles and Ferguson paid the accusation no mind, and life went on.

I chose to plaster a smile on my face whenever I spoke to the Mean Girls from that point forward. I would have to play the game, pretend I did not know their intentions, ignore the things they did to try to enrage me, brush off the rumors and nasty comments others continued to run back and tell me one of them said. It was a strategy I had used often over the years, one that made many people believe that I was afraid of them. In reality, I was afraid of myself.

As always, summer arrived in the nick of time. It was my second week off, and I had begun to do what I always did on my breaks: write, go to the spa, and frequent the gym. I had already lost three pounds and was feeling motivated. Right before I was about to leave my apartment to spend an hour on the treadmill, my phone rang. It was Ms. Davis, one of "the favorites."

"Hey, girl!" I said. "How's summer treating you?"

"Uh, can't complain," she replied. "Listen, I'm just going to get straight to it. I need to tell you something."

Seriously? What now? Whatever it was, I really didn't want to hear it, but I felt it must have been important for Ms. Davis to call me.

"What is it?" I asked.

"You were investigated," she replied. "Someone filed a report against you. She must have bragged about it because word got out and I'm just hearing about it now. Remember when she lied and told people you threatened her? Well, she filed a report. Don't worry, it was dismissed immediately. They don't have time for this foolishness."

Anything that involved an investigation sounded serious. My voice quavered as I tried to get more information. I knew the Mean Girls were low, but I never thought they would try to have me fired. I needed my job. We all needed our jobs. We all had bills to pay. They had no right. Didn't they know I had already beaten the odds? That I wasn't supposed to be here, making a decent salary with a master's degree under my belt? I was supposed to be a statistic, not successful! The idea that they would try to take something away from me that I had climbed hurdles to get made me hate them beyond measure. I hung up the phone enraged.

For several moments I sat on my bed feeling helpless. I couldn't fight them. I couldn't even curse them out. They'd definitely press criminal charges against me even if I said "peep."

"You will not break me!" Screaming this into my pillow was my only release.

On the first day back to school, the lump in my throat seemed to have found permanent housing. The investigation had been dismissed, but my paranoia was like the guy who keeps calling no matter how often you've asked him to lose your number. It was here to stay.

When it was time to pick up the keys to my classroom, which had been left in a big box in the main office before summer break, mine were the only ones that were "lost." They had been there when the school year ended. Each key was individually packaged in a small manila envelope with the room number written on it. In case you forgot what room you were assigned to for the year, the assignments for the entire school were posted right next to it.

I immediately panicked. I envisioned someone's taking my key, making a copy, and then planting things in the classroom to incriminate me. I burst into Giles's office.

"Why would you allow the keys to be in a pile like that for anyone to pick up?" I demanded. "Someone stole my key!"

Giles had never seen me so upset, and she didn't take kindly to a teacher's speaking to her in that fashion.

"Now, just calm down, Ms. Lewis," she said. "It could be misplaced. Or someone could've accidentally picked it up, and if so, they'll return it soon. And if it doesn't show up, Mousa has the master key and can open the classroom for you and make a copy for you." I didn't doubt that Mousa, the head custodian and a friend, would make a new copy for me. I just didn't want anyone else to have access to my classroom. And so I announced firmly to Giles, "I want my lock changed."

"What?" she replied, chuckling though clearly annoyed. "That's out of the question. What's the big issue? If you have anything of value, you shouldn't have it sitting around anyway. Either take it home with you or lock it up in the closets. No one will be able to steal from you that way, if that's what you're worried about."

"I'm not worried about what could be taken out of my room; I'm worried about what could be put in!"

Giles looked at me as if I were going crazy. I guess I was.

"Put in?" she demanded. "What on Earth would someone put in your room, Lewis?"

"Lord knows! I put nothing past these women!"

"I don't know where any of this is coming from." She shook her head. Then something seemed to click.

"What, the threat allegation?" she demanded. "You're letting that ruffle your feathers?"

"Of course I am. They investigated me!"

Giles rolled her eyes as if to say, "Oh, please."

"You know how many fake allegations they get every day?" she said. "Teachers lie about each other every day. Parents lie about teachers every day. It's not a big deal. They investigate, find the truth, and nothing happens if you didn't do anything. You have nothing to worry about."

"I don't care about other teachers. She lied about *me!*" I stormed out of her office before my eyes could betray me.

My classroom, as on every first day back for teachers, was spotless. The floor gleamed from the wax finish it had received over the summer. I carefully tried to move desks and chairs into clusters without scratching it. I had calmed down a bit and was getting into the groove of fixing up my classroom, decorating the walls and organizing the library, when Ms. Ferguson walked in, spreading her usual cheer around the school.

"Welcome back, Lewis! Just wanted to poke my head in and say hello."

It was hard not to like Ferguson; she always had a joke or syrupy compliment, but I was no longer feeling friendly toward any members of the administration. I felt betrayed by the fact that I had not been told about the allegation against me, and even more betrayed by the fact that nothing had been done about it.

"Hey," I replied. It wasn't a friendly "Hey."

"You O.K., Lewis? You don't seem like yourself today."

I laughed. "Should I be?"

Ferguson literally scratched her head to show her confusion and walked away.

Two of the Mean Girls walked past my classroom several times, each time looking inside so they could stare me down as if we were in high school. I stared back, looking angry and helpless. They smiled smugly. By the end of the day, after anyone who had taken my key would have had time to make a copy of it, the key had been anonymously thrown back into the box.

By the next day, I felt as if I were losing my mind. I dressed taking deep breaths as I put on my armor of makeup and casual attire. The Mean Girls played it cool, too. Sometimes they would smile at me, and then when no one was looking begin glaring at me as if we were characters in one of those cheesy teenage movies where the bitchy head cheerleader has it in for some seemingly innocent girl because she's prettier.

I always called them the Mean Girls because I pictured each of them taking notes on the *Heathers* as young teens, the movie that our generation's *Mean Girls* was inspired by.

One night I had a nightmare that I was sparring with Mike Tyson with my hands taped to my thighs. Everyone kept yelling, "Put your dukes up!" even though I couldn't move my dukes. Tyson danced around, faking jabs but never really trying to hit me, just moving close enough to make me flinch and duck. Finally he caught me with an uppercut so hard that my head spun around and my mouthpiece flew out of my mouth. I fell on the canvas. TKO.

On my way to our Monday faculty meeting, panic had swept over my body with such intensity that I could barely breathe. The tears I tried so hard not to shed gushed out like two waterfalls, eroding my mascara and depositing it in clumps on my cheeks.

I ducked into the first pre-K room I saw, which happened to be Ms. Halstead's. We weren't what you would call close friends, but she wasn't on the side of the enemy. She was in there with Ms. Robles, the parent coordinator, who also was friendly to me. Both had gotten a whiff of the bullying, and they were sympathetic as the tears poured from my eyes. Robles gathered up my few girlfriends in the school to come and comfort me, but their words couldn't help. I was being terrorized, and no one understood how emotionally devastating it was.

"Why are you letting her win, girl?" one friend asked.

"Aren't you a believer in Christ?" another added. "Trust in Him. Satan can't hurt you."

"Just what are you scared of exactly?" asked a third.

I was tired of being strong. I didn't understand why black women weren't afforded the opportunity to be weak. If this had been happening to a white girl, she would have been expected to cry hysterically.

I, on the other hand, was supposed to be a warrior. How could I not cry, though? This was my livelihood. The allegations, however, touched a nerve.

All my life, my mother and I struggled with the notion of permanency. We always felt unsafe, as a result of the rug's being pulled from underneath us when we got too comfortable with life. The most obvious example of this involved my dad and the breakup of my parents when I was five. We had to move into my grandmother's already full house in the projects, which was filled as much with chaos and mayhem as with love and laughter. Visits with my father were pretty consistent, usually every other weekend, until he decided to move to Baltimore, Maryland, four hours away. The news hit me like a brick, and it hurt more than I would've even expected, as I was definitely not a daddy's girl. Then the rug beneath us was tugged so hard that it knocked me backward. I was told that my father was going to prison for seventeen years.

By the time I got comfortable with not having a father figure, my mother decided to get married again, hoping to bring some sense of normalcy into my life. Suddenly I had a father and a stepbrother, and we were going to live happily ever after. That is, until my mother and my stepfather had a fight and my stepfather pulled out a gun and threw it on the bed a few inches from where she was sitting. The fighting continued until the day I pounced on him with my fifteen-year-old frame after overhearing him tell my mother that he was changing the locks on the door and she and I would be locked out of our home.

Because we all had moved into the apartment together, it was no more his place than my mom's. I was livid. Instead of him grabbing me to prevent my blows, he put his dukes in the air, ready to fight me, a girl a third his age and a third his size. Yet again the rug was pulled from beneath me, and we were back in my grandmother's place, carrying our physical and mental baggage of clothes and shame past an array of spectators who watched two people who seemed to have escaped stumble back up stairwells stinking of urine to Apartment 1B.

Eventually, after my stepfather forced my mother to take him to court to regain our apartment, we moved back to our old place and he was moved out. But the idea of stability was long gone from my mind until a few years later, when my mother landed a job as director of a child development center. It was just the two of us, and money was abundant, abundant enough for me to consider attending Fordham, knowing that my mother could pay for what my loans could not cover.

Life was good again for several years until the day she was fired for blowing the whistle on board members who were extorting money from the center. The Department of Investigation told her that because she wasn't a city employee she would not be protected by whistle-blower protection laws, adding that if she didn't name names, she would be charged with obstructing an investigation. As she expected, the board fired her weeks later. We were devastated at the thought of my having to leave Fordham for lack of funds.

By then, there was another man she had begun seeing, who would eventually become my second stepfather. He agreed to pay for my tuition for the next two years while my mother successfully fought the firing and was reinstated. I finished college and at the age of twenty-one was accepted into the Teaching Fellowship program. So you can understand why my mother cried tears of joy when she learned of my acceptance. At an early age I had won something that she had strived for her entire life: a chance for stability. So you can imagine my emotions when that stability seemed threatened.

I was scared, but I was also angry. This mess had begun to make me fall out of love with the profession. The months just seemed to drift by. I had become numb and indifferent. Gradually, I just began to fade out.

6

The Thrill Is Gone

was beginning to feel as invisible as the children I taught. My needs
didn't matter to the system any more than theirs did. I was a shell of a
teacher, not even half the teacher I used to be. It was becoming clearer to
me how some teachers become those dreaded educators who just collect
paychecks. I wasn't there yet, but I feared that I was getting close.

The blow was even harder being a teacher of color because of my desire to serve the children of my community. I had *it*—the passion, the
creativity, the knowledge, the commitment, the connection to my community, the potential to actually make a difference. I had proven it, time
and time again, but my ability to affect this community of parents and
students was continually blocked by people and policies that didn't have
their best interests at heart. Everywhere I turned, something or someone
seemed to be in the way of my performing my job effectively. The best
teachers were happy teachers. How could I instill in students the spirit to
achieve while employed under a system that seemed to have been created
to destroy my own spirit?

In addition to feeling fear, anger, and anxiety, I felt worn. This profession ages you in ways other professions do not. During the ten years I
taught, I found a bedbug on my desk, caught ringworm twice and con-
junctivitis three times, and would have caught lice the year the Gonza-
lez family enrolled if it weren't for my 3c corkscrew curls. Teaching in
the South Bronx made my allergies flare to new heights, and each year I
caught colds and different strains of flu from my students.

My feet were destroyed from all the unsupportive flat shoes I had worn, and my hands felt as if I were in the early stages of arthritis from all the typing, grading, writing, and cutting I had done over the years. I ditched working out five days a week and eventually stopped all together, which when combined with the food selections in the neighborhood added an extra thirty pounds to my frame. At thirty-one years old, I began to see why so many teachers in their forties and fifties were so overweight.

Worst of all was the impact on my memory, my attention span, and my ability to concentrate. I couldn't keep my mind on one subject. I couldn't read a book straight through; I would get bored after twenty pages. Often after reading a page, I would realize that I didn't have a clue as to what I had just read. I now knew how many of my kids felt. I began to feel like a contestant on the show *Wipeout*, where the players get doused with water and hit with padded hands while trying to jump on spinning wheels. The only difference was that if those players didn't make it to the finish line, they still got applause and a pat on the back.

While my body and spirit were breaking down, the neighborhood was being built up. Jackhammers roared seemingly around the clock. The new buildings were beautiful, albeit cheaply built. Some were condos or pricey rentals with gyms and other amenities. The South Bronx, a.k.a. SoBro, was emerging as a new, trendy alternative for those who could not afford Harlem or Williamsburg prices. Not that the changes did anything to address the area's real problems. An expensive apartment building with fish tanks and clubhouses would do little to help the winos on the block to sober up, or lost boys to stop shooting up, or children to stop giving up.

The housing projects near many of these new buildings were still home to their same issues, and the children still brought these issues back into the classroom. Children were still being neglected. I had students whose hair had not been washed and whose teeth had not been brushed in weeks. Many reeked from the buildup of plaque on their teeth and oil and sweat in hair that had not been shampooed. I cannot tell you how many fights some of the more offensive body odors sparked. It's difficult to have students work in groups when there are several students whom no one wants to touch or even sit next to because they and their clothes smell so terrible.

Still, there were no solutions to these unfortunate realities. White men with intentions to kill were shooting up schools and shooting unarmed men for selling cigarettes and buying Skittles in neighborhoods that were not their own, yet many Americans mustered some level of empathy. These terrorists were labeled "mentally ill," victims of bullying, outcasts of society. Police officers were merely defending themselves from big black monsters, even when they were armed or weighed more. Still, our black and brown mothers and grandmothers who were failing their children were demonized; they were never offered sympathy, just judgmental opinions, and visits from ACS, Administration for Children's Services. When neglect turned into violence, they most definitely could have their children taken away, which made sense, because their children weren't safe in their care. However, I still found it ironic. There was an irony in the fact that black mothers' children were being taken away because of a tradition of violence first developed by black slave mothers in an effort to keep their children from being sold away. We demonized black mothers who carried on the tradition of neglecting their own children, a wrong first learned by slave women who were never given the permission to be mothers first but instead milk nurses and mammies to white children, servants to white mistresses, bed warmers for their masters, and manly field hands alongside their own men. While some seemingly unfit mothers were first generation in their failure to care for their children, the abuse and neglect were usually cyclical in nature and could most probably be traced back for generations. Slavery ended in 1865. That's only one hundred and fifty years ago. To put it another way, black people were enslaved in this country longer than we have been free. I couldn't help but wonder why these connections had never been taught in schools. Such kinds of teaching had great healing potential, in my opinion. But what do I know?

One year, a little girl cried in my arms about having to wear dirty clothes to school every day. Tasha's white uniform shirt had turned to gray and had stains all over it. She told me that she lived with her ailing aunt, who couldn't really take care of her, and that her mother came around only when she felt like it. She was ten, but because she was underdeveloped for her age she looked like a much younger child.

Tasha was so little that her aunt did not allow her outside on her own except to go to school. The laundromat was out of the question, and so she had no choice but to wash her own clothes by hand. Before I knew it, I was offering to wash her uniforms for her, and a plan was hatched. She would bring me her clothes in her book bag, and I would transfer them into my own bag during lunchtime.

After I washed the clothes, I would bring them back at the end of the week and we would reverse the process. But before I could do anything, I needed to get permission. I wrote a note to the aunt, trying to be as tactful as possible.

Dear Ms. Hyatt,

I am terribly sorry to hear that you have been bed-ridden from declining health. Tasha told me that you have been feeling very sick lately and I hope for a speedy recovery. I also totally understand your concern about her going to the laundromat alone. If it would be of any help to you, I would be more than willing to wash Tasha's uniform for her; I have a washer and dryer on my apartment floor and it wouldn't be an inconvenience.

Sincerely,
Ms. Lewis

The next day, Tasha came to school with an immaculate white uniform shirt. Still, I was disgusted by the idea that these problems were not supposedly *our* problems, and that many teachers saw their roles as pedagogical only so would've been complacent with Tasha's being an intellectual dirtbag. They would not be evaluated on Tasha's improvement in hygiene, only her test scores.

Teachers were all but helpless in the situation. Who's going to call ACS on a parent for sending a child to school with a dirty uniform shirt? Writing a letter was definitely too bold for most. Teachers became numb to these scenarios and usually fell into one of two categories: Either they understood that families were poor and so accepted the fact that they probably could afford only one uniform shirt, or they stopped caring about the children because, "Hey, if she doesn't care about her own child, why should I?"

While I understood that Tasha's family could afford only one shirt, I didn't like how easy it would be for teachers to just throw their hands up, for their ability to equate poverty with filth. I knew more than anyone that being poor didn't mean being dirty. But many teachers who came from different socioeconomic backgrounds could not understand how much deeper a filthy child was. They believed it simply to be an economic thing.

I wrote the letter to Ms. Hyatt because I knew better. Tasha's aunt somehow managed to get her a clean shirt by the next day. If it were that simple, why didn't she do it before? Had she not paid attention to the child enough to realize that her shirt was dirty? Had she not cared? Instances like this were what made the other half of teachers demonize our parents. But as I stated earlier, if Americans could find a way to forgive mass murderers, I definitely could find empathy for Tasha's aunt, who had probably learned neglectful behavior from her own parents, or suffered from depression, or PTSD, or some other 'hood mental illness, because there were plenty out there that no one cared enough about to even discuss, let alone do anything about. Even to those who may have factored in mental illness as the culprit, it was just accepted, no different from the acceptance of crazy homeless men on New York City streets. No one cared enough. And we were teachers of pedagogy, not politicians, policy-makers, or social workers. I was in the wrong lane if I really wanted to make a difference in what mattered.

Powerless, we did what we could. In stepping in to help students like Tasha, I was not unique. I can think of several teachers who have had a positive impact on the lives of children who have been made to feel invisible.

Ms. Gutierrez, my home girl, took her best-behaved students on trips every other Saturday. She raised money to buy tickets so they could see Broadway shows like *The Lion King*. When Sonia Sotomayor was appointed to the U.S. Supreme Court, Ms. Gutierrez wrote to her, mentioning that she was a fellow alumna of Cardinal Spellman High School in the Bronx and saying how proud she was to see a fellow Puerto Riqueña receive such an honor and how great a role model she was to the black and brown children of the South Bronx. Ms. Gutierrez was eventually invited to take her students to Washington, D.C., to meet the new Supreme Court justice.

Ms. Owens could also see students who might otherwise have felt invisible. She could see that one of her students, Frankie, had clothes so worn that she brought him clothes every fall and spring for four years. In first grade, when she saw the holes in his pants, she gathered a bunch of her son's hand-me-downs and gave them to him. As her son continued to grow out of his clothes, she packed them up to give to Frankie the next year, and she continued to do that until Frankie graduated.

Ms. Davis was yet another teacher who truly saw her students. Through her affiliations with black fraternities and sororities, she wangled many opportunities for them, including summer camp, mentorships, and scholarships. She felt that the kids we taught deserved the same opportunities that she had received when she was young, and she used her Greek connection and her own dollars to make this happen.

Illnesses of all kinds persisted. The number of children with learning and behavioral disabilities that required medication seemed to be increasing. Record numbers of black and brown boys were being diagnosed with ADD, ADHD, and autism. And thanks to technology, the attention spans of all children were getting shorter, making it even harder for them to read. Media outlets overstimulated our children's brains with rapid-fire changing images that zipped across the screen every five to six seconds, causing them to have extreme attention deficits. Our modern culture of instant gratification made it increasingly more difficult for them to do anything that required effort or time. After children had spent a day writing one-line Facebook statuses and Twitter tweets, writing a paragraph seemed as hard as writing a novel.

As a result of this overstimulation, teachers had to make learning unbelievably fun all the time, even though we didn't have computers in our classroom, or Smart Boards—interactive whiteboards that were touch-screen sensitive, thereby enabling teachers and students to write with stylus pens, text that could subsequently be erased electronically. It was more convenient and came with engaging technology, could play music and movies, pretty much the best teaching tool ever developed. Smart Boards had been around for years but were often lacking in schools in poor areas with small budgets. Even when schools in these neighborhoods finally received funding, the upkeep was expensive. When they broke down or needed replacement parts, schools in the 'hood were pretty much out of luck. Some schools would take months, even years to find the replacements needed, making them fixtures in the classroom that could not be used, along with many outdated, warranty-expired computers that often sat in the back of the room for decorative purposes. There were a few laptop carts that could be rolled from class to class throughout the day, but the batteries died easily, and as a result of the desire of certain children to lash out at inanimate objects, at least a third of them would be broken.

We'd beg some parents to check their children's homework. In some cases, we'd beg parents to just make sure their kids *did* their homework. "He told me he didn't have any homework" was the standard response, even after we explained that there was homework every day. Many children didn't come to school with bookbags at all, and their parents would sometimes blame the children for walking out of the door without one, even when those children were only six or seven years of age.

A younger child with a parent who suffered from mental illness or a substance-abuse problem responded very differently from the way an older child would. Reyna, a young girl whose father was an alcoholic and whose mother, a battered wife, suffered from severe depression, literally became mute for a few years. She was sweet and she aimed to please, but she decided not to speak, resorting to pointing, nodding, and shrugging when she wanted to communicate. She made herself as invisible as possible, hiding all of her feelings, trying not to be noticed, hoping to disappear, kind of the way I had that night in my bedroom as a little girl.

Once during a parent–teacher conference, while I was trying to explain to her mother why her daughter was barely passing, the woman actually tuned out. As she sat there like a figure in a wax museum, her soul seemed to leave her body while Reyna clung to her back and cried uncontrollably, as if trying to hide herself behind a wall.

I rubbed Reyna's back but could not console her, given that all she wanted was a mother's touch. Eventually, she opened up and began speaking to me in whispers, but she shut down again the following year, only this time she became indifferent. She stopped doing her homework and she no longer cared about the consequences.

We would call Administration for Children's Services, but there were too many such cases in the city for the agency to step in. A child would have to be beaten or sexually abused for anyone to take notice. By the time Reyna had gone off to middle school, she was what the kids called emo, wearing all black and dark eyeliner and streaking her hair with bright turquoise, green, or orange. This would be fine if she were doing well in school. Unfortunately, she wasn't even *in* school on the days I bumped into her on the street. Now her invisibility showed itself through her empty classroom seat.

When Isaac was put in my fifth-grade class, his former teachers all told me he was a behavior problem. According to them, he had run amok since kindergarten. No one knew exactly what was wrong with his mother, but we knew she had emotional problems. She was an avid smoker of weed, which I'm sure didn't help. Whenever she came to school to discuss Isaac, she redirected the conversation to government conspiracies.

This was especially awkward when she brought Isaac with her. I would smile and nod, pretending that I agreed with everything she said. The look on his face suggested that he knew better. Even a ten-year-old who couldn't read knew there was something terribly wrong with conversation about "new world orders" and secret silicon chip implants during a parent–teacher conference.

Isaac started out as a behavior problem, acting out to get the attention he didn't get at home. By the time he reached fifth grade, he stopped being a behavior problem in school. He would simply put his head down on the desk and pretend that he wasn't even in the room.

After I was assigned to be a SETSS teacher, I saw even more students with problems. SETSS stands for Special Education Teacher Support Services. As the SETSS teacher, I pulled students out of their general-education classes for one period of small-group instruction.

One of my SETSS students was Selena. She was only in first grade, but she was brilliant. She read beautifully and her level of comprehension was far above her grade level. Still, she was considered a special-education child in need of one period of support a day.

SETSS was designed to serve students with academic delays, of which she had none. But because Selena had spent her entire kindergarten and first-grade years not in a classroom but in the assistant principal's office, my administration decided that she would get extra help via SETSS.

She and I developed a strong bond, and she enjoyed spending time with me. The problem was, I had other SETSS students. While it would have been more useful for me to see Selena alone, I had no choice but to see her in a classroom along with my other SETSS students. This was a nightmare. Selena craved attention so much that she preferred to disrupt an entire class rather than share her teacher with other children. I tried to praise her by treating even her most insignificant achievement as a herculean feat, but all my good efforts were destroyed if I said so much as two words to another child.

The assumption was that being in a group of eight students would provide Selena with more attention than her being in the standard class of twenty-five. But the only thing that would have worked would have been for her to have one teacher for the entire day.

I wasn't surprised to learn that Selena's father was in jail. Many of the students had fathers and even mothers in jail. My father was in jail, serving a longer sentence than most people I knew who were also in prison. I also wasn't shocked to learn that she lived not with her mother but with her grandmother. Many of our students lived with their grandparents.

What exacerbated Selena's emotional problems was the fact that she lived with her maternal grandmother while her half-siblings lived with their mom in a better neighborhood in the North Bronx. The half-siblings also had the pleasure of living with their father. It was the perfect nuclear family for them, while Selena lived with neither her mother nor her incarcerated father. Her mother was very involved in her schooling and would answer the phone whenever I called. She would even pick Selena up after school every day and drop her off at the grandmother's apartment. She clearly loved her daughter, but the ache inside Selena would never be filled as long as she was forced to live away from her mother.

In any case, Selena made my group sessions a disaster. I tried every possible incentive I could think of to make her better behaved. I let her use the whiteboard to write down her answers instead of a notebook like everyone else. I gave her jobs like book distributor. When I collected children for these sessions, I picked her up first and dropped her off last so that she could spend the most time with me. Still, she made sure I could not pay attention to anyone but her during the entire forty-five-minute period.

Finally, I resorted to punishment.

"Selena, I need to be able to conduct my group," I told her. "You know the work, they don't. If you would just do your classwork and not run around in the halls during your normal class time, you would get the highest scores. These kids really need my help to read. If you can't behave while you're here with them, I'll just stop picking you up."

In response, Selena ran off screaming but was caught by Ms. Myles, the District 75 teacher I shared the classroom with, as she headed out the door. I put her on my lap and held her arms to her body so she couldn't run off. I rubbed her back while I rocked her slowly back to calmness. She continued to scream through her tears. "Get off me!" she yelled. "You're not my teacher anymore!"

I held her face and forced her to look at me. "Shhh. I'm not leaving you," I said to her. Still rocking her, I hugged her tightly and whispered the same words in her ear over and over until she finally tired herself out and grew limp in my arms. "I see you," I said softly. "I won't stop seeing you."

Anthony liked being rocked too. He was in first grade and had a twin sister named Amina. Both had trouble adjusting to pre-kindergarten, often running out of their classrooms to find each other. By kindergarten, however, Amina marched cheerfully into her classroom and Anthony was still feeling anxiety, making it apparent that the problem was more than new-school jitters. When the eighth week came and Anthony was crying for his mommy as much as he had on the first day of school, the school's guidance counselor got involved.

Every morning Anthony would try to run out of the classroom and hold onto his mother for dear life, hyperventilating when he was pulled away. He was inconsolable. His mother would let him stay home or pick him up early because he was in a constant state of panic, as if afraid that he would never see her again. He caused so much commotion that we decided he should be picked up for SETSS the first thing in the morning, in an effort to help him ease into a classroom atmosphere.

Every day I had to rip him from his mother's arms and let him cry on my lap until he exhausted himself and fell asleep. When he woke up, we would do some work. By the time we were finished, he would let me take him by the hand and walk him to his regular classroom, where he would be fine for the rest of the day.

Anthony didn't know the letter *A* when I showed it to him, even though he was in first grade. Eventually, it became clear that he didn't have a learning disability but had simply been mentally absent from his first two years of school. In two months, he learned all of his letters, short and long vowel sounds, and even CVC (consonant-vowel-consonant) words. After three months he was reading entire paragraphs.

Anthony read better than some of my third-graders with disabilities, and he was only six. I never saw a child advance so quickly. He was extremely intelligent, but no one had known it as a result of his crying fits and absenteeism. By the second year, we thought things would improve even further. But just the opposite happened. Anthony got worse. When he left school the previous year for summer vacation, his crying fits had ceased. By September, they had returned and were even more intense.

It was my job to pry him off his mother every morning, and still he would wriggle away and beg to say goodbye one more time. He would still ask me if he would ever see her again. He would pace around the classroom holding his head in his hands with a look of utter terror on his face. Sometimes, he would just sit on the floor and cry, his head buried in his hands. "Please, let me talk to my mother," he would whimper.

His mother said she planned to get him evaluated by a doctor. But instead, she simply kept him out of school for days on end. I tried to explain to her that she could be charged with educational neglect, and she would bring him in for a day or two, but he would be absent again by midweek. One day, he stopped coming at all. When the school's family worker visited the home, there was no one there. Finally, the school got a call from a school out of state saying that he had been enrolled there. I never saw him again.

The teachers would scoff in disgust at these examples of poor parenting. My emotions vacillated, ranging anywhere from embarrassment to pity to rage—not so much toward the parent but for what had brought us to this point.

The neighborhood seemed to be getting worse as well, despite all the beautiful new buildings. The projects, of course, endured. And despite official statistics indicating that crime was declining, it seemed to be on the rise.

One summer I bumped into a parent of a student in the street and asked her how summer was treating her.

"Oh, this is bullet-dodging season," she replied matter-of-factly.

One summer a four-year-old boy was killed by cross-fire during a memorial basketball tournament for yet another child victim of gun violence. The shooter was a former District 75 student, one of many troubled boys who go directly from the school system to the prison system. In that same week, four people were injured at another basketball tournament, this one at Rucker Park in Harlem just a few miles away. Later the following school year, another former District 75 student was shot and killed by a police officer when the student tried to raise his gun after being told to freeze.

Buses filled with white tourists from Europe and Australia parked in front of our school to learn about the "Real Bronx," courtesy of a tourist company whose very name mocked the everyday struggle on the streets. Community leaders rightfully bashed the company for providing foreigners the opportunity to laugh at our pain. They complained that the tour presented an inaccurate depiction of the South Bronx, something I did not agree with. Gawking at our problems was wrong. But to say that the tour gave a distorted view of what was happening in the neighborhood would be asking people to close their eyes and pretend that they didn't see the run-down buildings and the drunks begging for change on the corner.

Whether crime was down, as Mayor Michael R. Bloomberg's administration insisted, or not made no difference to me. Finding only a single bullet in the gutter right outside my school was all I needed to be terrified that one day a stray bullet would come flying through the window.

One morning, body parts of a mutilated woman were found in a garbage bag on the street outside our school, prompting the police to block off the street for the entire day. It didn't happen once a week, or even once a month; it happened only one time. That didn't make our reality any brighter, nor did it make the woman's death any less tragic.

It wasn't on every lunch break that I witnessed a high-speed car chase that ended with the suspect's being cornered by several police cars, pulled out of the driver's seat, thrown to the ground, and cuffed directly in front of my school either, but the problem was that it happened at all. I promise you that a schoolteacher in Mamaroneck could never say she saw the same.

One afternoon I heard gunshots a few feet from my classroom window. I had heard gunshots before, but never while in a school building. Gunshots were usually reserved for nighttime, and I began to wonder if I had heard correctly. Growing up in Edenwald Projects, however, one learns the difference between fireworks, a car's backfiring, and actual gunshots. I knew a shot when I heard one, and from the sound of it, two people or two groups of people had exchanged bullets just blocks from the school.

I had been on my way out of my classroom, prepared to pick up my last group for the day. After hearing the shots, I hurried to the main office to tell Giles. When I reached her office, everyone there was already staring out the window, watching a procession of police cars with blaring sirens race down the street. Helicopters whirred overhead. It was nearly dismissal time, so Giles got on the loudspeaker to issue a "shelter in" directive. Ever since the fatal shootings at Sandy Hook Elementary School in Connecticut, schools across the city had increased the frequency of these drills. Because this threat was not in the building but outside, the children could roam around in the school but could not leave. Nor could parents enter. We tried to distract the students by teaching, but it's hard to teach when helicopters are circling overhead looking for shooters on the loose.

With crime in the community so prevalent, I should have realized that many of my students would be involved in crime at some point in their lives. My cute little elementary school children were growing up into young men and women and would eventually be forced to make a choice. They would have to decide whether to live a life that followed the rules or one that did not. But whose rules? Mainstream American rules or 'hood rules?

When I was a teenager, we listened to Biggie's "Ten Crack Commandments," a playbook for dealers that warned hustlers not to extend credit to their consumers and not to get "high on your own supply." Today, a plethora of songs reference the code of the streets, including "Chiraq" by Meek Mill, from Philadelphia. Meek raps about Chicago, aka Chiraq, in this particular song, a city notable for the high number of homicides of people of color. "Niggas know the rules in my 'hood, if you touch me, you get murked," Meek warns. "We ain't with that back and forth, it ain't no rap, we hittin' first."

In short, Meek's song warns his adversaries that he will not waste time fighting in the street. Any form of disrespect will result in homicide. Meek's threat, like that of many rappers who still talk about the codes of the street in their songs years after their financial success, may have been just talk, but the rules still applied to those still running in the streets. 'Hood rules are so embedded in the culture that several rap songs have the term "hood rules" in their titles, among them "Hood Rules" by the Houston rapper K-Rino, "Hood Rules Apply" by the R&B singer Trey Songz, and "Hood Rules Apply" by Team Invasion, a song on Volume Two of a series of mix tapes called—what else? "Hood Rules Apply." The basic message is never snitch, be loyal, don't get caught, trust no one, and always, always "keep shit real"—that is, be honest to those who deserve the truth and never pretend to be more than what you are.

Asking a student to tell on another student was, for many, the equivalent of telling him to break the law. I understood. I lived by this rule for years and struggle even today to ignore my first instincts whenever I feel disrespected. Luckily, I never came to blows. Except once.

In Kennedy High School, I ran with a few girls from my gifted program who were also black and from low-income neighborhoods. Although we were good girls who didn't get into trouble, and although I had never been in a fight in my entire life, one day one of our enemies jumped one of my friends when she was alone. We weren't fighters, but 'hood rules applied to us nonetheless. There would be no chickening out.

We came to school dressed for battle every day: hair tied up, faces greased, wearing sweats and Timberland boots. Looking silly and unlike ourselves, we waited for something more to happen. After the third day of my looking like this, Sarah Foster finally asked, "What the heck is going on?"

"Girls wanna fight us," I replied.

"So?"

"So? We're ready."

"You want to fight them?"

"Of course not, silly. Since when have you seen me looking like this?"

"Well, then, why would you?"

I loved Sarah for keeping her shit real too. She was genuinely confused and had no qualms about admitting so. I paused at her question, though, baffled at how she could not understand my fighting obligation. I realized that she didn't live by the same code. I decide to educate her.

"Because, girl, there is no other option."

"Yes, there is! Run!"

Of course I didn't run. One day after I had gotten off the bus, I decided to wait at the stop for my friend Natyla so she didn't have to walk up the hill to our school by herself. I had already felt guilty for not going along with the rest of the crew to another girl's house who was present the day she had been jumped. This girl, whom we believed to be a friend of ours, stood there and watched her supposed friend fight eight girls alone. My friends decided to pay her a visit, and I had already been home. Once I was home, I was in for the night, my mother's standard rule. I could not just leave my apartment whenever I pleased like many of my friends. I also wasn't trying to sneak out, because my mother would have lost her mind. I declined. My ballsy friends walked right up to this girl's door and told her mother to go fetch her own daughter. Her mother, as one would expect mothers to do, protected her daughter, and my friends never got the revenge they had desired.

I had to make it up to Natyla and be her protector moving forward. Given that I was the tallest girl in the group, it only made sense that I would walk with Natyla to the school every day after we got off the bus. We didn't have cell phones then, so I would have to tell her my plan on the bus. But she wasn't on the bus that day. I figured she might be late for school, so I stood at the bus stop and waited for the next one to arrive. There I was, donned in official fight attire, my greasy face glistening in the sun, when the same girl whom my friends had harassed the night before stepped off the bus. She looked scared because I was much bigger than she, but as 'hood rules applied, she wouldn't back down. She assumed I had been waiting for her. She dropped her book bag to the ground and put up her hands. My confused expression allowed her to acknowledge her error; I was not waiting there to fight her; however, she could not back down now and neither could I. A crowd was already forming.

Suddenly the fight was on. My opponent fought like a girl, which entails her attempting not to actually hurt me but to ugly me. She pulled my hair in hopes of ripping it out, scratched at my face in hopes of scarring it, and attempted to yank off my father's chain that I wore around my neck, but she couldn't because it was "that good shit." My dad ran with the Italians before he was locked up, and his jewelry wasn't like the cheap, hollowed-out chains that brothers were buying on Fordham Road. Several times she tried to run away, making the battle more a game of cat and mouse than an actual fight.

Running around in the cold, the sun's bright light reflecting on mounds of snow, chasing a girl in heavy boots and thick sweatpants, I got hot, and as luck would have it, my nose started to bleed. My mother would later tell me that it was God paying me back for trying to be a thug. Knowing she hadn't even tried to punch me, the girl was more surprised than I was at the tiny drop of blood that stained my shirt.

By the next week she had told everyone that she'd beaten my ass and then brought her mother in to see the principal in an effort to keep me from fighting her again. I was told that if I fought the girl again, I would be dropped from my program. She knew I was in a gifted program and would be concerned about such matters. My opponent had broken two rules: snitching, by telling her parent, and lying about her "victory." I devised a plan to prove she had lied, one that didn't end in my suspension. I made sure everyone knew how afraid of me she really was by standing next to her every time I saw her in the halls and singing "Shook Ones" by Mobb Deep. *Shook* meant scared, and the words went like this:

Son, you shook, 'cause ain't no such thing as half-way crooks,
Scared to death but scared to look, you shook.

The girl would stand there mutely while her friends nudged her to do something. It didn't make any sense. A girl who could kick my ass shouldn't stand for my taunting her in public. Without fighting, I had still managed to play by the rules I had been given, both in school and in the streets.

———————

I can't say my life would be the same if I'd stayed living in the projects for my entire childhood. I would have had a different set of laws to abide by. When I was eighteen and in college, I went back to Edenwald to visit my grandmother and bumped into a couple of my former classmates from elementary school. Both girls were pushing baby strollers with toddlers walking alongside them. We embraced and they asked what was going on in my life. I told them I was going to Fordham. They were impressed. But they were also confused as to why I hadn't had any children yet. While I didn't think they should be ashamed for having children early, I was surprised at their expectation that I should have had multiple kids by the age of eighteen. The fact that they had had children already wasn't surprising to me; we all were having sex. Too often, the ones who raise their noses in judgment of teenage moms would be moms too if they hadn't had abortions. I salute girls who make the brave decision to keep their children when they too, are still children. However, these girls seemed to not be fazed by their age. They did not panic at the idea of being teenage mothers. Whatever fears they had about having children were no different from those the average woman in her twenties or thirties would have. Their comment about my lack of children confirmed for me that their realities were expected of them. *I* was the anomaly, not they. They weren't teenage mothers; I was a childless woman. In their world, it was I who had broken the rules.

Teaching in the 'hood made me realize that my mother had not followed typical protocol, her journey resulting less from strategic decisions and more as a consequence of a series of serendipitous events. She was born in Edenwald Projects and would ordinarily have followed the path that many of her siblings and friends had followed. But she was lucky enough to have discovered a different path. She stumbled upon education thanks to my grandmother, who forced my mother to continue her schooling simply out of fear that she would lose my grandfather's Social Security checks if my mother weren't officially listed as a dependent.

When choosing a major, my mother decided on early childhood education, based simply on the fact that she liked babies. She thought that teaching toddlers meant making multicolored hand prints and playing dress-up. In school she learned how much more went into teaching young children and how crucial learning was in the first few years of a child's life. She kept learning, earning an associate's degree at Bronx Community College, where she met my father, and then bachelor's and master's degrees at Lehman and City College. She applied everything that she learned to me from the moment she learned of life in her womb.

As a result, I was ahead of my peers since conception. My mother surrounded me with books from the time I was a baby. She spoke to me not in baby talk but in complete sentences. She asked me questions, taught me to think critically, and exposed me to new things. From birth, she instilled in me the value of an education and made sure I took my education seriously.

By the time I graduated from high school, she was the only still-attending parent at our school's teacher conferences. In addition, she never stopped asking God to protect me, my brain, and my path. If it weren't for her stumbling upon the truth of education's ability to set one free, I don't know where or who I would be right now.

I could predict success for a handful of my students who lived in the housing projects near the school. They each had a different set of rules from that of most of the other children who lived in their neighborhood. Each of their families had a different culture that was responsible for their children's guaranteed success.

Gabby was a first-generation Dominican American. Her mother, who didn't speak English, was a single parent, raising Gabby and her two sisters alone. Like many immigrant parents, however, their mother had certain expectations for her daughters. Although the mother couldn't speak English, she spoke and wrote fluent Spanish, as did Gabby and her sisters. Education was *extremely* important in their household, and Gabby's homework was always complete. Many parents would argue that they valued education but offered no meaningful consequences or solutions when their children misbehaved, lost focus, or lacked work ethic. There was a learned helplessness that many of the parents seemed to develop when their children did not give their all:

> "He wouldn't stop playing his video games. I told him if he waited until ten to start his homework that he'd be sleepy."

> "I told him to buy pencils with the money I gave him, but he wanted to spend it on candy."

> "I wanted her to go to school today, but she didn't feel like it."

While I would get frustrated at these answers, I would be even more frustrated that my role as "teacher" was so minimal in the lives of my students and their parents. At best, I would try to reach the parent, but if I made the attempt and nothing was done on their end, the required "parental engagement" that teachers were supposed to attempt was fulfilled. I was on a schedule, and I was to follow what I was told to do in that schedule. As long as the attempt was made, there wasn't any more that administration could ask us to do. Trying to change the psyche of parents would have to be done on my own time, of which I had none. Sometimes teachers who really felt there was nothing they could do given their constraints developed the same attitude of learned helplessness that many of their students and parents of those students displayed. Between the parents, kids, and teachers, learned helplessness can easily become a part of a school culture for those who allow it.

But not Gabby. If she didn't understand something, she called me or Casey to explain it to her. If she had a doctor's appointment, she made sure she'd tell us in advance. If she was sick, she always had a note. Gabby made sure she was always accountable because good grades were a high priority in her household.

Jordan's culture was church. Though many of my African American students considered themselves Christians and many went to church on Sundays, Jordan's family went to church not only every Sunday but also several times during the week. Jordan attended Bible class and, if you remember, brought her little green Bible to class every day. She had such high expectations for herself and her family that she would fall apart whenever she did anything wrong.

Earlier that year she had had a breakdown for hitting a little girl—four years earlier. The pang of guilt came over her in the middle of gym class, probably after witnessing a scuffle between two kids. I told her to forgive herself because she had already been forgiven by God.

If everyone in the world had a moral compass like Jordan's, we would all be skipping through meadows, picking sunflowers, and enjoying world peace. Is it any wonder that Jordan was an exceptionally well-behaved child who tried her best in every subject?

Laila wore her hair in dreadlocks. She was the only girl in the entire school with locks. She may have been the only girl in the entire community with them, which was remarkable. Locks was a natural style that did not try to mask or change the coarseness of one's hair. But many little girls had their hair relaxed by the time they were in fifth grade.

Laila told me she had taken African dance at Alvin Ailey since she was five, and so I used her in one of my African dance numbers. She also informed me that her older brother had traveled to Africa the previous year with his school. I wasn't surprised when Laila went on to a charter school the following year. What Laila had that many others children did not was knowledge of self.

Some of the other girls would ask her why she had her hair dreaded. She would reply, "Because I like it." The other African American children were confused as to why she kept her hair "nappy"; these students usually commented on how pretty Hispanic hair was. Some flat-out admitted to wanting to be Hispanic and wishing they had lighter skin and thinner hair "like the Spanish people." Even though there were Hispanic children who resembled them, that group's heritage was seemingly ignored. In the minds of the black children I taught, all Hispanic people were lighter than they.

Laila's family empowered her by providing her with a different perspective on blackness, one that was often missing in poverty-stricken communities. It should be no surprise that she was one of the most advanced students in the entire grade.

One of the children I will always remember the most was Ali. Ali was a champion student, and I wanted him out of the public school system. He wanted it too. The seed was planted when the guidance counselor asked us if we had any overachievers in our classrooms who would like to apply to a prestigious private middle school. The chances of getting in were slim to none, she said, but it was worth a try. Ali and I looked at each other immediately. There was no one else in the class whom I would even have considered.

Ali's parents were Gambian immigrants who spoke English but still had trouble communicating with teachers. Ali was the oldest of several siblings, and at the age of ten he handled a lot of his own school business. Every morning he came to school with a cup of tea and a buttered roll or an egg-and-cheese sandwich with turkey bacon from the local *halal* spot. "No pork on my fork," he would remind me as I let him eat during the first five minutes of class.

I had several nicknames for him, one of which was Old Man, because he was such an old soul, I guess from having so many responsibilities at an early age. Once, I had to stop him from taking prescription pills during class, because it was illegal for a student to administer his own medication.

"But I have to take this every six hours for two weeks," he explained in his usual logical way. "It's just antibiotics."

"Ali, a teacher cannot be aware of a child taking medication," I replied. "Do you understand?"

He did. Five minutes later he asked me if he could go to the bathroom. I let him go.

Although it's a cliché, I also called him "champ" because the word was so fitting. He wanted to win in everything and could not stand defeat. If he was weak in any area, he worked tirelessly to become strong in it. His work ethic was tremendous, and as a result he excelled in every subject, leaving him bored because he was finished with his work ahead of the rest of the class.

Ali's family wasn't strict and didn't punish him to encourage him to do his work. It was just expected that he would perform well. He was an exceptionally bright child and did his homework without anyone's having to tell him to do so. His mother and aunts came to every single parent–teacher conference of his and his cousins' school careers and they answered their phones when we teachers called. Sometimes they didn't have anyone to help out with the babies who were still in diapers so they brought all of them with them. These outstanding women graced our school halls in their beautiful printed dresses and ornate *hijabs* to cover their heads with several younger children in tow while Ali and his scholar cousins, heads held high, led the way. Ali's women family and I were very close, and they often asked me if they could set me up with one of the family's "good Muslim men." They recognized me as one of their own, even though we were culturally quite different in appearance. We were family.

After our counselor talked to my class, I called Ali's parents to tell them about the opportunity of enrolling Ali in a private school. The family's plan was for Ali to study the Quran in Gambia for five years after fifth grade, but they trusted his teacher and agreed to let him take the required test.

Unfortunately, there was no one to take Ali to lower Manhattan, where the required test would be administered. His mother had several young children to take care of at home, and his father spent much of his time working or traveling back to Africa, where he also worked. While Ali was independent, he was not *that* independent.

"Ms. Lewis, can you take me?" he asked the next day.

It never crossed my mind, not that I wouldn't want to, but because I thought it was out of bounds for me to take a student anywhere alone. He assured me his mother would approve.

"She'll let you," he promised. "She trusts you."

I asked his mother if I could take him downtown for the test, and she was perfectly fine with the idea. Ali had to report to the school by 7:45 A.M., which meant that we had to leave by 6:45 to get there by train. As mature as he was, I expected him to be late, but he was in front of the school fifteen minutes early, drinking his tea and eating his egg, cheese, and turkey bacon sandwich by the time I arrived.

Though Ali had made it to the interview that followed the exam, he came to me with tears in his eyes after he showed me the letter of rejection, which he had already opened and read on his own. He wanted the opportunity to attend a better school so badly that I decided to explore other possibilities, but to no avail, other than that an incredible bond developed among teacher, student, and family.

I had been wrong to think that a prestigious private Catholic school would enthusiastically open its doors to a poor little black boy who also happened to be Muslim. And while his grades were great, he would have had to be beyond exceptional to be considered for a full scholarship, which he would have needed in order to attend.

Finally, one school accepted him. I took him to visit one day when our school wasn't in session so he could check it out. When I came back to pick him up, he told me that all the children were black, the instruction was horrible, and the building needed renovation. The children almost didn't get lunch because the kitchen staff never showed up. Luckily a teacher ordered pizza.

Needless to say, my Ali ended up in Gambia. I'm counting down the years he has left there, praying that his parents' phone numbers don't change and hoping that they have kept mine.

I could cite countless examples of children who were successful despite living in an impoverished neighborhood, but in almost every instance at least one distinctive ingredient helped them rise above the rest. There were only a few instances in which that ingredient was absent, yet a child still managed to come to school, get straight A's, and not present behavioral problems.

Eric was such a child. His parents were addicts, forcing him and his sister to live with his aunt in a homeless shelter. Although he moved from shelter to shelter and from school to school, he still managed to be the highest-scoring student in every school he attended. Eric was seemingly unaffected by his disorganized home life. In school, he was the most polite, the most loving, and the most considerate of all my students that particular year. He did well in every subject and had an enormous vocabulary. But children like Eric were rare. Living in a succession of shelters, having crack-addicted parents, and fighting simply to survive usually meant that a student would struggle both academically and emotionally. He should not be used as proof as to why socioeconomic conditions do not affect student achievement. It was possible that a child in his shoes could still be successful, but not *probable*.

Rebellious Reggie was in prison. I learned of this when I ran into the aunt who had raised him. After we greeted each other with our usual hugs and kisses, she gave me the bad news. I wasn't surprised. Neither was she. She'd done all that she could have. She had lost all control.

"Ms. Lewis, he has a lot of pain. He doesn't care if he lives or dies. And he's bigger than me, so I can't keep him inside. I'm just an old woman at this point. What control do I have?"

Reggie was troubled, and he had chosen the adjective *rebellious* for our icebreaker on the first day of school for a reason. Reggie followed the rules of the street, the rules that said to get it any way you can. Discovering what had happened to Reggie, I Googled the names of many of the boys I was concerned would one day end up in jail. Reggie wasn't the first and he wouldn't be the last. Suddenly, I thought of Lorenzo.

As I typed his name, I hesitated. I almost expected to find him in some criminal database. I wasn't sure if I could bear finding out. Optimistically, I thought of the relief I would feel if I didn't see his name. With one final click, I realized I should have gone with my gut feeling. Lorenzo was awaiting trial for a very serious felony, the penalty for which could send him away for many years.

What if I had never broken my ankle? What if when Trey asked to leave, I had just let him go? Maybe Lorenzo would have had an alternate path in life if he had never been placed in D75 but in general education as I had planned on eventually doing. What could his path have been?

Then again, how much impact could I have made in only one year when my main obligation was to teach kids to read and write and do some math? I was at best a facilitator that guided their thinking, one who asked them to think critically about historical information, literature, and mathematical problems. I gave them real-world problems as much as I could, given my constraints, which did wonders for some students, as in the case of Sydney. But how much lasting impression had I even made on *her*? Who's to say that when she went to junior high school she didn't revert to her old ways? What if she had a teacher who secretly hated black people, or simply didn't feel it was his/her responsibility to promote black beauty? What if he or she didn't even know that Sydney had issues with body image because she hadn't opened up to him, or her confidence had tricked her teachers into assuming she always believed she was beautiful? What if she had been rejected by a boy who had self-hatred issues, who couldn't see her beauty because he was mentally enslaved like so many of our youth still were? What real power did I have over ensuring that *any* of my kids would survive?

Without the support system to maintain these positive changes, my children were subject to lose *it*, lose what they had gained while with me. They say teachers can change lives, but the system made no guarantees. The framework for teaching in community schools in urban neighborhoods followed the same blueprint as any other teaching framework in any suburb in New York. We worked magic from 8:00 A.M. to 3:00 P.M., give or take. We clocked in and we clocked out. For the Lorenzos and Reggies of the world, that wasn't enough. We were failing them, myself included.

When the master gives you something you take it. He gave you a name. It's a nice name.

from *Roots*, the miniseries

Business models were increasingly being applied to education—all of our work had begun to be about proving that we obeyed the machine. While six hours a day was still a limited time for kids who truly needed life support, it had at least been time in which we were allowed to have some control. Previously, the amount of control a teacher had over the way she instructed students and ran her classroom varied from school to school, as I had experienced. However, these business models were beginning to be implemented department-wide, and even principals were losing control over how their schools should be run. It had become apparent that I would soon lose my identity. Some schools in the city provided rules to all of their teachers, such as forcing students to call their teachers by their first names. Soon, we were following the progressive-school wave, and many public schools began coming up with their own progressive ideas, such as forcing teachers to be called "Coach" or whatever cutesy idea they had come up with. Other schools kicked in full dress codes for their teachers as though we worked in corporate offices. We had also lost rights to our own style and our own language. Classrooms had to look uniform, sometimes down to the color scheme, often down to where everything could be found: all bulletin boards had to have the same kinds of information in the same exact areas of the room. We couldn't just put up student work anymore; we had to put it up exactly the way every teacher put it up, very similar to charter-school philosophy. This didn't help with student achievement—it was just another method of control. Having the rooms all look exactly the same meant that principals could know exactly where to look for things when they came in to observe their teachers. The frequency of their visits was increasing; therefore, our classrooms had to be modeled with observations, not children, in mind. All our "aims" had to be written the same. Some schools even told their teachers where the verbs needed to be located. For instance, if a school demanded the phrasing "How can I analyze a text using annotation procedures?" a teacher who wanted to write, "How can I use annotation procedures to analyze a text?" would have to change it in her lesson plan.

People with real thinking brains and ability to teach were no longer needed because we were no longer in control of our own minds and bodies. Teachers in some schools were requiring their teachers to write out scripts of exactly what they were going to say to the students, word for word, while others continued to have teachers instruct out of scripted textbooks that wrote, "Say this: . . ." and "Tell students: . . ." These scripts offered word-for-word recitations for a teacher to follow.

Schools were also telling their teachers and students how to speak to one another. Schools required chanting of school mantras in all the school classrooms. It seemed slightly cultish to me, although I understood the point. I didn't have an issue with what schools would require us to say so much as what wasn't required that we say. School mantras were never *bad*; in fact, they promoted perseverance and high expectations, things kids needed to hear. However, none of those chants would ever be "Black is beautiful" or anything relative to what my black and brown students specifically needed to hear. Students learned and recited quotations, none of which would ever be from Malcom X or Marcus Garvey, Angela Davis or Nina Simone. We were all supposed to be the same, but that meant losing my own self and assimilating into what those up top believed suited our school. In order to belong to a school culture, many black teachers across the city had to lose their own. When teachers didn't follow the rules they were expected to abide by, the whip was cracked and they were beaten into submission. It didn't matter if teachers were successful in moving students or not; it was becoming increasingly important to do so in the fashion that you were told. Ironically, as we moved toward less-teacher-centered classrooms and pushed for more student-centered ones, the city became more oppressive on its members, more policy-driven, providing us with minimal choice. While we were required to give students opportunities for them to be able to think more critically, we were told not to think but to listen to the city's direction.

A network consultant met with all of us teachers one day and asked us, "What is your brand?"

"Our brand?" one of the teachers inquired sarcastically.

"Yes, when the quality reviewers come in, they'll be wanting to know what your school brand is. Here's an example: When you go into Target, how do you know you're in Target?"

"There's a big red bull's-eye on everything—on the walls, on the shopping bags, the bathroom sign."

"Exactly, so, what is *your* brand? What lets anyone walking in know you belong to this school?"

We sat there and thought about the sheer absurdity of comparing a school building to a major retail corporation. We had been branded all right. We were property of New York City. I dreamed of plotting my escape.

And at the point when I didn't think things could possibly get worse, the city decided that student test scores would soon be affecting our evaluations. The Measure of Student Learning (MOSL) would be the new system by which all teachers in the city would be rated. Forty percent of our rating would be based on test scores. Students would have to take the state exams, the MOSL exam, and tons of practice exams that monitored their progress. If students failed, we would be responsible. Teachers resented the fact that we were being told exactly what to do but then would be blamed if *their* plans didn't work.

The kids, many of whom were already uninterested in school, became even more disenchanted. The only schools whose students stood a chance of passing the exams were those in which many of the children were already above grade level, specifically schools that weren't in poverty-stricken communities. It was evident that teachers like me and students like mine were being set up to fail.

Before the first state exam was administered, letters were sent to parents, preparing them for what school officials knew would be a disaster. In simple language, the letters told parents that their children would fail. Children who normally passed with a grade of 3 or 4, which meant that they were performing at or above grade level, were at risk of failing with a 1. The letter told parents not to be alarmed if their children received a 1 because only the students with Lexile scores that fell within the lowest percentage of level 1's would be held back.

When the first new state exams were administered, I was assigned to proctor a group that had the directions read to them, and so I had a chance to skim through the test booklet. The readings were definitely challenging, and my special-education students would surely struggle to read the passages included, as would the lowest-performing general-education students. But it was the questions that were the real problem. In both the math and English exams, several questions were obviously written to trip up the kids.

In the English exam, instead of using terms that would have been appropriate for a ten-year-old, questions posed were at times convoluted and seemingly intentionally confusing. Several students raised their hands and told me that they didn't understand the questions being asked.

The same happened on the math test. The exam focused more on language than on mathematical reasoning. As I looked over the shoulder of many students, I saw that they had gotten an answer wrong that I knew they would have gotten right had it not been for the way the question was phrased.

The exams were also too long, something that we knew would be a problem even before the testing period began. Parents across the city made mad dashes to get their children "504 letters" from their doctors, letters that would allow a student with learning or emotional problems to have extra time to finish an exam. But even with extra time, many struggled to finish the exams within the allotted period. Those who didn't receive extra time struggled the most. The readings were much longer than they were accustomed to, and often boring to boot. Overall, the tests were less about measuring children's ability to read and comprehend and more about testing their stamina and distractability. I had to keep students from falling asleep the entire time.

There were other problems, notably when it came to reading and understanding passages of text. Not only were the passages too long, the questions required the students to re-read the passages over and over. Traditionally, a few sentences would have been plucked out of a passage, and the student would be asked to identify the purpose of those sentences. For example, was the purpose stating the main idea? Describing a character? Foreshadowing? Irony? But in these exams, the approach was flipped. A typical question: "Which paragraph foreshadows the events to come?" Students then had a choice between A (lines 5–20), B (lines 25–35), C (lines 42–54), or D (lines 60–72). This meant that four paragraphs had to be re-read in order for a student to answer a single question. And so it would go for most of the exam.

By the time they had read these paragraphs all over again, many students complained, they had forgotten even what the question had asked them. Students were being tested on their working memory as opposed to comprehension.

Students were also subjected to questions that had no single right answer. After the reading exam, several teachers gathered to ask one another what the answers were to questions that seemed to have more than one answer. We all agreed that certain questions had at least two possible correct answers.

And there was another problem. During the math exam, a student raised his hand and said he could not find the answer to a specific question. I told him to do the best he could, but I remembered the question so I could see if this was another case of intentional confusion.

When the test was over and I brought back all the material to the testing room, I tried the math problem the student had mentioned, and, as he had insisted, the answer was not provided. Several teachers complained of the same thing. We later found out that these questions were included only as some kind of experiment and the results would not be counted. Unfortunately, the students did not know this and spent valuable time on these questions, trying to find the right answers. Some panicked and spent as long as twenty minutes on a question that had no answer.

Predictably, children across the city failed the state tests miserably. It seemed to be all a part of the plan.

Teaching in the twenty-first century was becoming one of the most hated professions of all time. A colleague and I began playing around on Google one day, typing in partial searches to see what was the most popular. We started with letters, then began writing sentence starters like, "Why," which was followed up with "do we yawn?" or "am I so tired?" Eventually we typed in "I don't want to t—" which finished with "teach" as the number two search result. "I can't stand t—" returned "teenagers" as the number one search and "teaching anymore" as number two. If we typed, "Help, I don't want to—," "teach anymore" was higher in the search results than "be gay," "be married," or "be pregnant."

———————

By this point in my teaching career it was becoming increasingly clear that I would soon become one of the nasty, miserable old women in my school if I didn't do something fast. I had to do something else with my life or else I would lose my soul.

For starters, I had to get my "plus 30," an additional thirty academic credits that would help boost my salary. I found a master's program in school-building leadership and decided to go for it. For the first time, I contemplated the possibility of being a principal or a coach, someone who wasn't in the classroom.

Then I heard about a leadership program from the city's Office of New Schools. Under the program, individuals were hand-picked to become principals and placed in schools within a year. I applied and got an interview, along with a chance to critique a teacher whose work was highlighted in a five-minute video.

I realized very quickly that I was supposed to destroy a teacher based solely on a five-minute snapshot of her performance. First, I was asked to give her a letter grade. Then I was asked to determine whether I would consider her effective and whether I would hire her in my school. I subsequently learned that those selected for this leadership program would be hired to take over "failing schools," schools that had been closed based on test scores. Here, more or less, was my response:

"Honestly, I wouldn't rate someone after only watching five minutes of her lesson, but since I must, I would give her a B. She gave her mini-lesson, which was clear while informative, and her students seem to comprehend it. She gave them a group activity in which all members participated and were engaged in thought-provoking discussion, and she asked them higher-order-thinking questions which they were all able to answer.

"I know I can't say she was perfect, but to say that there were blatantly obvious errors would be a lie. I'm sure I could find something that she could have improved on if I were truly looking to find something negative, but nothing in her lesson appeared to be a red flag. As for whether

I would hire her to teach in my school, I don't really think five minutes would be enough time observing her practices to say.

"If I had to note anything, it would be that she didn't engage every single one of her students. There were maybe three or four who were quiet or seemed to be watching the clock. However, since this was junior high, that should be expected. I was an exceptional student my entire school career, but there were times, especially in junior high, when I would sometimes tune out."

Needless to say, I was not invited to the next round of interviews. I was glad, though. I couldn't imagine pushing an administrator out of a job and making her a scapegoat for society's ills. By now, schools were closing throughout major cities in the Northeast. These were always black and Hispanic schools. Some of them probably deserved to close. But I knew the majority of so-called bad schools were the by-product of bad politicians, bad public policy, and, most important, poverty. If school leadership was in the cards for me, this wasn't the route to take. I would still be controlled.

A group of us teachers, mostly teachers of color, began to go to the local karaoke spot, the Bruckner Bar & Grill, to release, through heavy-handed drinks and raucous behavior, some of the stress we were experiencing. We were all in our late twenties and early thirties, had all taken the bull by the horns and tackled careers at tender ages, and had lived seemingly independent lives—or so we thought—for years. This new phase of education had all of us feeling like we were twelve years old again. We had mastered teaching and changed lives and all of a sudden could be rated as merely "developing" according to a piece of paper. I had an out-of-classroom position by the time many of these changes had taken place, but that was not promised in following years. I still felt the insane pressures of my colleagues and was angered that the entire city was subject to micromanagement. The Bruckner Bar & Grill was our release. It eased a bit of our angst, at least temporarily.

We took turns bolting obscenities and gyrating to an eclectic collection of irrepressible, law-breaking, maniacal outlandishness. We picked artists known for being crass, vulgar, and absurd. No beautiful ballads were chosen. Though Beyoncé had tons, we opted for songs that allowed her alter ego, Sasha Fierce, to be wild, like "Ring the Alarm" or "Crazy in Love." We cursed along with Biggie, Nas, Pac, and Jay. We got dark with

Nirvana and irresponsibly indifferent with Icona Pop. We were tired and beaten, weary and broken, from all the rules, expectations, and pointed fingers. We were sick of being told by people who in some cases had never set foot in the classroom and who were out of touch with our students' realities how to close the achievement gap while no one intended on closing the poverty sinkhole. So we put up our middle fingers and said "Fuck it" for the night. I never left a karaoke night without requesting Jay Z and Rihanna's "Run This Town," a battle cry that gave us back our power, temporarily fooling us into believing that we had control over what was happening in our own lives.

> Life's a game but it's not fair,
> I break the rules so I don't care,
> So I keep doing my own thing,
> Walking tall against the rain,
> Victory's within the mile,
> Almost there don't give up now,
> Only thing that's on my mind, is who's gonna run this town
>   tonight?

———————————

I had no particular plan, but I knew a plan had to be hatched. I didn't need to run this city—politics wasn't my thing. But at the very least, I needed to have a say over my own life. It was time to say goodbye.

Giles's office, as usual, was open. She was playing the fiftieth anniversary of the March on Washington on the Smart Board. President Obama was giving a very King-inspired speech, eloquently written and spoken as usual despite the horrible rainy weather.

I had found a new position. It wasn't the end of the rainbow, but it was a step toward my fulfilling my long-term goal, which was to own my own destiny—that is, to make my own decisions. I would found my own school. Most important, that school would allow students of color better opportunities to own their own fates as well. I was nowhere near reaching this goal, but I couldn't begin the process as long as I stayed where I was. I couldn't make plans for the future with a broken spirit. I needed a change, a fresh start.

Giles stretched back in her principal's chair as I walked in, almost as if she knew what I was about to say. I walked in reluctantly, not so much afraid of her response but rather concerned that I might hurt her feelings. Giles had been good to me, and I loved the passion she brought to her school. If it wasn't for the Mean Girls, I would've stayed at the Old School forever, or at least until I started my own. Giles had taught me so much about what leadership in our communities was supposed to look like. If only she didn't have to comply with the system, it would have been a perfect place for me. I came to the realization that I needed to be uncomfortable in order to move into the next phase in my life. She deserved a face-to-face conversation, as painful as the prospect was for me. She must have noticed my hesitance, because in her usual jovial fashion, she welcomed me with an inviting smile.

After about an hour of hanging out in her office, talking about life, moving on, and next steps, we embraced and finally bid our farewells. I was a big girl now who would fend for myself by any means necessary. Rather than burn a bridge, I used it to walk out of her office and toward new beginnings that drizzly day with more than raindrops on my cheek. However, as I continued to walk home, I couldn't help feeling as though I had been cleansed. The seed within me that had been denied the chance to sprout because of horrible policies, envious women, and my self-doubt were slowly washing away with each drop. In the end, all that was left was me in my own skin to choose.

Epilogue: The Greatest Love of All

It was a balmy summer evening in August. Omar had prepared his usual basil shrimp and mushroom *risotto* dish, plating it to perfection the way a chef at an upscale restaurant would, with splashes of sauce spattered in a very Jackson Pollock sort of way. Though it wasn't his turn to cook, he had decided to let me off the hook after I had spent an entire day reading up on nonprofit legalese for my new business venture. A friend of mine and I were opening our own school, one that spoke to the needs of children of African descent living in urban communities. His much-needed consideration came right on time; I was famished.

"Did you guys incorporate yet?" he yelled over the running water he used to rinse the wine glasses.

"Not yet, we're thinking backward, completing our mission statement, core values and all that information first and then deciding on a name. We have some thoughts, but nothing set in stone as of yet."

"That's cool. Maybe we can discuss the names over dinner. I'd love to hear your ideas."

It was the same dish he made for me the first time I had invited him over for dinner, showing up with eco-friendly shopping bags from Whole Foods and a crisp sauvignon that paired well with the savory dish. He had me at first bite.

There was much I found intriguing about Omar. He was a New Yorker like me, someone who'd been raised in the 'hood and who possessed a deep sense of pride in where he came from. My mother loved him immediately, saying we were "cut from the same cloth," that we were perfect for each other. She would tell me that the best kind of love was one that allowed you to love yourself first.

A strong intellectual brother, tall, broad-shouldered, with dark bronzed skin, he was my equal in both stature and wit. I had nothing to be ashamed of with him and had no reason to feel the need to impress or dumb myself down, as I had done on more than one occasion with failed relationships not worthy of being discussed in these pages. With Omar, I could be me. Everything about him was soothingly familiar.

Both of us had had to learn to love ourselves first before we could truly find happiness with another human being. By the time we met, we were both ripe fruit ready to be plucked, eager to move into commitment, into building a lasting foundation. We both were ready to take on the world, strong in our convictions, understanding of what was necessary to survive. We had both woken up, him in his own life, which contained his business and a daughter whom he absolutely adored, I in my career, one that continued to evolve since I left the Old School. I was preparing myself for a life in education that actually valued my beliefs and the needs of black and brown children. We had both experienced being under another's control and we had both learned how vital it was for us to own our own destinies. We inhabited the same island of truth. Equipped with the proper gear, we set off together to explore and to claim our lives as our own. It took both of us the whole of our lives to figure out. I glanced up at the pictures of my students Sydney, Lorenzo, and Reggie in their frames and shivered at the thought of students' learning to control their own destinies early on in their school careers. It didn't have to take a third of a lifetime to discover, if only they were taught to love themselves and own their own power the minute they entered a classroom. If only that instruction never stopped but instead followed them past the day they graduated from college and continued to echo in their minds as they prepared secure lives full of happiness and success for themselves. Omar tapped me on the shoulder, interrupting my daydream. He held two glasses. He kissed me gently as he handed me one.

"A toast to real love," he said, raising his glass to mine, "the love that comes from within. May it find itself in the hearts of those we hold dear to us, especially our children, because without it, nothing can grow."

I took a hearty swig, emptying my glass and ingesting both its contents and the promise in those words as if some magical elixir.

ESE SELECT TITLES FROM EMPIRE STATE EDITIONS

Allen Jones with Mark Naison, *The Rat That Got Away: A Bronx Memoir*

Janet Grossbach Mayer, *As Bad as They Say? Three Decades of Teaching in the Bronx*

William Seraile, *Angels of Mercy: White Women and the History of New York's Colored Orphan Asylum*

Andrew J. Sparberg, *From a Nickel to a Token: The Journey from Board of Transportation to MTA*

Daniel Campo, *The Accidental Playground: Brooklyn Waterfront Narratives of the Undesigned and Unplanned*

John Waldman, *Heartbeats in the Muck: The History, Sea Life, and Environment of New York Harbor, Revised Edition*

John Waldman (ed.), *Still the Same Hawk: Reflections on Nature and New York*

Howard Eugene Johnson with Wendy Johnson, *A Dancer in the Revolution: Stretch Johnson, Harlem Communist at the Cotton Club*. Foreword by Mark D. Naison

Joseph B. Raskin, *The Routes Not Taken: A Trip Through New York City's Unbuilt Subway System*

Phillip Deery, *Red Apple: Communism and McCarthyism in Cold War New York*

North Brother Island: The Last Unknown Place in New York City. Photographs by Christopher Payne, A History by Randall Mason, Essay by Robert Sullivan

Stephen Miller, *Walking New York: Reflections of American Writers from Walt Whitman to Teju Cole*

Tom Glynn, *Reading Publics: New York City's Public Libraries, 1754–1911*

Greg Donaldson, *The Ville: Cops and Kids in Urban America, Updated Edition*. With a new epilogue by the author, Foreword by Mark D. Naison

David Borkowski, *A Shot Story: From Juvie to Ph.D.*

Craig Saper, *The Amazing Adventures of Bob Brown: A Real-Life Zelig Who Wrote His Way Through the 20th Century*

R. Scott Hanson, *City of Gods: Religious Freedom, Immigration, and Pluralism in Flushing, Queens*. Foreword by Martin E. Marty

See www.empirestateeditions.com for a complete list.